MOSES IN THE LETTER TO THE HEBREWS

SOCIETY
OF BIBLICAL
LITERATURE

DISSERTATION SERIES

edited by
Howard Clark Kee

Number 42

MOSES IN THE LETTER TO THE HEBREWS
by
Mary Rose D'Angelo

Mary Rose D'Angelo

MOSES IN
THE LETTER
TO THE HEBREWS

Scholars Press

Distributed by
Scholars Press
PO Box 5207
Missoula, Montana 59806

MOSES IN THE LETTER TO THE HEBREWS

Mary Rose D'Angelo

The Iliff School of Theology

Ph.D., 1976
Yale University

Adviser:
Rowan A. Greer

Library of Congress Cataloging in Publication Data

D'Angelo, Mary Rose.
  Moses in the letter to the Hebrews.

  (Society of Biblical Literature. Dissertation series ; no.
42)
  Originally presented as the author's thesis, Yale, 1976.
  Bibliography: p.
  1. Moses.   2. Bible.   N.T.   Hebrews—Criticism,
interpretation, etc. I. American Academy of Religion.
II. Title. III. Series.
BS580.M6D33   1978   227'.87'06   78-12917
ISBN 0-89130-265-4
ISBN 0-89130-333-2 pbk.

Printed in the United States of America
1 2 3 4 5

Edwards Brothers, Inc.
Ann Arbor, MI 48106

TABLE OF CONTENTS

ABBREVIATIONS

AB   Anchor Bible.

ANF   Ante-Nicene Fathers.

Aland   K. Aland *et al.*, *The Greek New Testament* (United Bible Societies, 2nd ed.).

ARNA   *Aboth de Rabbi Nathan*, Version A.

ARNB   *Aboth de Rabbi Nathan*, Version B.

BDB   G. Brown, S. R. Driver and C. A. Briggs, *A Hebrew and English Lexicon* (Oxford, 1968).

CCL   Corpus Christianorum, series Latina.

GCS   Die griechischen christlichen Schriftsteller der ersten drei jährbunderte.

JE   *Jewish Encyclopedia.*

ICC   The International Critical Commentary on the Holy Scriptures of the Old and New Testaments.

Loeb   The Loeb Classical Library.

LSJ   J. G. Liddell, R. Scott *et al.*, *A Greek-English Lexicon* (Oxford, 1968).

LXX   The Septuagint.

MT   The Masoretic Text.

Nestle   E. Nestle, ed., *Novum Testamentum Graece* (25th ed.).

NPNF   Nicene and Post-Nicene Fathers.

NTS   *New Testament Studies.*

PG   Patrologia graeca.

PL   Patrologia latina.

RSV   Revised Standard Version.

SC   Sources Chrétiens.

St. Ev.   *Studia Evangelica.*

Soncino   The Soncino Press editions of the Midrash
            Rabbah and the Babylonian Talmud (London, 1939
            and 1948).

TDNT   G. Kittel and G. Friedrich, *A Theological
            Dictionary of the New Testament* (Grand Rapids,
            MI, 1964).

Tg.   Targum.

Other works have been abbreviated by the author and,
where necessary, by shortened title after their first
appearance in the notes.

PREFACE

In presenting this study to the reader I am impelled to acknowledge both that its errors are the result of my own limitations and that whatever contribution it may make owes much to the wisdom and kindness of many friends and colleagues.

The Iliff School of Theology has borne much of the cost of preparing the manuscript for publication and Regina Harness, Lorna Kuyk, Gretchen Hawley and Kent H. Richards lent their patient cooperation to that task. The study was done under the auspices of Yale University and is indebted to the comradely interest of many who were my fellow students there, especially of Francine J. Cardman. The hospitality and assistance of E. Ann Matter and Kathleen M. Nilles made it possible for me to complete the text amid many distractions. Professors Nils A. Dahl and Wayne A. Meeks have given me much guidance and encouragement from the inception of the project. I wish in particular to acknowledge my debt to the advice and teaching of Professor Judah Goldin and to the members of his class in Midrash and Talmud. A special note of thanks goes to Alan Cooper for his early tutoring and more recent criticism. Since the completion of the dissertation, advice and the encouragement to publish have come from my three gracious readers, Professors Dahl, Meeks and Goldin as well as from Professor Paul Minear, under whose tutelage I first did a study of Hebrews. No sufficient acknowledgement could be made here of the assistance of my teacher and friend Professor Rowan Allan Greer, for the study has been formed at every point by our continuing conversation. But it must be said that he has offered to the thesis not only his patient attention and kind encouragement, but also its most pithy formulation: "Ask not what Moses can do for Hebrews; ask what Hebrews can do for Moses."

Mary Rose D'Angelo
Denver, Colorado
June 1979

ix

INTRODUCTION

In recent years scholarly studies of the New Testament have been accustomed to speaking of a "Moses-Christology" in describing one of the various Christologies of the New Testament authors. The term implies an understanding of the formation of New Testament Christology in which the expectation of a prophet like Moses or of the eschatological return of Moses himself has become a model for explaining the person of Jesus and his mission. Presumably the New Testament author's view of Moses, or the view of Moses taken by the community from which that author springs or by the Judaism to which the author or community is related, determines the main lines of this aspect of the book's Christology. Thus, the conception "Moses-Christology" becomes a methodological tool, a reconstruction of popular expectation which can be used to explain the Christology of the Christian author, or at least certain aspects of it.[1]

Indeed, a careful look at the Christology often reveals traits of the Old Testament or first-century figures of Moses; there is a correspondence between Moses and Christ in almost every book of the New Testament in which Moses is treated. And it is also the case that the reconstruction of contemporary Moses traditions and expectations often succeeds in illuminating the Christologies of the New Testament. But the variety of such reconstructions makes it difficult to speak with confidence of any fully coherent Moses expectations. And all the reconstructions remain hypothetical, at least in their application to traditions which may have shaped New Testament views. The variety of such pictures should remind us to take into account the selective role of both the tradition of the

---

[1]An impressive example of the way in which this approach can assist in the illumination of well-defined aspects of the text is the study of Wayne Atherton Meeks, *The Prophet-King: Moses Traditions and the Johannine Christology* (Leiden: E. J. Brill, 1967).

author's community and the creative work of the author. Their
hypothetical character demands that we recognize the impact of
the fulfillment upon the expectation; the path from expectation
to fulfillment is not a one-way street.

In the case of Moses, the relationship between expectation
and fulfillment, or between non-Christian and Christian
pictures, is complicated by at least two additional factors.
First, the figure of Moses is different from other figures or
constructs we use to explain the evolution of Christology.
Unlike Elijah, "the heavenly son of man," the messianic high
priest, the Davidic Messiah or even the prophet like Moses,
Moses himself is not primarily one, or even the, option of
eschatological expectation, but is primarily a figure so
determinative in the history that no theologian who is in any
way the heir of Judaism can avoid coming to terms with his role
in the tradition as a whole. Thus Moses is important for the
New Testament writers in more ways than as a model in the
formation of their Christology, and the commentator must widen
the horizons to include other factors involved in a writer's
positive understanding of the Christian dispensation.

In the second place, the authors of the New Testament have
already come to the point at which expectation is being supplanted in its determinative role in the Christology by apologetic. At least in the Pauline writings, Christ has supplanted
the role of Torah in Judaism, and the problematic relationship
between Christ and the mediator of the Torah represents a
major focus in the debate between Christianity and Judaism.

Thus in dealing with the texts of the New Testament, it
becomes possible and perhaps more useful to prescind from the
question of the role of expectation in the development of a
"Moses-Christology" and to look at the correspondences between
Christ and Moses in order to see how an understanding of Christ,
of Christianity and of the relation of Christianity to Judaism
has shaped an author's understanding of Moses. If Moses has
contributed to New Testament Christologies, so also has Christ
determined "Mosesologies" of the Christian authors. The
commentator who chooses to reflect upon the genesis of the
Christian Moses reverses the usual process, tracing the effect
of fulfillment upon expectation to show how the New Testament

author's Christology moves in and out among the texts and traditions which discuss Moses, selecting and exposing them in such a way as to present a Moses who is conformed to Christ.

Lest this description prejudice the independence of the traditions about Moses, let me point out that it is indeed possible to construct and even simply to point to varieties of independent "Mosesologies" which like Christologies, can be described as "high" and "low." Each has favored a series of crucial texts and has developed a tradition of interpretation. But the selection and integration of texts and traditions about Moses depends upon the author's Christology: an author with a low Christology emphasizes the texts and traditions which will produce a correspondingly low picture of Moses; a high Christology may not necessarily produce a correspondingly high picture of Moses, but the texts and traditions which would supply such a picture must be treated.

This view of the New Testament texts is, like any other, hypothetical, a tool for explaining them. Its usefulness can be best described by seeing how it accounts for the differences in New Testament pictures of Moses. The Lukan Moses demonstrates a peculiarly Christian reworking of a "low Mosesology;" the Pauline and Johannine versions of Moses show two Christian ways of dealing with a high picture of Moses.

Luke's view of Moses in Acts 7.20-40 is illustrative of the workings of his Christology upon the portrait of Moses as well as of the expectation of the prophet like Moses upon the Christology. The prophecy in Dt. 18.15 is explicitly brought into play in this text (Acts 7.37) and is clearly one of the dominant themes in Luke's Christology. The last direct description of Jesus in Luke's gospel is the description given by the (still unenlightened) disciples at Emmaus: "a prophet mighty in word and work." In keeping with the miraculous character of Jesus' ministry in Luke, the signs and wonders of Egypt and the wilderness are emphasized in Moses' prophetic career (7.36). Although the sojourn of Moses on the mountain is mentioned, no mystical character is given to it. Rather, it is emphasized throughout the whole account that Moses' revelation came to him through the hand of an angel. Moses then did not speak directly with God; the view of him is a "low" view as "a prophet, like one of the other prophets."

The distinctive picture which governs Luke's "Mosesology"
is a picture of Moses as martyr which is dominated by Ex. 2.14.
Moses is primarily the prophet sent to his people whom they
reject with the words: "who has made you ruler and judge?"
The prophet who is like Moses is the prophet who is rejected.
Moses' sojourn on the mountain is significant chiefly as the
occasion of Israel's defection. Everything in the account of
Moses' life as it stands in Acts 7.20-40 is taken from the
scriptures or the traditional accounts, but this particular
account could never have been given without the understanding
that the prophet like Moses was Jesus, the leader and savior
rejected by Israel and exalted by God.[2]

In contrast to the "low" picture of Moses the prophet-
martyr is the higher view of Moses as prophet-mystic. It
invokes and responds to a group of Old Testament texts which
raise the question about the unique status of Moses' prophecy
as a result of his unique vision of God. Exodus 33-34, Nu.
12.6-8 and Dt. 34.5-10 make various and sometimes contradictory statements about the prophecy of Moses. Exodus 33-34
contains at least two stories about the vision of Moses, which
have been worked together so as to produce a not entirely
coherent whole. The first, Ex. 33.7-11, is an account of
Moses' habitual intercourse with God in the tent pitched outside the camp; this account concludes with the statement, "The
Lord spoke with Moses face to face, as a man speaks with his
friend." This is immediately followed by a story which
appears to introduce either a contradiction or a qualification
of that statement. In Ex. 33.12 ff, Moses demands a sign of
God's favor toward himself and Israel, as an assurance that the
covenantal presence of God with Israel is to be reinstated:
he asks to see God's glory (Ex. 33.18). To this request God
replies that he shall indeed have the vision, but in it he
will be able to see God's back only, and not his face (33.20-
23). In Ex. 34.1-7 the preparations of the lawgiving are recounted; they include not only the cutting of the tablets, but
also Moses' ascent of the mountain and vision of God's glory,
accompanied by God's pronouncement of his oracular name (34.6-7)

---

[2]5.31; cf. 1.22-23; 2.23-24, 36; 3.15.

as a prelude to the second lawgiving (34.8-28). At the close
of his second interview with God, Moses descends from the
mount with his face glorified from the glory of God "while he
was speaking with him" (34.29). His fellow Israelites are unable to bear the glorious visage of Moses as they were unable
to bear the sound of the words and the sight of the fire on
Sinai. Moses then begins to wear a veil which he removes only
to speak with the Lord in the tent--i.e. face to face (cf.
33.11), and to deliver his dicta to Israel (34.34-35).

Nu. 12.6-8 is a praise of Moses in which God says that he
speaks with Moses "mouth to mouth," differently from the other
prophets who see in a mirror or lens and in riddles, while
with Moses he speaks in a vision (or clear sight) and he
beholds his image (or, according to the LXX, his glory). While
this may not have originated as a reflection of Exodus 33-34,
the tradition of interpretation certainly understands it as
such. Dt. 34.10 does seem to be a reference to the vision of
Exodus: "There did not arise another prophet in Israel like
Moses whom the Lord knew face to face."

The reconciliation and exposition of these texts is a
major concern of the rabbinic sources; they seem always to
engender a "high" view of Moses, or at least a debate over
such a view. Entwined into this debate with the passages already mentioned are the texts and the discussion involving the
ascent of Moses as prototypical for mystic ascent (Ex. 19.3,
Lev. 1.1). The picture of Moses that they always evoke is the
picture of Moses at the foot of the mountain, his face aflame
with the glory of God. Perhaps the dangers of exalting Moses
are somewhat mitigated for the interpreters of the tradition
by the close relationship of the glory bestowed on Moses and
the loving munificence of God's covenantal relationship with
Israel. The glorious (though hidden) face of Moses is the
sign of the healed covenant.

Thus for New Testament authors, the glory of Moses' face
at once raises not only the question of the meaning of Moses
himself, but also of his ministry, of the law that he wrote
and of the covenant of which he is mediator and guarantor.

That "Moses the Mystic" is one of the portraits in Paul's
gallery is clear from his handling of this constellation of

texts in 2 Co. 3.7-18 and 1 Co. 13.12; but it is equally clear that Paul's selection of this portrait is motivated by his Christology and that the portrait is then radically revised by the image of Christ.

In 2 Co. 3.3-4.6 Paul puts before us the visage of Moses transfigured by the glory of the vision of God granted to him when he received the stone tablets engraved by the finger of God. He remarks, precisely as the account in Exodus 34 relates, that the Israelites were unable to bear this glory, so Moses put a veil on his face. But Paul's interpretation of this move of Moses is very peculiar: πρὸς τὸ μὴ ἀτενίσαι τοὺς υἱοὺς τοῦ Ἰσραὴλ εἰς τὸ τέλος τοῦ καταργουμένου (2 Co. 3.13). It is usually translated so as to give the impression that Moses hid his face so that the Jews would not be able to tell when the passing glory faded from it (RSV: "so that the Israelites might not see the end of the fading splendor");[3] presumably the veil was an attempt to keep them in line. But the formulation is a difficult one, and can certainly be read otherwise.

For one thing, πρὸς τὸ μὴ ἀτενίσαι can just as well intend result as purpose. Further, τὸ τέλος τοῦ καταργουμένου cannot mean the end of the glory, for the participle is neuter (see 3.11), but must mean "the end of the passing thing that was glorified" (3.10-11) as opposed to the "abiding thing." It is not absolutely necessary to specify neuter antecedents for the two participles, but two hypothetical antecedents can be suggested. If Paul is thinking in terms of the text of Exodus, he may be opposing the glorified face (τὸ πρόσωπον) of Moses who was to die, to the glorified face of Christ who abides. If, however, he is thinking in the context of his own argument, he is more likely to be thinking of (the covenant of) the letter (τὸ γράμμα) as opposed to (that of) the spirit (τὸ πνεῦμα).[4]

_____

[3]All citations are taken from the RSV unless the sense requires a retranslation. The exception to this is citations marked LXX. These have been directly translated from the Septuagint.

[4]Cf. *Song of Songs Rabbah* I.2-4, where it said that when the people refused to hear for themselves and had Moses for their mediator, they became liable to forget the law: "They said,'Just as Moses, being flesh and blood, is transitory, so

If one selects the latter alternative and rereads the verse, it begins to sound a bit more familiar: "...Moses put a veil upon his face so that the sons of Israel did not perceive the *telos* of the passing letter (of the law)...that in Christ it is passing away." Paul then is restating what he said in Ro. 10.4: "For Christ is the *telos* of the law" and the two statements are functionally identical. That Christ is the *telos* of the law is a principle of exegesis; the law can all and only be read as referring to Christ. Presumably then had Moses not veiled his face the sons of Israel would have been able to read the law unto its end, i.e. to know that it refers to Christ.[5] How and why can Paul think that this is so? The clues to this part of Paul's argument lie hidden chiefly in 2 Co. 3.18. There Paul is discussing our (Christian) vision and transformation in contrast to that of Moses:

> For we all with unveiled faces *gazing through the mirror* on the glory of the Lord, on the very image, are being transformed from glory to glory....

This description combines images from Ex. 34.29 ff, in which we are told that Moses unveiled his face only while he spoke with God, with Nu. 12.6-8, where it is said of Moses that "not in a mirror or in dark speeches," does God speak with him, "but mouth to mouth, in clear sight (or in a straight lens) and not in riddles, and the image of the Lord he sees." The "image" which Moses sees is in the LXX translated as the "glory" of the Lord: i.e. the LXX reads the verse as a reference to the vision of God's glory granted to Moses according to Exodus 33-34.[6]

---

his teaching is transitory.'"

[5]J. Héring also takes this position on the verse, for differing and more complex reasons. See Jean Héring, *The Second Epistle of Saint Paul to the Corinthians* (London: Epworth Press, 1967), 25-26.

[6]As do *Siphre Bemidbar*, the Targums and other significant rabbinic witnesses. Coupled with the evidence given by Paul's use, these suggest that at an early point, Nu. 12.6-8 must have been referred to Exodus 33-34 as a matter of course. Paul's reference and interpretation cannot be explained by his reliance on the LXX. Possibly he is influenced by some specific representative of the tradition; more likely, he relies on what appears to be the simple sense of the text, derived from a holistic view of scripture and attested by most of his contemporaries.

Paul's interpretation of Nu. 12.8 in 1 Co. 13.12 casts
further light on the way in which he is using the mirror
imagery here. There he applies the difference between the
other prophets' vision and Moses' vision to our vision now
and in the future: "Now we see through a mirror, in a riddle,
but then face to face." In 1 Co. 13.12 the word translated by
"mirror" is ἔσοπτρον; in 2 Co. 3.18 another compound,
κατοπτριζόμενοι, is used. The latter's standard meaning in the
middle voice is simple "look/gaze in a mirror," and that
meaning is appropriate to 2 Co. 3.18. But the word can and
does here convey something different from gazing on one's own
image. As in 1 Co. 13.12, the mirror is the means of a vision;
Paul seems to want to say that we gaze through the mirror (or
lens) onto the true image.[7]

And for Paul the image as the glory of God has but a
single meaning: 2 Co. 4.4 "the glory of Christ who is the
image of God." If then the glory equals the image equals
Christ, the vision of God's glory which Moses saw was also
Christ, and the glory which was reflected on his face was also
the glory of Christ. Thus at the Jews' rejection of that
glory, he was forced to veil it, giving them only the law but
not the key which would enable them to read it to its end.

In this passage the point of comparison slides about. In
2 Co. 3.12-13, Paul and Moses are being compared or rather
contrasted as preachers of the gospel; Paul and his fellow
apostles ("we") are *not* like Moses, who veiled his face. But
in 3.18, Paul and his hearers ("we all")[8] are like Moses; we
all, apostles and believers, gaze with unveiled face upon the
glory of the Lord, like Moses who unveiled his face to speak
face to face with the Lord in the tent. But here, if Moses is
compared to Paul and to ourselves, he is also likened to
Christ, conformed to Christ on the soteriological and theological level as the Lukan narrative of Moses' life is transformed

---

[7]On this meaning, see R. Bultmann, *Der Zweite Brief an
die Korinther* (Göttingen: Vandenhoeck and Ruprecht, 1976), 93-
97. Note especially his examples from Philo. *Leg. All.* III.
101 is perhaps the most illuminating of these.

[8]Accepting the reading of the Nestle text. On the
application of the verse, see Bultmann, 93.

on the pattern of Jesus' life. The pattern Paul suggests is
not that what happened to Moses must also have happened to
Jesus; it is rather that the mission and person of Moses derive
from that of Jesus. The difference between Paul and Moses is
finally not that Moses is an unsuccessful Paul, but that Paul's
proclamation admits us all to the vision of Moses: for us the
enlightenment of the knowledge of the glory of God shines in
the face of Christ, as for Israel it shone reflected from the
face of Moses.

At this point we can return to 3.11 and the opposition
between what remains and what passes. In view of the function
of Christ and Moses it matters little whether the opposition
is between the face of Christ who abides and the face of Moses
who was destined to die, or between the spirit and the letter,
for it is possible and perhaps necessary to read it both ways.
If indeed "the Lord is the spirit" (3.17)[9] for Paul, there is
little doubt that Moses is the letter; so that "that which
passes" in verse 13 can be the glorified face of Moses, and
still in verse 14 can be the letter that passes away in Christ.

In addition to the functional conformity between Christ
and Moses another radical revision has been wrought upon Moses
by the Christological reworking of these texts. Moses' vision
as the vision of Christ has made him a Christian. Paul's
Moses is *Saint* Moses the Mystic.

Paul's high Christology in which Jesus is explained as the
preexistent incarnate image of God is, then, set to work upon
Moses the Mystic and his vision of God:

1) Moses' vision is explained as a vision of Christ;

2) Moses' glorification is explained as his conformity
to Christ;

3) Moses himself becomes a Christian.

Thus the picture of Moses is considerably higher than the
Lukan Moses, with whom God always deals through an angel, but

---

[9]On the problem of identifying the Lord, i.e., Christ,
and the spirit, see Héring's summary, 26. He points to the
opinion which would explain 3.17 as an equivalent of "the end
of the law is Christ"--"the Lord is the spirit," i.e., of the
law. However, 1. Co. 15.45 suggests that a more concrete identification is also implied. See also Bultmann, 99, who
emphasizes the exegetical character of the comment, referring
the reader to Ro. 8.16.

at no point does Paul say with *Midrash Tehillim*: "Moses, a
man, the God" (Ps. 90.1).[10]

The Gospel of John also uses the vision of Moses as a
background against which to explicate the person of Christ and
the meaning of the old covenant. Although the Christology of
John and his understanding of the law throw into relief
different aspects of the vision, the glory of the vision is
its keynote here also:

> 1.14 And the Word became flesh and tented among us and
> we beheld his glory,
> glory as of the only one of the father,
> full of grace and truth;

> .16 of his fullness we have all received,
> grace for grace;

> .17 for the law was given through Moses,
> grace and truth came through Jesus Christ;

> .18 no one has at any time seen God;
> the only God who is in the bosom
> of the father,
> he has made him known.

Behind these verses lie some decisions about the vision
of Moses. According to John, Moses did not see God when he
saw the glory of God, as indeed no one has at any time seen
God. Yet he did see the glory of the only God, God the
revealer, the Word who is God. Like Paul, John understands
the vision as the source of the law, and as Paul uses the
word "dispensation" (διακονία) to indicate the parallel
between old and new, John uses the word "grace" (χάρις, apparently a translation of חסד).[11] For John, new is related to
old as the fulness, fulfillment of the old; as the truth of
which the old is the shadow. Moses saw the one whose fullness
made our true grace, true covenant; of that fullness, he could
only relate the law. But all that he wrote, he wrote about
him, and even the works which he did in the redemption of
Israel find their truth only in that fullness.

Thus Paul and John on the one hand and Luke on the other

---

[10]*Midrash Tehillim*, 90.5; tr. William G. Braude, *The
Midrash on Psalms*, Vol. 2, Yale Judaica Series VI (New Haven:
Yale University Press, 1959), 88-89.

[11]On this and on the discussion of John as a whole, see
below, chapter four, 183-186.

all treat Moses as conformed to Christ in his person and mission. But the letter to the Hebrews goes one step farther. The cosmological theory of this author makes this conforming an explicit, even a deliberate move. For Hebrews, it is never the case that Jesus is like Moses, like Melchizedech, like the high priest on Yom Kippur, like Isaac; rather, it is always the case that all these are "likened to the son of God" (7.3).

Hebrews then is an ideal subject for an examination of the workings of Christology as a principle of interpretation of the scripture within the New Testament. Indeed, the present study began not from the recognition of the principle, but from an interest in the text of the letter and the role of Moses in the author's theological reflection; the observations put forward here arose from attempts (now long abandoned) to account for all allusions to Moses in the text, and through them for the letter's Christology.

The study in its present form has instead attempted to discover a coherent, though by no means comprehensive, picture of Moses in the thought of the author of Hebrews, and has done so by attempting to answer the questions raised by three passages in the letter. Two of them are major and direct references to Moses, 11.23-27 and 3.1-6. The third is the long central section of the letter (8.1-10.18) where Moses is mentioned specifically in 8.5 and 9.19 and where the description of the tabernacle and its service is related to Moses' vision.

Chapter one will examine Hebrews' version of the life of Moses in 11.23-27, focusing on formal characteristics, the function of the passage and its relation to other traditional interpretations of the same period of Moses' life. The version of Moses' early life which is given by these verses is a portrait of "Moses the Martyr," the example of faith as *endurance*, the virtue of martyrs. It is highly formal in character; its function is clearly parenetic and it relies on a tradition of interpretation which treats the scriptural text in an inclusive and holistic fashion. However, on all these levels, it shows the distinctive creative hand of the author of Hebrews, particularly in Moses' conformity to Christ;

for Hebrews, Moses' sufferings are not merely the unconscious
witness of the fate of Jesus, but even a Christian martyrdom,
a sharing in the reproach of Christ undertaken for his sake in
view of the recompense. In the light of this portrait some
suggestions will be made about the objective nature of faith
for Hebrews, and a major question will be raised about the
function of Moses in this letter. The question is: How did
Moses become a Christian?

To answer this question, we shall turn to the comparison
between Christ and Moses in Hebrews 3.1-6. This crucial
discussion of the relationship between Moses and Christ will
be examined in the three central chapters of the study, each
of which will focus upon the author's use of scripture. Chapter two will deal with the Christological testimonies in 3.1-6,
chapter three with Nu. 12.7 in the history of interpretation
and chapter four with the comparison of the glory of Moses and
the glory of Christ.

In keeping with the thesis of this study, chapter two
will assert that the structure of the argument in 3.1-6 is
supplied by a Christological oracle, a composite oracle about
the messiah, the royal priest, and his faithful house, which
is cited in 3.2 by a reference to 1 Chr. 17.14 ff and used in
midrashic fashion to express the relationship between Christ
and the people of God. It will be observed that the context
of this oracle establishes for the word πιστός (usually translated "faithful") the double meaning "appointed/faithful," and
sheds some light on Hebrews' use of the word "house" to denote
both people and dwelling of God. It should be noted that this
chapter does not attempt to explain the Christology of Hebrews
by this oracle, but rather asserts that the use of the oracle
can only be fully understood in the light of Hebrews'
Christology.

The third chapter will make some observations about the
career of Nu. 12.7 in the tradition of interpretation,
suggesting that as God's particular testimony to Moses and
especially to the unique immediacy of his vision of God, the
text functions principally in a "high" doctrine of Moses the
mystic. Elaboration of the theme in interpretation focuses
the association of the text with Moses' vision of the giving

of Torah and the use of the text to prove Moses' superiority
to the angels. The tradition supports the meaning "appointed/
faithful" for πιστός in Nu. 12.7 also, as well as suggesting
that the various applications of "house" (to the world, the
sanctuary and the people) are connected by this tradition which
says that Moses entered God's house, the heavens, prevailed
over the heavenly *familia* (the angels) and carried off the law
of fire. Thus the tradition illumines the peculiar structure
of Hebrews, which compares Christ first to the angels, then
to Moses, their superior. Neither the history of Nu. 12.7,
however, nor that of the Christological oracle explains the
comparison between Moses and Christ, nor does it intimate how
Moses became a Christian. For light upon these questions, we
turn to an examination of the point upon which the comparison
is made in 3.1-6; the glory of Christ and the glory of Moses.

Examining the comparison in the argument of Hebrews,
chapter four identifies Moses' glory (3.3) as the glorified
face of Moses described in Ex. 34.29 ff, and suggests that the
divine artificer argument used in 3.3 and 4 implies that the
glory of Moses is related to the glory of Christ as house to
builder, i.e. that when Moses saw the glory of God in Exodus
34, he beheld Christ, the effulgence of his glory, and his face
shone from his speaking with him. In support of this suggestion we shall then examine the sources that would make such
a theological decision possible for Hebrews, the Christological position of Hebrews in the first chapter of the letter
and the theological function of the vision and glory of Moses
in Philo and John. All three areas lead to the conclusion
that the glory that Moses saw and wore was the glory of Christ,
the seeable of the Unseen God. Thus Moses serves a theological function in the Christology of Hebrews; like the angels,
his role is to assist in the articulation of the Christology,
of Christ's relation to God. The exegetical implications of
Moses' vision as the source of the law are then sketched in
the thought of Paul and John, and questions raised about
Hebrews' application of the vision as an exegetical principle.

The final chapter of this study will turn to Hebrews'
interpretation of the law under the rubric of Ex. 25.40,
cited in He. 8.5, an examination placing Hebrews in a high

tradition which applies that verse to the whole of the (cultic) law making it a revelation of unseen realities on the grounds of Moses' vision of the Unseen. By examining the antitypical details of the law according to Hebrews' account of them, the chapter concludes that for this author the *typos* that Moses saw on the mountain was the *teleiosis* of Christ, the passage of Christ across the veil, and the same vision that conformed him to the glory and the suffering of Christ. This conviction of Hebrews is then shown to be integral to the dispensational view of the letter, which describes the law as imperfect, but still salvific.

In conclusion, we shall sketch some of the implications of the study for scholarly understanding of the New Testament Christology and of the use of the scripture by New Testament authors and raise some questions about the possibility of preserving the paradigmatic character of their exegetical enterprise and the theological function of Moses' vision of God.

This very limited study ought to be introduced by many disclaimers; questions of introduction to the letter to the Hebrews have not been directly addressed at any point, and apologies are owed to the scholarly endeavors of so many commentators whose great contributions my ignorance has slighted. However, existential pressures require that one such issue be addressed before we turn to the body of this study. This commentator wishes to acknowledge that although she is acquainted with Ruth Hoppin's study *Priscilla: Author of the Epistle to the Hebrews*,[12] she is unable to be convinced that the author of the letter can be identified with any known figure of the early church, and the attractive alternative of referring to the unknown author as "she" seemed to add to the distractions of an already complex treatment. The study therefore resorts to the unhappy expedient of avoiding the pronoun in reference to the author of Hebrews wherever

---

[12]*Priscilla, Author of the Epistle to the Hebrews and other essays* (New York: Exposition Press, 1969), 11-116. See the introduction (15) where Hoppin names Harnack as the earliest proponent of the theory and lists some more recent commentators who have held it (note 3).

possible. My apologies to reader and writer alike for the
lapses which have no doubt occurred, and for this awkward
compromise of an awkward age.[13]

---

[13]A second compromise lies in the decision to retain the
use of the masculine pronoun to refer to God as consistent
with the usage of the texts which will be discussed.

CHAPTER ONE

SAINT MOSES THE MARTYR:
THE LIFE OF MOSES IN HEBREWS 11.23-27

11.23 By faith Moses, when he was born, was hid for three
months by his parents, because they saw that the
child was beautiful; and they were not afraid of
the king's edict.

.24 By faith Moses, when he was grown up, refused to be
called the son of Pharoah's daughter,

.25 choosing rather to share ill-treatment with the
people of God than to enjoy the fleeting pleasures
of sin.

.26 He considered abuse suffered for the Christ greater
wealth than the treasures of Egypt, for he looked
to the reward.

.27 By faith he left Egypt, not being afraid of the
anger of the king; for he endured as seeing him who
is invisible.

11.23 Πίστει Μωϋσῆς γεννηθεὶς ἐκρύβη τρίμηνον ὑπὸ τῶν
πατέρων αὐτοῦ, διότι εἶδον ἀστεῖον τὸ παιδίον,
καὶ οὐκ ἐφοβήθησαν τὸ διάταγμα τοῦ βασιλέως.

.24 Πίστει Μωϋσῆς μέγας γενόμενος ἠρνήσατο λέγεσθαι
υἱὸς θυγατρὸς Φαραώ,

.25 μᾶλλον ἑλόμενος συγκακουχεῖσθαι τῷ λαῷ τοῦ θεοῦ
ἢ πρόσκαιρον ἔχειν ἁμαρτίας ἀπόλαυσιν.

.26 μείζονα πλοῦτον ἡγησάμενος τῶν Αἰγύπτου θησαυρῶν
τὸν ὀνειδισμὸν τοῦ Χριστοῦ. ἀπέβλεπεν γὰρ εἰς
τὴν μισθαποδοσίαν.

.27 Πίστει κατέλιπεν Αἴγυπτον, μὴ φοβηθεὶς τὸν θυμὸν
τοῦ βασιλέως· τὸν γὰρ ἀόρατον ὡς ὁρῶν ἐκαρτέρησεν.

The portrait of Moses in 11.23-27 offers a particularly
advantageous starting point for this study. It is the longest,
and perhaps the only, direct treatment of Moses in the letter.
As a chronological narrative, a very condensed "life of Moses"
or "portrait of the prophet as a young man," it is easily
compared to the biblical stories and the narratives of later
writers in the "life of Moses" tradition. Because the passage
treats the early life of Moses, beginning here enables us to
follow the biblical chronology of Moses' life and to measure
the picture of Moses in Hebrews against it. Finally, the high
degree of formal definition in this passage makes its function

17

more readily identifiable and invites comparison with a variety
of other texts which are similar in form. For all of these
reasons, He. 11.23-27 is a passage in which the unique details
of Hebrews' portrait of Moses are thrown into high relief and
questions about his function in the letter are raised in an
acute fashion.

The highly formal character of the passage requires some
attention. This chapter will make a series of observations
about the relation of form, function and interpretation of the
scripture in chapter 11 of Hebrews. First, Hebrews 10.32-11.4
is a list of exempla, similar to other Jewish and Christian
lists but nearly identical in form and function to *1 Clement*
17-19, a list of examples attested by God. However, the list
in Hebrews differs from that of *1 Clement* in that the list of
those attested by God is made to function as a list of
witnesses as well. Second, the exemplum of Moses in 11.23-27
is a complete unit in which Moses is presented as the example
of endurance (καρτερία); however, the endurance (καρτερία) of
Moses is not the moral virtue of self-restraint preached by the
Hellenistic philosopher, but the martyr's endurance. Third,
the examination of the function of Moses in regard to the
rest of the chapter suggests that Hebrews' whole list be seen
as a martyrology, brought to completion by the example and the
saving deed of Christ. Fourth, examination of the use of the
scripture in 11.23-27 shows that the Old Testament texts to
which these verses refer have been selected by and accommodated
to the portrait of Moses as a martyr, and a Christian martyr
at that.

10.32-12.3, Form: a list of attested witnesses.

The eleventh chapter of Hebrews is a list of examples
illustrating the definition of faith in 11.1. Similar lists
occur in Sirach (44-50), 1 Maccabees 2, 4 Maccabees 16.20-23,
Wisdom 10, Acts 7, and *1 Clement* 4-6 (negative examples), 7,
10-12, 31, 45, 55. Philo casts two of his moral treatises in
the form of exemplary anecdotes (*De Virtutibus*, 198-225; *De
Praemiis et Poenis*, 7-78) and uses abbreviated lists as well
(*Legum Allegoria* II.53-59, III.228). The form is generally
taken to be a commonplace of Hellenistic parenesis, extensively

adopted and thoroughly adapted by Hellenistic Judaism.[1] Indeed,
the contribution of the Jewish community is so great that it
might be more accurate to speak of a combination of two forms,
the collection of moral exempla and a form which is actually a
résumé of the saving history summarized in the persons of God's
friends and prophets and illustrating a single aspect of God's
working in that history.[2] The sermon of Stephen in Acts 7, for
instance, in no way can be seen as a piece of moral teaching;
the overt function intended for it by the author of Luke-Acts
is probably best described as kerygmatic; its latent function
is clearly apologetic: the sermon seeks to convict the Jews
of the sin of rejection of God not merely in the present but in
their history. Most of these lists, however, combine the
functions of exhorting the readers to the particular virtue
exemplified (or the practice of virtue) and showing forth its
meaning in God's salvific plan.

Hebrews 11 and *1 Clement* 17-19: The testimony list.

The closest parallel to the list in Hebrews 11 is *1
Clement* 17-19. Without fully discussing the much debated
relationship of Hebrews and *1 Clement*, I would like to
suggest that Hebrews 11 and *1 Clement* 17-19 are related by a
common form which is of more significance than any putative
dependence.[3] Together, Hebrews 11 and *1 Clement* 17-19
represent a version of the exemplary list which might be
called a *testimony* list or a list of *attested examples*. The
form is distinguished by a specialized use of the word μαρτυρέω
to refer to testimony from God (taken from or discovered in the
scriptures) which guarantees the exemplary function of the

---

[1]Ceslaus Spicq, *L'Épitre aux Hébreux I, Introduction*
(Paris: J. Gabalda et Cie, 1952), 19-21. Cf. Otto Michel, *Der
Brief an die Hebräer* (Göttingen: Vandenhoeck and Ruprecht,
1955), 244-245.

[2]Spicq, II, *Commentaire*, 335-336. Cf. Ethelbert Stauffer,
Theology of the New Testament tr. John Marsh (London: SCM
Press LTD, 1955), 240-241; Hans Windisch, *Der Hebräerbrief*,
Handbuch zum Neuen Testament 14 (Tübingen: J. C. B. Mohr,
Second Edition, 1931), 98-99.

[3]On the formal relationship of the lists of *1 Clement* and
Hebrews 11, see Stauffer, 240; Michel, 245.

figures who are presented for the edification of the readers.[4]
Not only is the word used in this rather special sense in both
passages, but it also plays a formal role in their structure.
The form as distinguished by the use of this word consists in
1) a brief introduction to the list which explains it as a list
of those who exemplify the virtue and are "attested" by God;
2) the series of exempla, explaining how each figure a) was
"attested" and b) exemplified the virtue; 3) a hortatory
conclusion, urging the reader to attend to these models who
were so highly "attested" and to press on to the goal which
they, presumably, have attained. A comparison of the two
passages is needed to clarify the common form and the highly
individual use to which Hebrews puts it. Since *1 Clement*
treats the form in a more straightforward manner, it is easier
to use it as the standard of comparison.

1) *Introduction*: Both lists open with a reference to the
exempla as "attested" by God.

1 Clement	Hebrews
Let us become imitators of those who preached the coming of Christ...the prophets and those who were *attested*.	By it the ancients *received testimony*.[5]

2) *Exempla*. The individual exempla are formally, but not
rigidly, constructed. *1 Clement* 17-18 contains four exempla
whose form consists of a) the name of the example; b) the
attestation, in the first and the last examples referred to by
the word μαρτυρέω; c) the words of the example which demonstrate his humility.[6] Thus:

---

[4]This formulation is my own and is intended only to
convey the reference of the word in these two passages. But
see: Michel, 249-250, 253; also Spicq II, 240; George Wesley
Buchanan, *To the Hebrews:* AB 36 (Garden City, New York:
Doubleday and Company, Inc., 1973), 183.

[5]RSV, "For by it, men of old received divine approval."
In order to make clear the function of the vocabulary, I have
used my own translation of citations from Hebrews and *1 Clement*
in this section.

[6]For a similar but less detailed analysis of the form of
the passage see: Robert M. Grant and Holt H. Graham, *The
Apostolic Fathers* II: *First and Second Clement* (New York:
Thomas Nelson and Sons, 1965), 40.

a) Abraham

b) was greatly *attested* (ἐμαρτυρήθη μεγάλως) and was
    called a friend of God

c) and says, gazing upon the glory of God and humbling
    himself: "But I am earth and ashes" (*1 Cl*.17.2).

The form of the exempla in Hebrews differs from that in
1 Clement and is further modified as it continues. The formal
pattern seems to be that of the first two exempla. Each of
these a) begins with the word πίστει; b) gives the model's
name; c) refers to the occasion on which the model's faith was
proven; d) alludes to God's *witness* to the example:

a) By faith

b) Enoch

c) was translated so that he did not see death and "he
    was not found, because God had translated him"
    (Gn. 5.24).

d) But before his translation, *he is attested* "to have
    pleased God" (Gn. 5.24 LXX); but without faith it is
    impossible to please him. For the one who draws near
    to God must believe that he exists and is the rewarder
    of those that seek him (He. 11.5-6).

However, this pattern is modified after the first two examples,
and this modification affects the testimony.

In *1 Clement* and the first two exempla in Hebrews, the
testimonies given to the saints are scriptural allusions, at
times explicitly introduced by the word μαρτυρέω, usually in
the passive. God is always understood to be the witness. Very
often the testimony is a highly traditional, almost stereo-
typical, way of referring to the model: Abraham the friend of
God (*1 Cl*. 17.2); Moses faithful in all God's house (*1 Cl*.
17.5); Abel the righteous (He. 11.4). The testimony which the
model receives from God guarantees the exemplary function of
that figure, because the praise God gives assures the reader
that the model is worthy of being followed. The testimony,
however, does not necessarily acclaim the virtue the model here
exemplifies: *1 Clement*--they were greatly attested, but they
had humility, so follow their example; Hebrews--their faith
made them righteous, which brought them God's testimony, so
have faith. Hebrews appears to lose interest in this function
of the testimony after 11.6, so the question is raised: how
is Hebrews using the scriptural testimonies, and should they

be regarded as testimonies at all? Other questions follow
from it: How is the chapter related to "testimony lists"
(i.e. lists of scriptural citations based upon a theological
theme)? Was there a Jewish or Jewish-Christian *Vorlage* and if
so, how is the chapter related to it?[7] These last questions
are beyond the scope of this study and can be postponed with
the assertion that the author, whether using sources or
traditions, exercises a creative, purposeful and selective
interpretation.

   3) *Conclusion*. Each list concludes with a summary
underlining the point of the exempla.

1 Clement 19.1	Hebrews 11.39

The humility and submission through obedience of so many and such great models, *attested* in this way, has made better not only us but also the generations before us.	and all these, *though attested* through faith did not receive the promise...

τῶν τοσούτων οὖν καὶ τοιούτων οὕτως <u>μεμαρτυρημένων</u> τὸ ταπεινόφρον καὶ τὸ ὑποδεὲς διὰ τῆς ὑπακοῆς οὐ μόνον ἡμᾶς, ἀλλὰ καὶ τῆς πρὸ ἡμῶν γενεᾶς βελτίους ἐποιήσεν.	καὶ οὗτοι πάντες <u>μαρτυρηθέν-</u> <u>τες</u> διὰ τῆς πίστεως οὐκ ἐκομίσαντο τὴν ἐπαγγελίαν...

The exhortation then urges the readers on to the goal, using
the athletic metaphor for the moral life:

1 Clement 19.2	Hebrews 12.1

...let us race on for the goal of peace handed down to us from the beginning...	...let us run with perseverance the race that is set before us...

and directs their sights to a heavenly example:

1 Clement 19.2,3	Hebrews 12.2,3

...and let us gaze upon the father and creator.... Let us look upon him with the understanding and contemplate with the eyes of the soul his long-suffering purpose.	...looking (onward) to Jesus the pioneer and perfecter of our faith.... Consider him who endured from sinners such hostility against himself....

The function of the last two features of the conclusions will
be considered below. Before we go on, however, it is necessary

---

[7]See Windisch, 98-99.

to note the questions raised by one feature of the references
to *attestation* in *1 Clement* 19.1 and Hebrews 11.39.

In both passages, the reference to the testimony is filled
out by an instrumental phrase which can be read in a variety of
ways. In *1 Clement* 19.1 "through obedience" (διὰ τῆς ὑπακοῆς)
can be read in any of three ways: 1) as modifying the humility
and submission: "obedient humility and submission;"[8] 2) as the
cause of their attestation: "humility and submission attested
through their obedience;" and 3) as the means of our improve-
ment: "made us better through (our) obedience" (i.e., to
their example).[9] In Hebrews 11.39 the phrase "through faith"
(διὰ τῆς πίστεως) can be read either "attested by faith" or
"did not receive the promise through their faith." This
multiplicity of meanings appears intentional; the writers
conclude by urging their readers to note that faith or obedient
submission and humility got the models their testimony, and
also was part of God's saving plan. But on the last point,
1 Clement and Hebrews differ in such a way as to raise another
major question about Hebrews' interpretation of the scripture.

Both Hebrews and *1 Clement* have a highly dispensational
view of salvation history; that is, both emphasize the continuity between old and new, seeing in each era of revelation a
dispensation of God's saving grace, although the former is
incomplete, a shadow of the new, perfect and final dispensation. For *1 Clement* the examples preach the coming of Christ
(17.1); they improve not only the Christian reader of the
scripture but also the earlier generations to whom they also
preached (19.1). Hebrews also regards the old dispensation,
even the old laws of worship, as an efficacious means of
grace and forgiveness, but imperfect, incomplete. Perhaps the
use of a list of Old Testament saints as exemplary presupposes

---

[8]Graham (in Grant and Graham, *First and Second Clement*,
42) translates: "The humility and obedient submission...."
Cf. Annie Jaubert, *Clément de Rome, Épitre aux Corinthiens*
SC 167 (Paris: Desclée et Cie, 1971), 133: "...tant d'humilité et de soumission dans l'obéisance...."

[9]Hippolyte Hemmer, *Les Pères Apostoliques* II, *Clément de
Rome, Épitre aux Corinthiens, Homélie du IIe Siècle* (Paris,
1926), 45, suggested this possibility: "L'humilité, l'abaisse-
ment de si grands et si saints personnages qui ont récu un
témoignage pareil nous a rendus meilleurs par l'obéissance...."

this dispensational view of salvation. However, in Hebrews 11.
39 the dispensational view seems to be superseded by other
more pressing concerns. The point of the examples according to
this verse is not that they improved those of every generation
who received their message, or that they were glorious each
in his/her own generation (Si. 44.1; cf. Wis. 7.27). Rather,
the point of the examples is that despite the testimony they
received, despite their faith and obedience, they did *not*
receive the unseen, hoped-for promise, but their perfection had
to wait on ours. It seems that their dispensation is *unlike*
ours. Hebrews' ultimate interest is not in the positive
exemplary function of the models, but rather the letter seeks
to build upon that function. The saints are not only attested,
witnessed to, by God, but also they are his *witnesses*;[10] their
faith is indeed for us also "the substance of, argument for,
things hoped for; the pledge, the proof, of things not seen."

The form transformed: Hebrews 10.32-12.3 as a "cloud of
witnesses."

Earlier in the discussion it was mentioned that *1 Clement*
uses the form in a more straightforward fashion than does
Hebrews. The differences between *1 Clement* and Hebrews in this
regard are functional differences and now that the common form
has been somewhat clarified, it is necessary to consider the
peculiar character of Hebrews' list of attested witnesses.

In order to underline the common form we have been
speaking of Hebrews 11 as if it were the complete formal unit,
with 11.2 as the introduction and 11.39-40 as the conclusion.
In fact the formal unit extends beyond these limits (as we
have already intimated); the exhortation actually begins in
10.32 and conludes in 12.3 with a transition to a new
exhortation. The character of the witness list in Hebrews can
only be understood by taking the full exhortation into account.

The introductory material begins in 10.32 with a call to
remember their early endurance and in the face of that memory
to call up hope and perseverance that they may "receive the

---

[10]Otto Küss, *Der Brief an die Hebräer* (Regensburg, 1966),
166. Cf. also 171, 180, 185; also Michel, 287-288, and Windisch, 101, where he speaks of the examples as "Glaubenzeugen."

promise" (κομίσησθε τὴν ἐπαγγελίαν). This exhortation is
undergirded with a citation from the scripture (Hab. 2.3-4) the
center of which is the dictum, "My just man shall live by
faith." To this is added a definition of faith: "faith is the
substance of things hoped for, the pledge of things not seen."
(RSV "assurance of things hoped for, conviction of things not
seen.") The exempla are then given; they are intended as
illustrations of both the citation and the definition. The
first two or three figures (Abel, Enoch and Noah) are care-
fully, even laboriously described in these terms. But as the
testimony is dropped, the exempla begin to focus on the
saving events of the history rather than on the person and
character of the models. Not each example, but each event is
introduced with the words "by faith." Thus the case of
Abraham is not only a summary of his life, character and faith,
but also a capsule history of the promise, touching upon his
call and sojourn in 7-10, upon the conception of Isaac in 11-
12, the delay in fulfillment in 13-16 and the binding of Isaac
in 17-19. The shift puts the exemplary behavior of the models
in a new perspective; it becomes less significant that their
deeds were proven to have been examples of faith than that
their deeds testify to the content of our faith. Their
yearning is a witness to a heavenly homeland ("for if they
were remembering the one from which they went out, they had
the opportunity to return " 11.16). Their martyrdoms were
the testimony of a better resurrection (11.35-38). Indeed, the
dispensational view of Hebrews turns out to be more acute
than that of *1 Clement* precisely because in Hebrews the
saints have not yet received the promise, for their perfection
awaits ours, which is still held out, and the coming of Christ
which these witnesses preach is also in the future for their
Christian hearers (10.37, 12.26-28). Thus the real hortatory
conclusion of the list regards them less as attested than as
witnesses: they are exemplary figures because their faith in
what they did not or did not yet see is attested by God in the
scriptures. But because they, though attested died without
having received the promise, they are something more: they
are "a cloud of witnesses" (12.1) to the "better thing which
God had foreseen for us" (11.40).

One final difference between Hebrews' handling of the form and that of *1 Clement* should be noted. In *1 Clement* also the treatment of examples of humility extends beyond the boundaries we have assumed. *1 Clement* 16 presents Christ as the great example of humility; 19.2-3 makes the transition to an exhortation to peace, using God as the example. This peace, which should be the result of their humility, is then authorized by the exemplary peace and order of God's creation (*1 Cl.* 20). Creation and the example of Christ also appear in Hebrews 10.32-12.3, but in Hebrews, they are more fully integrated into the formal list of examples. The whole passage becomes the story of the role of faith in the salvation history in the Bible as the author of Hebrews knows it, beginning with creation and ending with the witness of the Maccabees.[11] This whole is then surmounted with the climactic example of Christ, the pioneer and perfecter of faith, its beginning and end, who is not merely the last step in that history, the final example, but embraces the whole of it, who is the meaning of the history as he is its end. Thus the substantive meaning of faith is underlined here also; not only does the faith of the saints offer a basis for ours, but their faith and ours alike is founded and brought to completion on and by Christ.

Hebrews 10.32-12.3 is then an exhortation to faith made through an exemplary list of attested witnesses, whose lives, deeds and deaths proclaim the meaning of the history of which they are the summation by faith. Hebrews' attested examples are not merely famous men who inspire the reader by their faithful, even heroic example. They are also witnesses who seek to convince, who give their evidence (πίστις) for the role of faith in the salvation history, for the unseen and hoped for recompense on which they secured the conduct of their lives. Thus the function of the witness list in Hebrews 11 has been clarified and we can now turn to the exemplum of Moses and ask how Moses in Hebrews 11.23-27 fulfills the dual role of attested example and exemplary witness.

---

[11] It is not absolutely certain that 11.35 refers to the Maccabean martyrs, but it is very likely; cf. Buchanan, 203.

The form of Hebrews 11.23-27: Moses the Martyr, example of endurance.

The formal exemplum of Moses as example and witness of faith consists in Hebrews 11.23-27; 28 and the verses which follow seem to belong to another formal unit. Both external evidence and the selection of Old Testament texts testify to this.[12] However, the most convincing argument for regarding this passage as a unit is the recognition of the internal structure of the passage and its homiletic function. The life (or faith) of Moses is presented in three parallel statements in these verses, each of which a) beings with the words "By faith" (πίστει); b) describes an event in the life of Moses in which his faith is demonstrated; c) concludes with a comment upon the role of faith in that event:

.23 a. By faith
      b. Moses, when he had been born, was hidden for three months by his parents
      c. because they saw that the child was goodly and did not fear the decree of the king.

.24 a. By faith
      b. Moses, when he had grown up, refused to be called the son of Pharoah's daughter
.25   choosing rather to be maltreated with the people of God than to have the fleeting pleasure of sin,
.26   esteeming as greater wealth than the treasures of Egypt the opprobrium of Christ,
      c. for he looked away to the reward.

.27 a. By faith
      b. he abandoned Egypt, not fearing the wrath of the king
      c. for as seeing the unseen, he endured.

The last climactic comment, "he endured" (ἐκαρτέρησεν), is the clue to Moses' exemplary function; 11.23-27 presents to us an example of endurance: Moses the Martyr.

The vocabulary of Hellenistic moral teaching and the martyr's choice.

Both the vocabulary and the concepts of Hebrews 11.23-27 reflect the milieu of Jewish-Hellenistic moral teaching and

---

[12]On the selection and treatment of Old Testament texts as evincing the functional unity of the passage see below, 62. John Chrysostom is one commentator who divides the passage after 11.27.

especially the martyr tradition of Jewish Hellenism. This background is strongly suggested by both the expressions used to set out the moral choice and the function of the word "endure" in the passage and in that tradition.

In verses 24-26 the choice of Moses is emphasized with two expressions which underline the context of moral teaching: "he chose rather (μαλλὸν ἑλόμενος)...the fleeting pleasure of sin (πρόσκαιρον...ἀμαρτίας ἀπόλαυσιν)." Both expressions help to place the choice of Moses in the light of the moral choice between greater and lesser end. In Christian and Jewish literature they have an even more clearly defined context.

The word "fleeting" (πρόσκαιρον, "temporary, passing, ephemeral") occurs in the New Testament only in the context of trial and persecution.[13] In the LXX it is used exclusively in 4 Macc. 15.2,8,23. There the mother of the seven martyrs sets aside a fleeting safety (πρόσκαιρον σωτηρίαν) for her children and her own fleeting mother-love (πρόσκαιρον φιλοτεκνίαν) for "religion which saves to eternal life" (ἐυσέβειαν...τὴν σῴζουσαν εἰς αἰωνίαν ζωήν). In this passage the word "fleeting" operates in a way that is central to the exemplary function of the book, the posing of the dilemma within which the moral choice must be made: "the mother, when two choices were proposed to her, religion and the fleeting safety of her sons, loved rather (μᾶλλον ἠγάπησεν) religion" (4 Macc. 15.2). This same context of choice between a temporal and an eternal good appears in He. 11.25, "having chosen rather to be maltreated with the people of God than to have the fleeting pleasure of sin."

The same choice is presented to Joseph according to Josephus, who uses an expression synonymous to Hebrews' "fleeting pleasure." Recounting the story of Joseph and the wife of Potiphar, he presents Joseph's choice as the choice of a martyr:

> and he chose rather (μᾶλλον εἵλετο) to suffer unjustly, even to endure the most extreme penalty (ὑπομένειν τι τῶν χαλεπωτέρων) than to take the pleasure of the present (τῶν παρόντων ἀπολαύειν) upon which indulgence he knew that he would be justly condemned by his conscience.[14]

---

[13] He. 11.25, 1 Co. 4.17-18, Mk. 4.21 par.

[14] *Jewish Antiquities* II.50. Translation is my own.

As the drama progresses this vocabulary recurs and the exact
words with which the choice of Moses is described in Hebrews
also appear in Josephus' account of Joseph. As Joseph remon-
strates with the wife of Potiphar, he contrasts for her the
fleeting (πρόσκαιρον) enjoyment of lust and marriage which
brings a secure pleasure (ἀπόλαυσις). Josephus' use of these
words underlines for us certai.. aspects of their function:

1) Their context is parenetic: the whole passage is
couched in the standard language of Hellenistic moral teaching:
ὑπεμίμνησκε, παρεκάλει, μετανοίαν, διορθώσει, συνειδότος,
παρρησία, all occur, many of them more than once within a
short passage.

2) The significant words are used to set out the moral
choice both in describing the dilemma of Joseph and in recounting his attempt to persuade the woman.

3) The choice of Joseph and that of Potiphar's wife
differ in that Joseph chooses not between fleeting and enduring
pleasure, but between fleeting pleasure and punishment, perhaps
indeed the most dire penalty, endured for the doing of right.
This choice of suffering and foregoing of fleeting pleasure
belongs to the exemplary function of the martyr, and the
vocabulary used seems also to belong to that function.

Josephus also uses the word "pleasure" (ἀπόλαυσις) in
recounting an exemplary choice of Moses still closer to that
described in He. 11.24-27: Moses' decision to leave the
safety of Raguel's home and to join his persecuted brothers:

> I, who have secured for myself a life of ease, through
> my prowess and at thy will, thanks too to what Raguel
> my father-in-law left me, abandoning the enjoyment
> (ἀπόλαυσιν) of those good things, devoted myself to
> tribulations on behalf of this people (ἐμαυτὸν
> ἐπέδωκα ταῖς ὑπὲρ τούτων ταλαιπωρίαις). At first
> for their liberty and now for their salvation great
> are the toils I have undergone, opposing to every
> peril all the ardour of my soul.[15]

---

[15]*Ant.* IV.42 (Loeb IV, 495). My attention was called to
this passage by Windisch (103), who also remarks on other
parallels between Hebrews' vocabulary in this passage and that
of Josephus, Philo and 4 Maccabees. Although he notes the
character of the Moses passage as martyrological, he does
not explicitly make the connection with the vocabulary.

Here also Moses' choice is made between pleasure (ἀπόλαυσις) and misery.

Other uses of "pleasure" (ἀπόλαυσις, "pleasure, enjoyment, pleasurable benefit, fruition") also bear out some of these observations. In 1 Tim. 6.6, the word also occurs in a parenetic setting. *2 Clement* 10.3-4 outlines the moral choice underlining the transitory character of "pleasure:" the present pleasure; the promise to come (ἡ ἐνθάδε ἀπόλαυσις...ἡ μέλλουσα ἐπαγγελία). Finally 3 Macc. 7.16 employs it in the parenetic setting of exemplary martyr literature: the faithful who have survived persecution obtain the pleasure of safety (σωτηρίας ἀπόλαυσιν, "the enjoyment of salvation").

Thus the presence of the two words "fleeting" and "pleasure" helps to mark the passage as belonging to the milieu of Hellenistic parenesis; their function in setting out the exemplary moral choice of Moses further specifies the form of the parenesis as exemplary martyr literature. Still a third significant word, "he endured" (ἐκαρτέρησεν) confirms these two words in tying the passage into Jewish Hellenism and the martyr literature in particular. In fact, "he endured" is the most definitive of these distinctive words. As the final word of the whole exemplum, it functions as the summary statement: "as seeing the unseen, he endured." The author of Hebrews presents Moses as an example of the Hellenistic moral virtue of endurance (καρτερία). The understanding of this virtue in Hellenistic Judaism offers us further insight into the function of Moses in Hebrews' history of faith.

Philo's use of endurance (καρτερία) indicated its milieu in general moral teaching and especially its relationship to self-control (ἐγκράτεια) with which he frequently pairs it. For him the two words are either synonyms or very close complements. They are often predicated of the king or ruler, the ultimate example of the human being in the role of responsibility. This is particularly true in Philo's virtue lists. One of the lists headed by this pair is of particular interest: *De Vita Mosis* I.154 employs a virtue list as a summary of that wealth which Moses preferred to the "treasure-gathering of former rulers" (the pharoahs?).

In *De Iosepho*, Philo's comments on the "enduring power"

(τὸ καρτερικόν) and the self-control (ἐγκράτεια)[16] of the
statesman show how he conceives of them as synonymous: dominion over the desires and needs of the body gives one true
political freedom, for only the body can be seized and
subjected to the pressures of tyranny.[17] This conception makes
the pair appear frequently in the context of the standard
metaphorical representation of the moral life through the
athletic contest.

The role of this virtue in the explication of Moses'
flight is of particular interest to us. In *Leg. All.* III.11-14,
Philo makes a moral allegory (in his terminology, a "theory")
of Moses' flight which in some respects parallels He. 11.27:
for Philo, Moses does not flee, but, like a good athlete,
withdraws before "opinion, the leader of the passions--that
is Pharoah" (ἡγεμονίδος τῶν παθῶν δόξας φαραὼ)[18] to "reason,
the practitioner of endurance" (καρτερίας ἀσκητὴν λογισμόν).[19]
Josephus also sees the flight of Moses before Pharoah in terms
of endurance although he envisions that flight on a more
concrete level: Moses escaped from the plot of Pharoah by
departing "unequipped with provisions...for he despised (such
things) by endurance."[20] This agreement in the three very
disparate interpretations of Philo, Josephus and Hebrews
suggests that by some strange metonomy the flight of Moses
became a standard illustration of the virtue of endurance in
Jewish Hellenism. Even with this conclusion, Hebrews' interpretation seems to require a more specific content for this
virtue than self-control understood as moderation or even as
heroism: as the choice facing Moses is not between acquired
and natural wealth, or between fleeting pleasure and lasting
good, but between wealth in Egypt and maltreatment with the
people of God, so also his departure from Egypt ought to be

---

[16]*De Ios.* 54.

[17]*De Ios.* 68.

[18]*Leg. All.* III.13.

[19]*Leg. All.* III.10.

[20]*Ant.* II.256-257.

exemplary of more than a rational asceticism.

Endurance as the virtue of martyrs.

Something more must then be implied by "endurance" and
the LXX seems to provide the more specific content which is
needed to explain its import in He. 11.27. In the LXX,
excluding the Maccabean literature, the word is used only in
the form of the verb and that only four times. Twice it
clearly means "to suffer" (Job 2.9, Is. 42.14); twice more it
occurs in Sirach, once meaning "persevere" (12.15) and once,
interestingly enough, exhorting the one who decides to serve
the Lord "...prepare yourself for trial" (2.1-2).

In the Maccabean literature, however, the word appears
over twenty times and these various meanings appear to be
subsumed and transformed into a new context. Especially in
4 Maccabees, that tract for martyrdom as reasonable moral
action, it is evident that the LXX meaning "suffer" has been
combined with the Hellenistic virtue of self-control to make
endurance (καρτερία) *the* martyr-virtue. It is endurance-
perseverance which the martyrs prove in the tortures. As
the youths in defiance of the tyrant undergo his torments, they
warn him of the recompense: in the future he will endure
torment in retribution for the unjust torture to which they are
subjected.[21] Alongside this very Jewish expression of retribution, they hail the torture sessions under the Hellenizing
metaphor of the athletic games, even to the point of calling
them "the exercise of gymnasium rights" (γυμνασίαν), the sign
of enfranchisement in the Hellenistic city (4 Macc. 11.20).

The complex exemplary function of endurance is perhaps
clearest in 4 Macc. 16.14, which demonstrates its principal
aspects: it is at once exemplary and apologetic; it glorifies
the persecuted religion by presenting the very resistance of
its witnesses as exemplary of the highest virtues of the
persecuting culture. Thus for the sake of religion and by
the gift of its God, even the weakness of woman and child is
endowed with courage (ἀνδρεία) and self-control: "O mother,
o warrior of God on piety's behalf, though old and a woman,

---

[21] 4 Macc. 9.9. Cf. 9.30, 10.11.

on endurance's account (διὰ καρτερίαν) you have both conquered
a tyrant and been found in word and deed mightier than a hero"
(ἂν ἀνδρός).

In a similar tone, Hebrews presents the exemplum of Moses
the Martyr in 11.23-27, whose faith in the unseen God rescued
him at his birth and in his youth, defying first the edict of
Pharoah, then the wealth and status of Egypt, then the king's
wrath at the peril of his life. Like the Maccabean martyrs
he chose ill-treatment and reproach: "for as seeing the
unseen, he endured."

Moses the martyr, example of Christians.

The exemplary function of Moses' choice becomes clearer
when one examines its relation to the exhortation as a whole
and in particular to the hortatory introduction and conclusion
of the list. Comparison with these passages demonstrates
that Moses' choice is presented in such terms as to conform it
both to the situation of the "Hebrews" and to the deed of
Christ.

In 10.33-35, the author of Hebrews puts forth an appeal
to perseverance by calling up for the readers their past vigor
and fidelity. In the past they themselves struggled with
opprobrium (ὀνειδισμοῖς 10.33) and trials; they shared the
lot (κοινωνοὶ...γενηθέντες 10.33) of those who underwent such
sufferings; they suffered the loss of their goods (10.34).
All this they did out of their confidence (παρρησία 10.35)
which is placed in a better and abiding possession (10.34), a
great recompense (μισθαποδοσίαν 10.35). Thus their past
fidelity is described in terms of a martyr's heroism, and
Moses' trials and his choice are accommodated to this interpretation of their experience and choice.[22] He chose "ill-
treatment with the people of God" (11.25), he gave over "the
treasures of Egypt" (11.26), "he looked ahead to the reward"
(μισθαποδοσίαν 11.26). He even bore "the opprobrium of Christ"

---

[22]On the choice as a martyr's choice, cf. Theodoret, who
says that Moses was only able to make the choice to share his
kinsfolk's ill-treatment because he saw the *contest* master
(ἀγωνοθέτην) with the eyes of faith (*Interpretatio Epistulae
ad Hebraeos* PG 82.765).

(τὸν ὀνειδισμὸν τοῦ Χριστοῦ 11.26). This last phrase reflects
an extreme exemplary appropriation, for "the opprobrium of
Christ" is exactly what "the Hebrews" have suffered according
to 10.35: opprobrium because they were Christ's.

As Moses' exemplary function is molded to the situation
of the recipients (at least as the author envisages it), and
in particular to the choice that is set before them, so also
is it conformed to the climactic example of Jesus, the pioneer
and perfecter of faith (12.2). Like Moses sharing the ill-
treatment of the people of God, he set aside the joy proposed
for him (ἀντὶ τῆς προκειμένης χαρᾶς 12.2) to share in the
contest proposed for us (cf. 12.1, τὸν προκείμενον ἀγῶνα).[23]
Thus the choice of Moses is not only a model to be imitated,
but also the type of the choice of Christ.[24] Both Jesus and
Moses proclaim the character of our choice: it is a choice
between present pleasure and present pain endured for the sake
of a well-attested but unseen reward (11.27, 12.2).

Precisely in the choice set before him Moses illustrates
through his faith the definition "substance of things hoped
for, pledge of things not seen." Each of the three events in
the exemplum deals with a conflict in which the seen must be
weighed against the unseen (or the not-yet-seen, cf. 11.7).
This conflict is most fully developed in 11.24-26: Moses gave
over the good fortune which he already possessed as the son of
Pharoah's daughter for the sorry lot of God's people. Why?
Because he saw the treasure of Egypt as the benefits of sin
which are fleeting and looked ahead to the (unseen, but
lasting) recompense. He has the martyr's conviction which is
expressed by Paul: "...the things that are seen are fleeting,
but the things that are unseen are eternal..." (τὰ γὰρ
βλεπόμενα πρόσκαιρα, τὰ μὴ βλεπόμενα αἰώνια 2 Co. 4.17-18).
The trial of the present is light in comparison with the glory
that it brings; the one who suffers for God is certain of
unseen but lasting good.

---

[23]For the use of προκείμενος to present the martyr's
choice cf. 4 Macc. 15.2: μήτηρ, δυεῖν προκειμένων, "The
mother, when two choices were *proposed* to her...."

[24]Buchanan (208) also remarks on the likeness of Moses to
Christ in his choice.

This choice also lies behind the exemplary function of
the other exempla, although it is not always as clear as in
11.23-27.[25] But according to the exemplum of Moses, faith
in the unseen appears to be expressed or accomplished in some
kind of seeing. The final comment on each of the events is
not only a comment upon the role of faith in the event, but
also a suggestion of the role of a vision in that event:

.23 ...because they *saw* (εἶδον) that the child was
   beautiful...

.26 ...for he *looked ahead* (ἀπέβλεπεν) to the recompense.

.27 ...for as *seeing* the *unseen* (τὸν ἀόρατον ὡς ὁρῶν)
   he endured.

The deeds which are done, the choice which is made by faith are
grounded on or motivated by a vision of the unseen. Since
this theme is not prominent in the other exempla, the question
arises whether it is a peculiar feature of the author's
interpretation of the life of Moses.[26] Earlier in this
discussion the question of the author's hermeneutical method
was raised. Both of these questions should be illuminated by
an attempt to describe the exegesis which has produced this
author's version of the life of Moses.

The author's exegetical enterprise.

This brief literary and philological look at the story of
Moses in 11.23-27 identifies the passage formally as an
exemplum of faith as endurance, and the function of Moses as
the exemplary role of a martyr. The passage is shown to
function as a reinforcement of the exhortation in 10.32 ff.,
an anticipation of the Christological climax in 12.1-3 and an
illustration of the definition in 11.1. This complex function
of Moses the Martyr in the list of attested witnesses raises

---

[25]Buchanan (187-188) points out the functioning of the
theme in 11.3-7.

[26]C. K. Barrett has remarked the relationship between 11.
26b and 11.27b, noting that the two parallel comments must be
interpreted together and that when they are so interpreted they
testify to "an eschatological faith which is convinced of
future good because it knows that the good for which it hopes
already exists invisibly in God." See "The Eschatology of the
Epistle to the Hebrews," *The Background of the New Testament
and Its Eschatology*, ed. W. D. Davies and David Daube (Cambridge: At the University Press, 1956), 380 and 381.

some questions about the function of the list as a whole, as
well as leaving us with some questions about the story of
Moses.

The close conformity of the role of Moses to the situation
of the 'addressees and the climactic description of Christ in
12.2 lies precisely in the presentation of the martyr's choice.
Might this suggest that the word μάρτυς has already taken on
that specialized meaning "martyr" or "witness at the cost of
one's life" and that the list should be regarded as a sort of
early martyrology?[27] This could only be accurate if understood
in a figurative sense, as the figures involved witness by
death only in so far as they "died without receiving the
promise" (11.13, cf. 39). Further, some examples obviously
have or once had other exemplary functions; certain features
of the list might be interpreted as the remnants of lists
glorifying famous proselytes, such as those found in *Siphre*
and *Siphre Zuta*.[28] This question is far too complex to be
pursued within the confines of this study, and can claim our
attention for only passing observations.

However, a number of questions still remain about the
story of Moses, or the portrait of Moses as seen by and drawn
by the author of Hebrews. Why does the author focus on the
vision involved in Moses' faith? To what does Moses testify
as a witness? How is he attested? Seeking an answer to these
questions involves an attempt to describe more fully the
author's exegetical enterprise in 11.23-27. No direct
citations occur in these verses and the method must include
both midrashic techniques and traditions of a haggadic

---

[27]Windisch asserts that He. 11.36-38 is "ein reiner
Martyrerkatalog" and that the whole passage belongs to the
martyr-literature of Judaism and the early church. He also
notes that Moses is presented as a martyr (98). See also
Michel, 287-288, esp. n. 6 on 287. Against this is the opinion of Strathman (μάρτυς κτλ., *TDNT* IV, 486-495), who
would deny the technical martyrological meaning to the words
from this stem in both NT and contemporary Jewish sources.

[28]*Siphre Bemidbar Beha'alothka* 78, *Siphre Zuta
Beha'alothka* 10.29; *Siphre ad Numeros adjecto Siphre zutta*;
ed. H. S. Horowitz (Leipzig: Gesellschaft zur Förderung des
Wissenschaft des Judentums, 1918; reprint ed. Jerusalem:
Wahrmann Books, 1966), 72-73, 263-265.

character.[29]

Analyzing this allusive exegesis requires a number of steps. We shall take each event of the story as it stands in the letter, and attempt to discover which texts of the Old Testament are behind this interpretation, what traditions or line of traditions have contributed to it, and which interpretive step represents the particular viewpoint of Hebrews. The first of these steps is of considerable importance because the author uses the Old Testament text through partial quotations and verbal reminiscences.

11.23 The birth and preservation of Moses: faith trusting in the invisible through a visible sign.

   11.23 a) By faith

   b) Moses, when he was born, was hid for three months by his parents,

   c) because they saw that the child was beautiful; and they were not afraid of the king's edict.

   11.23 a) πίστει

   b) Μωϋσῆς γεννηθεὶς ἐκρύβη τρίμηνον ὑπὸ τῶν πατέρων αὐτοῦ

   c) διότι εἶδον ἀστεῖον τὸ παιδίον καὶ οὐκ εφοβήθησαν τὸ διάταγμα τοῦ βασιλέως.

The first event of faith in Hebrews' life of Moses is his birth and miraculous preservation, and the text which lies behind this account of it is Ex. 2.2, LXX:

...and seeing that he was beautiful, they hid him for three months.

...καὶ ἰδόντες αὐτὸ ἀστεῖον, ἐσκέπασεν αὐτὸ μῆνας τρεῖς.

This version differs somewhat from the MT:

...And she saw that he was good and she hid him for three months.

ותרא אותו כי-טוב הוא ותצפנהו שלשה ירחים...

The step from either text to the causal connection which Hebrews reads into it is very small. The use of the distinctive word αστεῖον and the plural verbs of the LXX seem to be the basis of Hebrews. However, that should not lead us to assume that the Greek text alone has contributed to Hebrews'

---

[29]See above, p.21-22.

explication of the event. Although ἀστεῖον is clearly crucial
to that explication, the Hebrew word which it represents, טוב,
also is the crux of rabbinic comments upon this text. Therefore from here on we shall refer to it by the word "goodly"
which can represent either text.

The rabbis see in this word: 1) a reflection upon Moses'
name; 2) that he was "good" or "fit" for prophecy; 3) that he
was born circumcised; 4) that the whole statement "that he was
good" (כי-טוב הוא) is a reference to Gn. 1.4 ("God saw the
light, that it was good," כי-טוב) and testifies to a display of
light which attended Moses upon his birth.[30] None of these
immediately explains Hebrews' interpretation of the event; the
first two seem to suggest a sort of prophetic insight on the
part of Moses' parents; the second two, portents of his
greatness surrounding his birth.

The Hellenistic tradition is also interested in this
comment and particularly in the distinctive word "goodly"
(ἀστεῖον). Philo's *De Vita Mosis* sees a causal connection
between the child's beauty and the parents' decision to risk
the attempt to save him:

> Now the child *from his birth* (γεννηθεὶς οὖν ὁ παῖς) had
> an appearance of more than ordinary *goodliness*
> (ἀστειότεραν ἢ κατ' ἰδιώτην), so that his parents, as
> long as they could, actually set at naught the procla-
> mations of the despot. In fact we are told that
> unknown to all but a few, he was kept at home...for
> *three* successive *months*.[31]

Philo here fixes upon a series of words and ideas very similar
to those which Hebrews finds significant. He extends the
interpretation of the verse somewhat by crediting Moses'
adoption by the daughter of Pharoah as well as his parents'
daring to this "goodliness" (...εὐγενῆ καὶ ἀστεῖον

---

[30] See *Ex. R.* 1.20, b. Sotah 12a. On Moses' having been
born circumcised, see also Pseudo-Philo, *Liber Antiquitatum
Biblicarum* 9.13,15.

[31] *Vita* I.2 (Loeb VI,281). The question of Hebrews'
dependence on Philo in any of these verses has been fully
discussed: see Ronald Williamson, *Philo and the Epistle to
the Hebrews* (Leiden: E. J. Brill, 1970), 469-479. In this
discussion it will be assumed that similarities between
Hebrews and other writers are evidence for a common tradition
of interpretation rather than of dependence.

ὀφθῆναι...).[32] So does Josephus, although without using the distinctive LXX word.[33] He comments, "...God had taken such great care in the formation of Moses that he caused him to be thought worthy of bringing up and providing for by all who had taken the most fatal resolutions against him."[34]

These comments appear to explain the word more as an indication of the extraordinary physical beauty of a hero favored by God than as a reference to some supernatural sign of divine favor, like those of the rabbinic literature. It is difficult to tell which interpretation is favored by Hebrews, but it is clear that the letter, with both traditions, interprets the peculiar word "goodly" (ἀστεῖον) as "signed by God's predilection."[35] Thus, "Moses, when he was born, was hidden three months by his parents because they saw that the child was ἀστεῖον, and at this sign of God's favor (or election) they did not fear the king's edict." Acts 7.20 is similar and still more ambiguous: "At this time (the time of the promise, Acts 7.17, and of the persecution, 7.19), Moses was born and was beautiful before God (ἀστεῖον τῷ θεῷ--divinely beautiful?[36] beautiful, i.e., pleasing, to God?). And he was brought up three months in his father's house." Acts seems not to have

---

[32]*Vita* 1.4.

[33]μεγεθοῦς τε ἔνεκα καὶ κάλλους *Ant*.II.224; μορφῇ τε θεῖον *Ant*. II.232; see also the description of the child's extraordinary beauty in *Ant*. II. 230-31.

[34]*Ant*. II. 225. The translation is that of William Whiston, *The Life and Works of Flavius Josephus* (Philadelphia: J. C. Winston, 1957), 76. It conveys the connection between Moses' physical beauty and his preservation, which is intended by the text.

[35]R. A. Greer has called my attention to the comment of Chrysostom on this verse. He interprets the child's beauty at birth as a visible sign, or rather work, of grace: "The very sight drew them on to faith...great was the Grace poured out on that righteous man...the Grace of God which also stirred up and strengthened that barbarian woman, the Egyptian, and took her and drew her on." *Homilies on the Epistle to the Hebrews*, tr. E. B. Pusey, revised Frederic Gardiner, NPNF 14 (New York: The Christian Literature Society, 1911), 483.

[36]Cf. Josephus *Ant*. II.224, μορφῇ τε θεῖον.

made the causal connection made by the others, but the
emphasis on ἀστεῖον suggests that the word is seen as a sign of
the divine favor, though possibly a sign which the parents
could not read.

Other traditions which do not rely on this word do emphasize the role of his parents' faith or obedience in Moses'
preservation. The tradition represented by pseudo-Philo
explains how Moses came to be born at all in such adverse
circumstances by magnifying the faith of Amram, his father, who
chose to reject the edict of the king ("...non acquiescam
praeceptis regis.")[37] Because of God's word in the covenant
he would maintain his part in the covenant, obeying the command
of creation to increase and multiply ("...ingrediens mulierem
meam accipiam et faciem filios ut amplificemus super terram").
Thus Amram chose the command of God over the decree of the
king.[38]

Josephus records a supernatural motive for the obedience
of Amram, a dream in which God tells him of the future greatness of the son who is to be born and reminds him of the
providence which has pursued the people from the time of
Abraham, who was alone when God called him.[39] God's exhortation in Josephus closely parallels the confession of Amram in
other sources. According to Josephus, faith also prompted
Amram to entrust Moses to the river in a basket:

> ...Amram, fearing that he would be detected and, incurring
> the king's wrath, would perish himself along with the
> young child and thus bring God's promise to naught,
> resolved to commit the salvation and protection of the
> child to Him, rather than to trust the uncertain chance
> of concealment and thereby endanger not only the child
> clandestinely reared, but himself also; assured that God
> would provide complete security that nothing should be
> falsified of that which he had spoken.[40]

---

[37]Pseudo-Philo 9.5; cf. *Sefer-ha-Zikranoth*, quoted and
translated in Renée Bloch, "Quelques aspects de la figure de
Moïse dans la tradition rabbinique," in *Moïse, l'Homme de
l'Alliance*, Cahiers Sioniens (Paris: Desclée et Cie, 1955),
111-113.

[38]9.4; see 9.3-6.

[39]*Ant.* II.210-216.

[40]*Ant.* II.219 (Loeb IV, 259).

His conviction of providence is the result of the dream-vision
preceding the birth of the child.[41]

Miriam "the prophetess" supplements her father's testimony
with a prophetic dream foretelling the birth and greatness of
Moses, according to *Mekilta*, pseudo-Philo and *Sefer ha-
Zikranoth*.[42] In other sources, her prophecy entirely supplants
his profession; still elsewhere, Amram's faith is less highly
thought of and she rebukes him for having decreed with the
elders of Israel that children ought not to be conceived in
the bondage of Egypt.[43]

These traditions about Amram's dream or Miriam's prophecy
attempt to explain how Moses came to be born at all, and then
how he survived under the decree of Pharoah. The basic
answer is "because of the faith of Amram, because he believed
the unseen providence of God, his plan and promises for Israel,
his law and word more powerful than the might of Pharoah."
Although both question and answer are more elaborate in all
these traditions than in Hebrews, they are similar. Indeed,
the fact that Hebrews fills in the "they" of the LXX Ex. 2.2
with "fathers" may indicate some knowledge of the traditions
about Amram.

How then was Moses preserved at his birth? By faith,
which though "it deals with things unseen, still through some
visible signs we are able to confide ourselves to it."[44] Since
his parents set greater store on the might of God to fulfill
his promises than on the might of Pharoah to fulfill his
decree, they hid him, because they saw he was goodly (ἀστεῖον)
--they saw on him the favor of God.

---

[41]*Ant.* II.212-215.

[42]*Mekilta Shirata* 10; Jacob K. Lauterbach, *Mekilta de-
Rabbi Ishmael* (Philadelphia: The Jewish Publication Society
of America, 1949), II, 55: cf. Pseudo-Philo, 9.10; *Sefer-ha-
Zikranoth* in Bloch, 108-109, also *Chronique de Moïse* in Bloch,
108.

[43]*Exodus Rabbah* 1.13.

[44]Aquinas, *Ad Hebraeos* 613: "...quod licet fides sit de
invisibilibus tamen per aliqua signa visibilia possumus niti
ad ipsam.

11.24-26 Moses rejoins his people: faith reckoning against the present the recompense which is not yet seen.

11.24 a) By faith

     b) Moses, when he had grown up, refused to be called the son of Pharoah's daughter,

.25   choosing rather to be maltreated with the people of God than to have the fleeting pleasure of sin,

.26   esteeming as greater wealth than the treasures of Egypt the opprobrium of Christ.

     c) for he looked ahead to the reward.

11.24 a) πίστει

     b) Μωϋσῆς μέγας γενόμενος ἠρνήσατο λέγεσθαι υἱὸς θυγατρὸς Φαραώ,

.25   μᾶλλον ἑλόμενος συγκακουχεῖσθαι τῷ λαῷ τοῦ θεοῦ ἢ πρόσκαιρον ἔχειν ἁμαρτίας ἀπόλαυσιν,

.26   μείζονα πλοῦτον ἡγησάμενος τῶν Αἰγύπτου θησαυρῶν τὸν ὀνειδισμὸν τοῦ Χριστοῦ·

     c) ἀπέβλεπεν γὰρ εἰς τὴν μισθαποδοσίαν.

The event of faith celebrated in 11.24-26 is an event of Moses' life which is not recorded in any direct fashion in the scriptures. The exegetical work which lies behind these verses is extremely complex, involving a number of interpretive steps.

The first step is represented by the assumption that Moses was called "the son of Pharoah's daughter" and that he thereby had access to the "fleeting pleasures of sin" (or perhaps, "the temporary enjoyment of its benefits"), that is, "the treasures of Egypt." Ex. 2.10 says "...he became her son...." For Philo this clearly means not only adoption, but also that Moses is Pharoah's heir.[45] Josephus concurs in this, as does the bulk of the tradition.[46] This assumption may reflect the rather stringent legal functioning of the Roman practice of *adoptio*, which placed the adopted person in the legal position of a natural son of the family, and would thus have made Moses the heir of Pharoah, who, as our sources hasten to explain, had no male heir of his own.[47] If this is indeed the legal background of their deduction, the stage is set for Moses' heroic

---

[45]*Vita* I.32, 149 ff.

[46]*Ant.* II.232; *Jub.* 47; *Tanchuma* תזריעה 155a.

[47]*Vita* I.12-13.

refusal, for a choice is automatically placed before him. The legal practice of *adoptio* destroyed the status of the adopted son in his natural family.[48]

How and when did Moses "refuse to be called the son of Pharoah's daughter?" The answer to this question is found in the allusion in 24: "when he had grown up." These words are taken from Ex. 2.11: "It happened after those many days that, *when he had grown up, Moses* (μεγας γενόμενος Μωϋσῆς) went out to his brothers, the sons of Israel. Looking upon their labor, he saw a man, an Egyptian, striking a certain Hebrew...." After He. 11.23 a Western variant[49] fills in the gap in Moses' history with a condensation of the LXX account of Moses' slaying of the Egyptian:

    a) By faith
    b) *when he had grown up Moses* slew the Egyptian
    c) *looking upon* the humiliation of his brothers.

    a) Πιστει
    b) μεγας γενομενος Μωυσης ανειλεν τον Αιγυπτον
    c) κατανοων την ταπεινωσιν των αδελφων αυτου.

Clearly some corrector felt that this incident explained or preceded Moses' rejection of his title.

This explanation can in part be discovered in the traditional interpretation of Ex. 2.11 ff. The statement that Moses *went out* to his brothers was generally understood to mean that he chose to disassociate himself from the ruling house of Egypt. The words for "he went out" receive particular attention in both Hebrew and Greek interpreters. *Exodus Rabbah* records a tradition that explains "he went out" (ויצא) in this fashion: Pharoah's daughter was so enamoured of Moses that she constrained him to remain continually within the palace,[50] but, says the Midrash,

---

[48]See *Oxford Classical Dictionary*, 1970, "ADOPTIO." However, the practice was limited to Roman citizens and the (presumably more widespread) Greek practices were less stringent (see article "ADOPTION, GREEK"), so this background cannot be assumed.

[49]D*, 1827, it. Cf. Nestle.

[50]*Ex. R.*1.26.

...HE WENT OUT UNTO HIS BRETHREN. This righteous man went out on two occasions and God recalled them one after another. *He went out on the second day*.... These were the two occasions.[51]

Ezechiel the Tragedian is more explicit:

When I reached full maturity
I went out of the royal house (for to works
anger drove me and the machination of the king).[52]

ἐπεὶ δὲ πλήρης κόλπος ἡμέρων παρῆν
ἐξῆλθον οἴκων βασιλικῶν· πρὸς ἔργα γὰρ
θύμος μ'ἄνωγε καὶ τέχνασμα βασιλεῶς.

Like *Exodus Rabbah* Ezechiel sees in the verse a statement that Moses left the royal palace. But he also supplies a motive from the second part of the verse: he was driven to depart by anger (his own? the king's?) and the king's machinations and he was driven to "works."

The "machination" or "cunning" of the king which drove Moses "to works" seems to be displayed in Ex. 1.10 where Pharoah says of Israel, "Come, let us *deal shrewdly* with them, lest they multiply.... And he set over them overseers *of the works* (τῶν ἔργων) that they might wrong them *in the works* (ἐν τοῖς ἔργοις)." Ezechiel has used this verse to interpret the second part of Ex. 2.11: "He went out to his brothers. Looking upon their labor (πόνον)...."[53] Philo similarly records that the forced labor which Pharoah exacted from the Hebrews angered Moses[54] and turned him from his former allegiance to his adoptive parents.[55] He did what he could for his brothers, interceding for them with the overseers and exhorting them to courage. His willingness to take up their cause ended in the slaying of the Egyptian, which earned for him the indignation

---

[51] *Ex. R.* 1.27 (Soncino, 34). Citations are Ex. 2.11, 13.

[52] Eusebius, *Praeparatio Evangelica* 9.28 (PG 21.737).

[53] Thus "works" are "the works" to which the Hebrews were put. In this case τέχνασμα βασιλέως might mean "the king's projects" rather than "the king's machinations." It is also possible that ἔργα is meant to refer to Moses' mighty acts on behalf of Israel, though this seems less likely.

[54] *Vita* I.40.

[55] *Vita* I.33.

and enmity of the king: "What he felt so strongly was not that one man had been killed by another whether justly or unjustly, but that his own daughter's son did not think with him...." This anger of the king which was directed against Moses because he "...loved those whom he (the king) rejected and pitied those to whom he was relentless and inexorable,"[56] finally drove Moses to "retire to the neighboring country of Arabia."[57]

The rabbinic tradition also elaborates the text "and he looked on their burdens" to show how Moses involved himself on behalf of his brothers: he sorted out the burdens so that they were suited in size to the bearer;[58] himself he shared in the bearing;[59] he got Pharoah to permit them the sabbath.[60]

Thus for the whole tradition of interpretation, when Moses grew up, he became aware of his kinsmen and their oppression; he went out and shared in the burdens that he saw, "choosing...to be maltreated (συγκακουχεῖσθαι; cf. Ex. 1.11 LXX ἵνα κακώσωσιν αὐτοὺς ἐν τοῖς ἔργοις) with the people of God." But even more directly related to this choice is the interpretation given to Ex. 2.12:

> AND HE SAW AN EGYPTIAN SMITING A HEBREW. R. Huna in the name of Bar Kappara said: Israel was redeemed on account of four things, one being that they did not change their names.[61]

The translator[62] seems to assume that this comment is misplaced here and that the really significant item with regard to Ex. 2.12 is rather "that there was no fornication among

---

[56]*Vita* I.45 (Loeb VI, 299).

[57]*Vita* I.47 (Loeb VI, 301).

[58]*Ex. R.* 1.27, cf. *Lev. R.* 37.2.

[59]*Ex. R.* 1.27.

[60]*Ex. R.* 1.28.

[61]*Ibid.* (Soncino, 35).

[62]S. M. Lehrman (*ibid.*) seems to think that this comment is simply a shorthand for the list of four reasons, only one of which—that they were never suspected of immorality—is relevant. He refers the reader to *S. of S. R.* IV.12.

them." This assumption is due to the haggadic creation which is attached to explain what else Moses saw.[63] But the comment does refer to our verse.   Moses saw an *Egyptian* smiting a *Hebrew*--because he was and was known as a *Hebrew*. Because Israel did not change their names (so as to be no longer known as *Hebrews*), the Holy One, blessed be He, redeemed them.[64] Hebrews 11.24 gives a similar interpretation of the incident, but refers it to Moses. Moses by his intervention on behalf of the Hebrew, his brother, confessed himself to be a Hebrew, one of the people of God, and denied that he was the "son of Pharoah's daughter," disassociating himself from his position of privilege. Thus his denial (ἠρνήσατο) is the martyr's confession (ὁμολογία) for he must flee in peril of his life.[65]

According to Hebrews, in so rejecting his title, Moses also gave up the "treasures of Egypt." Philo also emphasizes that Moses in throwing in his lot with his brothers rejected the benefits of his position. Introducing the slaying of the Egyptian he states that Moses valued his natural inheritance above that which he received from his adoptive parents, and in fact was eventually driven to renounce the latter since he could only enjoy it at the cost of complying in the impiety (ἀσέβημα) of the king.[66] In other words, he saw the benefits

---

[63]*Ex. R.* 1.28 records a piece of haggadah which explains Moses' slaying of the Egyptian as justice wrought upon a taskmaster who raped the wife of one of the Jewish officers. Apparently it is intended to show that they were never suspected of immorality.

[64]See the comment of *S. of S. R.* IV,12.1 (Soncino, 218-219):

> They did not change their names: as Reuben and Simeon they went down to Egypt, and as Reuben and Simeon they went up from it; they did not call Reuben Rufus, nor did they call Simeon Luliani, nor did they call Joseph Listis, or Benjamin Alexander.

The other two reasons are also helpful. "They did not change their language," and "They did not inform against each other." Note how *Ex. R.* 1.32 attempts to explain the application of "Egyptian" to Moses in Ex. 2.19.

[65]On the confessional context of this word, see Michel, 273.

[66]*Vita* I.32-33.

from his position as "the pleasures of sin." The summary on Moses as king reiterates this choice:

> For when he gave up the lordship of Egypt, because the sight of the iniquities committed in the land...led him to renounce completely his expected inheritance (lit. expectations) from the kinsfolk of his adoption....[67]

The "treasures of Egypt" emphasizes the fabulous wealth which Moses rejected to join his people in suffering. The treasures or treasuries[68] of Pharoah especially are a commonplace in rabbinic literature, even to the appearance of the Greek loan-word "thesaurioth." *Mekilta Shirata* depicts Pharoah bribing the Egyptians to pursue Israel: "I will open to you the treasuries of silver and gold and distribute among you precious stones and pearls."[69] The last extravagant phrase seems to be a stereotype; it occurs in the same story as *Mekilta Beshallah* with the Hebrew word for treasure, אוצרות.[70]

Why was Moses willing to give up these fabled treasures? Because "he looked ahead to the recompense," or as Hebrews says earlier in 11, because he believed "that God exists and is the rewarder of those who seek him." (11.6) Moses then was willing to look ahead to the reward that would come to the people of God for their endurance of oppression. For the Jewish interpreter who was Hebrews' contemporary, the reward for the oppression and the labors in which Moses had joined came very concretely when the Israelites despoiled the Egyptians. Philo presents this teaching with a very apologetic ring to it,[71] but it occurs also in *Jubilees*[72] and in Wisdom 10.17. In the latter, both tone and vocabulary are close to He. 11.26: "She (he) gave to the holy ones the recompense of

---

[67]*Vita* I.148-149 (Loeb VI, 353).

[68]Spicq wishes to identify them with granaries (see II. 358-359).

[69]*Mekilta Shirata* 7 (Lauterbach II, 55).

[70]*Mekilta Beshallah* 2 (Lauterbach I, 200).

[71]*Vita* I.25.

[72]*Jub.* 48.18.

their labors" (ἀπέδωκεν τοῖς ὁσίοις μισθὸν κόπων αὐτῶν). The
idea of course belongs to the central theme of Wisdom's
reflection on Egypt and Israel: that both Egypt and Israel get
their recompense and that it must be appropriate in each case.

Hebrews, like Wisdom, is concerned with God the rewarder
of all who seek him (indeed, the rewarder of all according to
their works) and must have been familiar with this interpretation. But to explain the "recompense" which Hebrews
envisages by the despoiling of the Egyptians or even by the
whole of the events of the exodus and entry is far too
constricting. For Moses prefers to the treasures of Egypt
not the booty from Egypt or even the bounty of the land of
Israel, nor even Torah, nor yet wisdom, that unfailing
treasure--but "the opprobrium of Christ."

The opprobrium of Christ.

The phrase "the opprobrium" or "the reproach of (the)
Christ" (τὸν ὀνειδισμὸν τοῦ Χριστοῦ) appears to be a reference
either to Ps. 68 LXX or to Ps. 88.51-52 LXX. In either case,
the phrase is not an exact quotation; in itself, it involves
some interpretation.

Psalm 68 uses the word "opprobrium" or "reproach"
(ὀνειδισμός) in a number of verses:

.8   ...for your sake I have borne *reproach*....

.10   because zeal for your house has consumed me
      and the *reproaches* of them that *reproached* you have
      fallen up upon me

.11   and I bowed down my soul with fasting
      and it became a *reproach* to me....

.20   but you know my *reproach*....
      before you are they all who oppress me

.21   *Reproach* has my soul expected, and misery....

The frequent use of this word in Ps. 68 LXX and the
frequent use of Ps. 68 as a source of New Testament theological
speculation, and especially of New Testament Christology,
favors the possibility that the phrase in some way originates
in Ps. 68 LXX. There seem to be three ways in which the
author of Hebrews could have derived the expression from
this psalm.

1) Of the verses above, only one verse which includes the significant word is cited in the New Testament. In Romans 15.3 Paul represents Christ as the example of the strong considering the weak: "For Christ did not please himself, but, as it is written, 'The reproaches of those who reproached thee fell on me.'" Possibly the author of Hebrews has applied this verse to Moses in a similar way: Moses declares in this verse that he has shared the burdens of his brothers the Hebrews. Because like Christ he chooses to share the suffering of the people of God, the reproach he bears is the reproach of Christ.

2) Possibly the author of Hebrews concentrates on v. 8 "...for your sake I have borne reproach..." or on verses 8 and 10 together and hears in them Moses speaking to Christ. Thus Moses says that he bears (shares)[73] the ill-treatment of his brothers for the sake of Christ--he bears the *reproach* of Christ.

3) As has been mentioned above, Ps. 68 is an important source of the Christological language of the New Testament, which most frequently ascribes the psalm to Jesus (or to David speaking in his person), especially to Jesus in his passion.[74] Thus the *prosopon* which the Christian reader hears in the psalm is Christ, and the reproach of which it speaks (cf. especially 20, "you know my reproach" and 21, "reproach my heart expected") is the reproach of Christ, that is, the reproach which he bore.

In any of these three cases, the reference to the psalm clearly belongs to the picture of Moses the martyr, who chose ill-treatment above the "fleeting pleasures of sin." The martyr theme in the psalm itself is very strong; Theodore of Mopsuestia,[75] who gives the only non-Christological interpre-

---

[73]Later Christian interpretation identifies this *reproach* as reproach *from* his brothers, adducing the parallel in Acts 7.23-29, which presents Moses as persecuted by his brothers, the Jews, as also was Christ; cf. Chrysostom, *Hom. in Ep. ad Hebr.* XXVI (PG 63.48).

[74]Ps. 69.22 in Mt. 27.34, 48; Mk. 15.36; Lk. 23.36; Jn. 19.29; also Ps. 69.5 in Jn. 15.25.

[75]Robert Devréesse, ed., *Le Commentaire de Théodore de Mopsueste sur les Psaumes* (I-LXXX), Studi e Testi (Vatican

interpretation of the Psalm among Christian authors, applies
it to the Maccabees, the pre-eminent examples of martyrdom.
Thus the phrase "the reproach of Christ" can be explained from
Psalm 68 LXX; yet none of these explanations is strikingly
satisfactory.

Psalm 88 LXX is less frequently used in the New Testament
as a Christological source although a number of references to
that Psalm do occur; and the word "reproach" (ὀνειδισμός) is
used only in the last two verses. The expression "the reproach
of Christ" (τὸν ὀνειδισμὸν τοῦ Χριστοῦ) could, however, have
been drawn word by word from 88.51-52, as an elliptical
summary of these two verses:

.51 Remember, O Lord, the *reproach* of your servants
    which I have borne in my bosom of many nations
.52 of which your enemies, O Lord, have *reproached*,
    of which they have *reproached* the exchange of
    your Christ.

.51 μνήσθητι, κύριε, τοῦ ὀνειδισμοῦ τῶν δούλων σου
    οὗ ὑπέσχον ἐν τῷ κόλπῳ μου πολλῶν ἐθνῶν
.52 οὗ ὠνείδισαν οἱ ἐχθροί σου κύριε
    οὗ ὠνείδισαν τὸ ἀντάλλαγμα τοῦ Χριστοῦ σου.

The difficult LXX Greek is a rendition of a Hebrew text
quite as difficult; thus the translation is somewhat problematic. If "the reproach of (the) Christ" refers to Psalm 88.
51-52, these verses must have told the author of Hebrews how
Moses chose "the reproach of Christ" over the wealth of Egypt.
I suggest that he has ascribed these two verses to Moses, who
in them declares:

...I have borne in my bosom the reproach with which
(the Egyptians) your enemies reproached (my brothers,
the Hebrews) your servants, because of the exchange-
price of Christ (to which they, or I, looked forward).[76]

If this is Hebrews' interpretation, it is peculiar to
Hebrews. No other interpreter ascribes the verses to Moses.
The rabbinic tradition identifies the speaker of the whole
psalm, Ethan the Ezrahite, with Abraham.[77] The Christian

City: Biblioteca Apostolica Vaticana, 1939), 447.

[76]Cf. Buchanan (197), who also tries to read the psalm as
the author of Hebrews might have read it.

[77]*Nu. R.* 19.3 (Soncino, 750).

tradition ascribes these particular verses (51-52) to Christ. The very difficult second line "which I have borne or kept in my bosom" is applied by Cyril not to the "reproach" of Christ but to the promises which the Christ held "for many nations." He seems to attach this last difficult phrase to the words "your servants" as does Jerome.[78] The verse is thus read: "Remember the reproach of your servants from among many nations." It is not clear to me how the author of Hebrews would have read these words. They admit of reference to the whole history of Israel, throughout which it bore the reproach of many nations, or to the nations with whom Israel had to fight during the exodus and entry; they also can be simply ignored or omitted.

The crux in the interpretation of this passage is the last verse: "of which your enemies, o Lord, have reproached the *exchange* of your Christ." The key word, "exchange" (ἀντάλλαγμα), is the difficulty.[79] It represents a radical change from the Hebrew text which reads: "the footsteps of your anointed." The rabbinic comments are of course based upon that Hebrew text. According to them, the time of the Messiah's *coming* will be a terrible time, a time of blaspheming and reviling.[80]

Among the interpreters of the Greek text, the most frequent explanation of "exchange" (ἀντάλλαγμα) seems to be "change of status." Origen finds the phrase obscure, but hazards:"perhaps the Lord's humanity."[81] Augustine's text appears to be based upon the LXX, for it reads *commutatio* here; in Augustine's understanding, Christ was reproached for his death, by which he was changed from temporal to eternal

---

[78]Cyril, *In Psalmum LXXXVIII* (PG 69.1217); Jerome, *Tractatus de Psalmo LXXXVIII* (CCL 78, 413). Actually the source of these comments is uncertain (see 411).

[79]See Michel (273); also Bruce who translates: "...wherewith they have reproached thy anointed by way of recompense" (320).

[80]*B. San.* 99b; *S. of S. R.* II,13.4.

[81]Origen, *Selecta in Psalmos* (PG 12.1549).

life, from Jews to Gentiles, from earth to heaven.[82] Eusebius
uses both the LXX and the text of Symmachus, which more nearly
represents the Hebrew. As a result he appears to interpret
the words "change" (ἀντάλλαγμα) and "footsteps" (τὰ ἴχνη)
together:

> ...the *passage* of the Christ of God and his *way* which
> was that of the passion and the *footsteps* of the
> dispensation of human life.

> τὴν γὰρ <u>πορείαν</u> τοῦ Χριστοῦ τοῦ θεοῦ καὶ τὴν <u>ὁδὸν</u>
> αὐτοῦ τὴν κατὰ τὸ πάθος τά τε <u>ἴχνη</u> τῆς κατὰ τὸν
> ἀνθρώπινον βίον οἰκονομίας.[83]

Cyril's reading of the verse interprets ἀντάλλαγμα as "exchange" more than "change": for him, these verses tell of
Christ's exchange of the synagogue of the Jews for the Church
of the once-reproached Gentiles.[84] Jerome's interpretation is
similar.[85]

The interpretation of Athanasius makes use of another
shade of meaning of ἀντάλλαγμα, of what is in fact the basic
meaning of the word: that which is given in exchange for, the
price of exchange:

> *Remember, o Lord, the reproach of your servants,*
> since *your enemies, o Lord, reproached* me, saying
> that the promises given *to the nations* concerning
> me were false. These were that they would be saved
> and *discharged of the debt* (ἀπαλλαγῆναι) of death
> and sin. But they *reproached* me looking toward my
> death.... For the *exchange-price* (ἀντάλλαγμα) *of*
> *your Christ they reproached*, it says. Now his
> *exchange-price* (ἀντάλλαγμα) would be his death and
> blood, the redemption-price (ἀντίλυτρον) given for
> the world's salvation.[86]

A similar interpretation is given in *De Titulis Psalmorum*:
"they reproached your son who has given himself as *barter*

---

[82]Augustine, *Enarratio in Psalmum LXXXVIII* (CCL 39.1243).

[83]PG 23.1121.

[84]Cyril, *In Psalmum LXXXVIII* (PG 69.1217).

[85]Jerome, *De Psalmo LXXXVIII* (CCL 78.113).

[86]Athanasius, *Expositio in Psalmum LXXXVIII* (PG 27.393).

(ἀντάλλαγμα) on behalf of your *Christ*ened people."[87]

These readings of the psalm have certain common features which are significant: first, the passage is generally interpreted in some way which points toward Christ's self-giving on behalf of the people of God; second, the exchange is principally interpreted as a change of status which incurred reproach--the turning from Jews to Gentiles, or the humiliation of the incarnation of the Word and/or the death of the Lord. Especially in so far as it is referred to the death of the Lord and even to the verbal abuse he suffered in the gospel accounts of the crucifixion, we may speculate on the identification of the reproaches in this verse with the reproach of the great passion psalm, 68 LXX. These Christian readings of Psalm 88.51-52 may provide us with a paradigm for the way in which the author of Hebrews would have read it. "They reproached the exchange of your Christ" ... "who instead of the joy proposed to him, endured the cross, despising the shame" (He. 12.2). Christ and Moses as martyrs have each the choice to exchange the joy they could have had to join the suffering and opprobrium borne by the people of God. But Christ as leader of our faith brings it also to perfection; in exchanging the joy he could have had for the cross "he has taken his seat at the right hand of God" (12.2). Moses by making this same exchange took upon himself the same reproach, and though he died without entering into the promise, still he saluted his hope from afar, "for he looked beyond the reward."

11.27 Moses leaves Egypt behind: faith seeing the Unseen.

    11.27   a. By faith

               b. he abandoned Egypt, not fearing the wrath of the king

               c. for as seeing the Unseen, he endured.

    11.27   a. Πίστει

               b. κατέλιπεν Αἴγυπτον, μὴ φοβηθεὶς τὸν θυμὸν τοῦ βασίλεως

               c. τὸν γὰρ ἀόρατον ὡς ὁρῶν ἐκαρτέρησεν.

---

[87]Once attributed to Athanasius but now generally credited to Hesychius (PG 27.1036).

To what incident does this event of Moses' faith refer?
When did Moses "abandon Egypt, not fearing the king?" Opinions
diverge on this point; both Moses' flight before Pharoah and
his departure from Egypt at the head of the people have been
adduced as the source of this comment.[88]

If Hebrews is referring to Moses' departure from Egypt as
the leader of Israel in the exodus, the statement should be
read: "because he was not afraid of the king's wrath, he
abandoned Egypt." The statement is in excellent harmony with
the description of the events in Exodus: Exodus 10-12 is
precisely an account of Moses' defiance of Pharoah in order to
bring the people out. Further, if this is the reference the
three events of the example mark the beginnings of three
forty-year periods of Moses' life: 11.23--Moses' birth to his
maturity in Egypt; 11.24-26--Moses' departure from the house
of Pharoah, his slaying of the Egyptian and his forty-year
sojourn in Midian; 11.27--his departure from Egypt through the
forty years wandering to his death. This pattern (which occurs
also in the Acts 7 account of Moses' life) is a standard one.[89]

If this is the reference, there is some slight disar-
rangement of the sequence; for after discussing Moses'
departure from Egypt in 11.27, the author returns in 11.28 to
Moses' institution of the Pasch. However, the interest of
the narrative has obviously shifted from Moses to the wilderness period and its events, and 11.28 can be seen as the
opening for this new interest. However, there are more serious
objections to this suggestion. First of all, the pattern is
left implicit in the text and is not spelled out as it is in
Acts. This would seem to tell against its being in any way
central to the organization of the passage, although the
possibility remains that it was central to an older text or
tradition which Hebrews (theologically so much more creative

---

[88]On this see F. F. Bruce, *The Epistle to the Hebrews*
(Grand Rapids, Michigan: Wm. B. Eerdmans, 1964), 321-322;
Spicq II, 359; Michel, 275. Most commentators seem to have
come to the conclusion that the verse is a midrashic para-
phrase of Ex. 2.14.

[89]On the forty-year pattern cf. Acts 7.23, 20, 36; also
the collection of material on that passage in Strack-Billerbeck
II, 679-680.

than Luke-Acts) has remade to its own purpose and virtually
obliterated. Secondly, there is no direct verbal reference to
the text of Exodus 10-12, as there has been in the other two
instances (although these are undeniably scanty). The only
reference to fear in the account of the exodus is found at
14.10: "...the Egyptians were marching against them and they
were in great fear." Moses then encourages them.

Neither does the biblical account mention the wrath of
Pharoah, but both Philo and Josephus mention his anger in their
descriptions of Moses' contest with Pharoah for permission to
"worship in the desert." Philo records that in response to
Moses' first request to leave, Pharoah "in the harshness and
ferocity and obstinacy of his temper (ὀργήν--anger) ordered the
overseers of the tasks to treat the people with contumely, for
showing slackness and laziness...."[90] Josephus spells out the
role of the king's anger at Moses all through his account of
the signs and plagues. Pharoah, at the display of the signs
which God had given Moses, "was wroth (ὁ δὲ ἀγανακτήσας) and
dubbed him a criminal, who had once escaped from servitude and
had now effected his return by fraud and was trying to impose
on him by juggleries and magic."[91] He also remarks that the
anger of the king turned against the people with the refusal
to supply them with straw and further remarks upon the
constancy of Moses in the face of both threats from the king
and the blame of the people.[92] Finally, Josephus tells us,
"Infuriated (ὀργισθείς) by this speech the king threatened to
behead him, should he ever again come and pester him on this
matter."[93] Thus both Philo and Josephus see Moses pitted
against the wrath of Pharoah in his attempt to bring the
people out. Philo remarks only on his anger as directed at the
people (an inference which is very close to the surface of the
text). Josephus, however, concentrates on the personal
contest between Moses and Pharoah.

---

[90] *Vita* I.89 (Loeb VI,323).

[91] *Ant.* II.284 (Loeb IV,289).

[92] *Ant.* II.288-290.

[93] *Ant.* II.310 (Loeb IV,299-301).

Although 11.27 does not seem to cite any part of these accounts, identifying Moses' departure from Egypt with the exodus does offer a concrete reference for one allusion in that verse. Moses is here declared to endure "as seeing the Unseen." If the wrath of the king is understood to be his opposition to the departure of Israel, what better explanation of the courage of Moses (that meek and stuttering man) than his vision of God unseen in the formless and unconsuming flame of the burning bush?

If, on the other hand, Hebrews is referring to the flight of Moses before Pharoah, the translation is somewhat more difficult: "By faith he abandoned Egypt (since? although?), he did not fear the wrath of the king," or possibly "not because he feared the wrath of the king." The sequence of events is, however, easier, at least at first sight: Moses was born and hidden; he cast his lot in with his people and slew the Egyptian; he fled before the wrath of Pharoah; he instituted the pasch, the "passage" (διαβατήρια) of Israel, that is the departure, and the "passage" of the angel on account of the sacrifice at once.[94]

However, Hebrews does not say that Moses fled before the wrath of Pharoah, but that he was *not* afraid of Pharoah's wrath. These few words ("not fearing"--μὴ φοβηθείς) are closest to a verbal reminiscence of any phrase in the verse. But they contradict the statement to which they appear to refer: "Moses was afraid" (ἐφοβήθη δὲ Μωϋσῆς) says Ex. 2.14, and then, "But Moses fled from the face of Pharoah and dwelt in the land of Midian" (ἀνέχώρησεν δὲ Μωϋσῆς ἀπὸ προσώπου Φαραω καὶ ᾤκησεν ἐν γῇ Μαδιαμ, 2.15).

Although the allusion would be a contradictory one, at least the text does speak of Moses' fear and also of the role of Pharoah ("Pharoah heard the thing and sought to kill Moses." Ex. 2.15). Philo elaborates on that role, stating that Moses has fled from Pharoah's wrath[95] explaining that wrath as

---

[94]The two events were certainly celebrated as one and the name "pasch" was translated as διαβητέρια and referred to both. See Philo, *De Specialibus Legibus* II.145-147.

[95]*Vita* I:49: "Now any other who was fleeing from the king's relentless wrath (ὀργὴν ἀμελίκητον)...." (Loeb VI,303).

thoroughly unjust: "...the king was indignant not because one
man had been slain by another...but because his own daughter's
son did not think with him and...loved those whom he rejected
and pitied those to whom he was relentless and inexorable."[96]
Ezechiel also records that it is "the wrath (ὀργήν) and the
machination of the king" which drove Moses out of the royal
residence and to the "works."[97]

Philo and Josephus both appear to handle this text (i.e.
Ex. 2.14-15) with an interpretation by contradiction, at least
in effect. Although Philo does not directly contradict it, by
an absolutely literal explanation he is able to absolve Moses
of any charge of cowardice:

> ...Moses does not fly before Pharoah, for that would
> be to run away and not return, but like an athlete
> taking an interval to regain his breath, 'withdraws'
> that is brings about a cessation of arms....[98]

As I suggested above, the flight of Moses from Egypt appears
in the Jewish-Hellenistic literature in a form that is at
least considerably softened. The Moses story which Josephus
and Artapanus represent avoids the slaying of the Egyptian.
For Josephus, the flight of Moses is a demonstration of his
cleverness in preventing the hand of the jealous king.[99]
Artapanus also ascribes Moses' downfall in Egypt to the jealousy of the king and also records a complicated plot against
him which finally depicts the flight as a demonstration of
Moses' superiority over his appointed assassin.[100] Philo, who
does retain the biblical account, describes Moses' flight as a
withdrawal or retreat.[101] All come as close as possible to
contradicting the text.

---

[96]*Vita* I.45 (Loeb VI, 299).

[97]Eusebius, *Praep. Ev.* 9.28 (PG 21.7).

[98]*Leg. All.* III.14 (Loeb I,301).

[99]*Ant.* II.254-255.

[100]Eusebius, *Praep. Ev.* 9.27 (PG 21.729-732).

[101]*Leg. All.* III.14; *Vita* I.47.

Although Philo and Josephus part company rather drastically in their attempts to serve up a palatable motive for Moses' flight, they do have one more thing in common: both refer to the flight as an illustration of Moses' *endurance* (καρτερία). Seemingly in the apologetic atmosphere of Jewish-Hellenistic preaching the flight of Moses has taken on a positive exemplary function.

In a different vein this is also true of the rabbinic tradition, which uses Moses' flight as an illustration that flight is justified and good when both necessity and opportunity present themselves.[102] This sense that "he who fights and runs away lives to fight another day" may indeed be part of the exemplary function in Josephus and Philo, as Philo's insistence on the "retreat" of the athlete suggests. But their interpretation implies more; seemingly for the Hellenistic writers, the flight of Moses from Egypt has come to equal his voluntary departure from Egypt, the place of comfort and security (cf. Nu. 11.4), of the pleasures and satisfactions of ease and of the senses. For Josephus, Moses despises this security to the point that by his endurance (καρτερία) he is able to despise even the necessity of provisioning himself for flight and thus is able to make good his escape.[103] This explanation of Egypt is, of course, familiar to the later Christian writers of all ages, and Theodoret, in explaining Moses' departure in the light of Hebrews 11.27, neatly explains that fear of the king was no motive in that abandoning of Egypt: "Egypt he abandoned in fear, but boldly hurled down the Egyptian."[104]

If Hebrews 11.27 refers to the flight of Moses, then Hebrews and Philo represent a still further extension of the exemplary function of Moses' flight. This voluntary departure from Egypt, which is still the consequence of the Egyptian's death, partakes of the rejection of the leadership of Egypt

---

[102]Cf. *Dt. R.* II.26-27.

[103]*Ant.* II.254-256.

[104]Theodoret, *Interpretatio Epist. ad Hebr.* (PG 82.765): τὴν μὲν Αἴγυπτον φοβηθεὶς κατέλιπε θαρσάλεως δὲ τὸν Ἀιγύπτιον κατηκόντισε.

and of its false wealth. His whole early life then leads up
to this renunciation of Egypt and its wealth for God and God's
people, a renunciation which is particularly exemplary of
restraint and endurance (ἐγκράτεια, καρτερίαι),[105] because
Moses set aside fabulous wealth for the hardship of flight.[106]
And, of course, this renunciation comes to its fulfillment only
when Moses leads out in defiance of Pharoah the people he
has joined at such a cost.

Philo and the function of Moses' departure from Egypt.

This view that the flight of Moses actually represents his
voluntary renunciation of Egypt enables Philo to interpret the
flight of Moses and his departure at the head of the people
together. Although he keeps the actual events distinct, they
turn out to have the same meaning. This is evident in different ways in the two places in his work where the flight is
given significant attention. *Leg. All.* III.14 which treats of
the flight in itself speaks of it as a retreat or a cessation
of arms in Moses' contest with Pharoah. Moses withdraws to
"reason, the practitioner of endurance"[107] to place himself
before God, to inquire what to do and to consider his own
strength, until he should be supplied with the virtue and the
divine oracles (λόγων θείων) which would enable him to win
his battle. Thus the flight of Moses from Egypt is an
extension of his encounter on Sinai as his encounter with
Pharoah and leadership of the exodus are its sequel. Moses
flees *to* the retreat on Sinai and *to* the oracles given him at
the bush, *to* his return to Egypt and *to* his final desolating
departure from it.

The interpretation of this sequence of events as a manifold event with a single meaning is more evident still in
Philo's epitome on Moses as king in *De Vita Mosis*.[108] Here
are tied together: 1) Moses' renunciation of the kingship of

---

[105]*Vita* I.154.

[106]Bruce, 321, n. 191.

[107]*Leg. All.* III.11.

[108]*Vita* I.148-162.

Egypt; 2) his flight; 3) his departure at the head of the
people. The opening of this section declares that Moses, when
he abandoned the lordship of Egypt because of "the sight of the
iniquities committed in the land and his own nobility of soul
and magnanimity of spirit and inborn hatred of evil"[109] was
rewarded with the leadership of Israel which he exercised in
the exodus. When this passage is compared with I. 40-45, it
becomes clear that for Philo Moses' flight, as the consequence
of his having joined sides with his people and slain the
Egyptian, means his renunciation of the kingship of Egypt and
is precisely what has made him fit to be the leader of the
exodus.

The whole epitome on Moses as king exhibits certain features which make it significant for the explication of Hebrews
11.23-27:

1) *Content*. The epitome opens with a) Moses' renunciation
of his claim to the rulership of Egypt, b) his forswearing of
his inheritance and c) his joining of his brothers. All of
these are understood as the implications of his slaying of the
Egyptian and his subsequent flight. Also implied are the
virtues which the deed required and which continued to grace
Moses' leadership in the monarchy which it won him. These
include: d) his attitude toward wealth, shown in his renunciation of his inheritance and continued after his assumption
of office: "he did not treasure up (οὐκ ἐθησαυρίσατο)[110] gold
and silver;" e) his liberal dispensation of virtuous deeds,
especially *restraint and endurance* (ἐγκράτειαι καὶ
καρτερίαι);[111] f) his contemplation of and entry into the
"eternal, unseen and non-bodily (ἀειδῆ καὶ ἀόρατον καὶ ἀσώματον)
exemplary being"[112] which enabled him to become the great
example that he is. This contemplative experience/habit
appears to refer both to Moses' entry into the cloud at Sinai

---

[109]*Vita* I.149 (Loeb VI,353).

[110]*Vita* I.152 (Loeb VI,355).

[111]*Vita* I.154.

[112]*Vita* I.158.

at the lawgiving and to his call when he was named a "god" to
Aaron.[113]

2) *Homiletic function*. The epitome's function is clearly
exemplary and parenetic:

> ...in himself and in his life displayed for all to see,
> he has set before us, like some well-wrought picture,
> a piece of work beautiful and god-like, a model for
> those who are willing to copy it.[114]

3) *Literary and theological function*. The epitome marks
the end of the events of Moses' life that took place in Egypt,
and at the same time gives the meaning of his life up to that
point. In the epitome, (and indeed in the events which lead
up to it) there are two strains of events: those of Moses'
miraculous, royal and ennobling nurture which fitted him for
the duties of monarchy, and the events by which he came into
possession of it: his flight from Egypt and then his departure
at the head of the people by which he renounced the false
kingship of Egypt. In both of these things he becomes not only
a model for all, but also a sharer in God's nature as posses-
sing all things, yet needing nothing[115] so that Moses'
dominion over his own person is extended also to the realities
of nature.[116]

The epitome on Moses as king provides us with a useful
comparison to the exemplum of Moses in He. 11.23-27 offering
some strong similarities in content and function against which
the character of the latter stands out in bold relief. In the
light of these observations about the epitome we can now
summarize our conclusions about Moses in Hebrews 11.

---

[113]*Vita* I.158: "For he was named god and king of the
whole nation" (Loeb VI.359). Presumably this refers to Ex.
4.16, "He shall speak for you to the people, and he shall be
a mouth for you and you shall be for him as God." Cf. 7.1.

[114]*Vita* I.158 (Loeb VI,354).

[115]*Vita* I.157 (Loeb VI, 357).

[116]*Vita* I.155-156.

Conclusions: Saint Moses the Martyr, example of Christian endurance.

The picture of Moses in 11.23-27 is a picture drawn out of a multiplicity of texts embellished with haggadic material and woven together with a subtle midrashic technique. It is characteristic of this passage and (as we shall see) of the author's technique that texts and traditions are used allusively in such a way as to include in their reference other texts and traditions. Thus, while it is probable that the author's bible is the LXX, interpretations which appear to depend on the Hebrew text ought not to be excluded from consideration as possible background for the interpretations Hebrews gives.[117] So also while it is virtually certain that 11.27 refers to Ex. 2.14, that does not exclude a reference to Exodus 3 and 10-14 under the same allusion. Here the method of Philo is an important parallel; while the two departures of Moses are neither muddled nor obscured in the epitome, they are brought together in such a fashion as to make clear that they have but one meaning: that Moses renounced Egypt. Another important point in regard to their method of interpretation can be noted in the way in which both speak of Moses' vision of God or vision of the Unseen. It is unnecessary either to distinguish completely or to identify absolutely the understanding which Hebrews and Philo give to the similar expressions which they use in regard to this notion.[118] In fact, for both Philo and Hebrews, the vision of God, whether understood as the habit of philosophic contemplation or the impetus of eschatological yearning[119] can be embodied in, exhibited in, the event at the burning bush, as the martyr's

---

[117]On Hebrews' modification of the LXX, see H. J. Combrink, "Some Thoughts on the Old Testament Citations in the Epistle to the Hebrews," *Neotestamentica 5* (Proceedings of the Fifth Meeting of Die Neuw Testamentiese Werkgemeenskap van Suid-Afrika, 1971), 22-36. Combrink emphasizes Christological motives for the alteration of the text of the LXX but gives no attention to the role of tradition and other texts.

[118]Williamson (475-476) distinguished them; Michel (273), Spicq (II,359), and Windisch (104) point to the similarity.

[119]Williamson ascribes the first view to Philo, the second to Hebrews (476).

renunciation of ease can be exhibited in the departure(s) by
which Moses abandoned Egypt.[120]

One is more readily convinced of the similarity in
methodology by the recognition of a certain similarity in the
picture produced by these two authors. For both Philo and
Hebrews, Moses is a child signed by divine favor, a man who
joins his own people, God's people, at the cost of power and
wealth and with an expectation of misery, a hero who defies
Pharoah at the risk of his own life, and who turns his back on
a life of ease and sin. This picture is produced not only by
a similar approach to the text but also by a functional similarity. Moses' function in both passages is exemplary. In the
light of their parenetic purpose, Moses' early life is explained as a process of endurance (resistance and survival) of and
separation from Egypt, the world of pleasure, persecution and
sin. Moses is made a model for those who must resist and yet
survive, for those who have not yet had to resist to the point
of bloodshed. But alongside this functional similarity there
appears a strong theological difference. For Philo the
martyr aspect of Moses' portrait is a detail in the much
stronger delineation of a moral hero, whereas for Hebrews, the
endurance that Moses' example urges upon the reader is not the
heroic self-control preached by the Hellenistic philosopher
and modeled by the ruler who first rules himself, but the
endurance that is the accompaniment and condition of the
martyr's confession, as also his renunciation is the renunciation of the one who shall not see what he has been promised
in this world. More significant than Moses' exemplary
renunciation of wealth and fame, more significant than his
defiance of the king, more significant even than his heroic
abandonment of Egypt is the recompense to which he looks and
the Unseen One upon whom he gazes. More important than his
exemplary fidelity is the faith by which he bears witness to
God, the rewarder of those who seek him, and to the promise
which he shall not inherit without us. The picture of Moses

---

[120]Spicq (II.359), Héring (105), and Bruce (320) refer
the phrase to the vision of the burning bush. Michel (275)
enters into the question of whether Moses ever saw God, extending the reference to Ex. 33.7-18.

in Hebrews is accommodated parenetically to the needs of the hearers, but also by the theological, specifically the soteriological view of Hebrews, which presents to us not a man who by his great virtue has come to share God's character and power, but a martyr, a saint conformed by suffering to Christ the savior who originates and perfects his sanctity.

The distinctiveness of the picture of Moses is underlined by the characterization of his choice: the choice of the opprobrium or reproach of Christ. Although examination of the phrase suggests its origin in an interpreation of Ps. 88.51-52 LXX, none of the traditions surrounding those verses is able to explain either the phrase itself or its application to Moses in the Hebrews' verse. This is hardly surprising, for we would expect the phrase to arise from Hebrews' own dispensational view of salvation. However, more than a conformity to Christ is claimed for Moses by this phrase. How could Moses have known to choose the opprobrium of Christ? The problem is articulated in Aquinas' comment on the verse: "*Improperium Christi*: id est pro fide Christi: eadem est enim fides antiquorum et nostra."[121] The distinctive feature of Hebrews' portrait of Moses is not that he is a "martyr" and "warrior for God" or even that he is conformed to Christ in his suffering and therefore also an example for Christians, but that he is a *Christian* martyr, a martyr *pro fide Christi*. The question then becomes: How did Moses become a Christian?[122]

---

[121]Aquinas, *Ad Hebraeos*, 615.

[122]Most commentators explain this phrase as envisaging the suffering of God's people who prefigure or are a type of the suffering of Christ (Spicq, II.358; Héring, 105; Michel, 273-274; Bruce, 320). But this explanation does not suffice; the verse implies that Moses chose this reproach because he knew it to be the reproach of Christ. I am expecially grateful to Mr. Greer for pressing this question in our discussion of the thesis.

CHAPTER TWO

JESUS OUR HIGH-PRIEST, CHRIST AS SON: THE CHRISTOLOGICAL TESTIMONIES OF 3.1-6

> ...it is evident that ·all the prophets declared con-
> cerning Christ, that it should come to pass at some
> time, that being born with a body of the race of
> David, He should build an eternal temple in honour
> of God which is called the Church and assemble all
> nations to the true worship of God. This is the
> faithful house, this is the everlasting temple; and
> if anyone hath not sacrificed in this, he will not
> have the reward of immortality. And since Christ
> was the builder of this great and eternal temple,
> he must also have an everlasting priesthood in it;
> and there can be no approach to the shrine of the
> temple and to the sight of God, except through him
> who built the temple.
>
> Lactantius
> Divine Institutes IV.14[1]

When Aquinas comments on He. 11.27, "eadem enim est fides eorum et nostra,"[2] he rightly assumes that the author of Hebrews considers the faith of all the exemplars to have been the Christian faith. But this comment is made about Moses, and with reason. While all the ancient witnesses are con-formed to Christ, while all recognize that they journey to a better homeland, while all look forward to a hope that they share with us, no one among them seems to know so clearly as Moses the nature and end of the contest which they witness. The faith of Moses and his martyrdom seem not to be "in a figure" (ἐν παραβολῇ) as was the resurrection of Isaac.[3] Rather Moses endured "as seeing the unseen."

Moses' Christian faith requires an explanation: how did he come to "look ahead to the reward" if indeed the reward is "the exchange of Christ"? The examination of 11.23-27 has

---

[1] ANF VII,113; tr. Rev. William Fletcher, DD (New York: the Christian Literature Company, 1896).

[2] *Ad Hebraeos* 615.

[3] Cf. 11.19.

already made it clear that the final answer cannot be found in the traditions which Hebrews is using but must originate in the thought of the author. The best explanation of the relationship of Moses to Christ is then likely to be found in the comparison of Christ and Moses in He. 3.1-6.

Hebrews 3.1-6 belongs to a larger division, 1.1-4.16, whose theme is "God has spoken through his son." These chapters seek to make an exhortative point by establishing the primacy of the revelation in Christ, a primacy based upon Christ's sonship. The first two chapters (1.4-2.18) declare Christ's message superior to and therefore more demanding than that of the angels (i.e. the law), because 1) he is in origin superior to the angels as the son of God (1.4-2.4) and 2) in the end, in the age to come, all will be subjected to him as son of man (2.5-2.16).

The argument proving that Christ is superior to the angels as son of God is used as the basis for a *qal wehomer*: if their message was guaranteed by punishment for every transgression and every disobedience, how much the less shall we escape punishment if we disregard the salvation spoken through the Lord (2.2)?

Chapters 3 and 4 appear to make up a second and parallel treatment of the superiority of the message of Christ to the Law.[4] They begin with a direct comparison between Christ and Moses in 3.1-6, the comparison with which we are concerned:

3.1   Therefore, holy brethren, who share in a heavenly call, consider Jesus, the apostle and high priest of our confession.

.2   He was faithful to him who appointed him, just as Moses also was faithful in God's house.

.3   Yet Jesus has been counted worthy of as much more glory than Moses as the builder of a house has more honor than the house.

.4   (For every house has a builder, but the builder of all things is God.)

.5   Now Moses was faithful in all God's house as a servant, to testify to the things that were to be spoken later,

---

[4]Cf. Michel, 92-93; Héring, 21; Buchanan, 57.

.6 but Christ was faithful over God's house as a son.
And we are his house, if we hold fast to our confidence and pride in our hope.

3.1 ὅθεν, ἀδελφοὶ ἅγιοι, κλήσεως ἐπουρανίου μέτοχοι,
κατανοήσατε τὸν ἀπόστολον καὶ ἀρχιερέα τῆς
ὁμολογίας ἡμῶν Ἰησοῦν,

.2 πιστὸν ὄντα τῷ ποιήσαντι αὐτόν, ὡς καὶ Μωϋσῆς ἐν
(ὅλῳ) τῷ οἴκῳ αὐτοῦ.

.3 πλείονος γὰρ οὗτος δόξης παρὰ Μωϋσῆν ἠξίωται καθ'
ὅσον πλείονα τιμὴν ἔχει τοῦ οἴκου ὁ κατασκευάσας
αὐτόν.

.4 πᾶς γὰρ οἶκος κατασκευάζεται ὑπό τινος, ὁ δὲ
πάντα κατασκευάσας θεός.

.5 καὶ Μωϋσῆς μὲν πιστὸς ἐν ὅλῳ τῷ οἴκῳ αὐτοῦ ὡς
θεράπων εἰς μαρτύριον τῶν λαληθησομένων,

.6 Χριστὸς δὲ ὡς υἱὸς ἐπὶ τὸν οἶκον αὐτοῦ· οὗ οἶκός
ἐσμεν ἡμεῖς, ἐὰν τὴν παρρησίαν καὶ τὸ καύχημα
τῆς ἐλπίδος κατάσχωμεν.

These verses set out the superiority of Christ to the earlier
messenger, Moses, who (like the angels) mediated at the giving
of the law (cf. Ga. 3.19 "ordained by the angels through the
hand of an intermediary."). But the form differs from that of
the comparison between Christ and the angels in 1.4-2.2.
Chapter 1 proceeds by comparing a series of citations praising
alternately Christ and the angels, while 3.1-6 appears to make
a comparison of Christ and Moses based on the single citation
from Numbers in praise of Moses, and the Christian confession
of Jesus as Son of God. We might have expected this comparison
to conclude with another *qal wehomer*. If it was necessary to
attend to the message Moses God's servant brought, how much
more necessary to attend to the message of the son and builder?
But this conclusion seems to have been put off by the intervention of a modified indicative/imperative: "And we are his
house, if we hold fast our confidence and pride in our hope"
(3.6). This exhortation is reinforced by a second more
direct imperative put across in the words of Psalm 95:

3.7 Therefore, as the Holy Spirit says;
"Today, when you hear his voice,

.8 do not harden your hearts as in the rebellion,
on the day of testing in the wilderness,

.9 where your fathers put me to the test
and saw my works for forty years.

.10 Therefore I was provoked with that generation

and said 'They always go astray in their hearts;
they have not known my ways.'
.11 As I swore in my wrath,
'They shall never enter my rest.'"

Ps. 95.7-11

In the exegesis the author of Hebrews gives to these
verses (3.11 ff.), "hold fast our confidence" comes to mean:
"do not rest till you rest." Moses' role appears to center not
on his mediation of the law with the angels but on his "leadership" of "those who left Egypt" (3.16), the "house of Jacob"
that "came out of Egypt" (cf. Ps. 114.1).

Although the argument flows persuasively enough, the passage raises a number of questions. Why is the passage struc-
turally different from the comparison with the angels? More
significant still, why is the point of the comparison so different? Why does the author draw attention to "the message
declared by angels" in 2.2, and conclude with praise of the
word of God in 4.12, yet make no reference to the law in the
comparison between Christ and Moses? Why, when Christ has already been declared greater than the angels, compare him with
Moses, a man, though a man of God?[5] What intrinsic connection
does the author see between 3.6 and the exhortation from Ps. 95
such that he can introduce the citation with "therefore" (διό)?
Finally, what has happened to the theme of Christ the High
Priest? Why is it introduced in 2.17-18, emphasized as if it
were the point of the argument in 3.1, then dropped until 4.14
where it is reintroduced, apparently arbitrarily?[6]

Most of these questions center upon the problem of Hebrews'
interpretation of the scripture. What texts are being invoked?
What do these texts suggest to the author? How are they accommodated to the author's purpose and theology? Commentators
have long explained 3.1-6 as a partial citation and

---

[5]Cf. Spicq II, 62. The solution he proposes merely makes
more acute the problem of why the theme of the high priest is
introduced in 2.17-18 and then dropped. The suggestion that
it is intended as a literary inclusion is weak, if the theme
does not progress within the inclusion. Michel attempts to
give a more satisfactory answer, which will be treated in
chapters 3 and 4 below.

[6]Michel seems to think 3.1-6 an excursus, spinning off
from the word "faithful" in 2.17. See 93 and n. 1.

interpretation of Nu. 12.7: "Not so with my servant Moses; he
is trusted with (LXX faithful in) all my house." While this
passage is clearly one of the texts the author had in mind,
He. 3.1-6 is a very complex midrashic treatment of a number
of texts and, like other treatments of Moses in the letter, it
is guided by the author's Christology rather than by any
inherited or contemporary picture of Moses. Before examining
the function of Nu. 12.7 and of Moses himself in the passage,
it is necessary to examine the structure of the passage and of
the Christological statements being made in its exegesis of the
scriptures. Chapters 3 and 4 of this study will deal with the
citation from Numbers and the comparison made upon the basis of
that citation. This chapter will make a series of assertions
about the Christology and the Christological testimonies
involved in 3.1-6. It will be helpful to make some of these
assertions explicit as a preface to the discussion.

First, I would assert that the text cited in He. 3.2 is
not Nu. 12.7 (although the allusion is present and held in
abeyance) but 1 Chr. 17.14, most probably according to the
Septuagint. The citation is a deliberate reference to the
Nathan oracle, which is introduced in order to structure the
comparison. Second, the Nathan oracle in the targums, the
midrashic tradition and especially in the LXX, is already
deeply involved with an oracle given to Eli in 1 Sam. 2.35
so that the two texts come to be regarded as twin testimonies
for the Davidic messiah and the messianic priest. So extensive
is the relating of the two texts that it becomes possible for
the author of Hebrews to find in them an oracular testimony to
the "royal priest," the major model for the Christology of the
letter. Thirdly, this complex oracle explains or at least is
part of the relationship of Christ, apostle and high priest,
and the pilgrim people of God which is his house. Finally, the
role of the oracle in the passage makes it clear that the
Christology controls the picture of Moses, and not the other
way around.

As can be seen from this brief summary, the discussion on
which we are about to embark is a rather convoluted one, and
involves a complicated process of tracing the relationship of
a variety of Old Testament texts to each other and to an

ongoing tradition as well as to the text of Hebrews. Therefore
the best route for the discussion seems to be a rather circu-
itous one. We shall begin with a suggestion made by another
commentator, Sverre Aalen,[7] and summarize his observations on
the relation of the text of Hebrews to the Nathan oracle. Then
we shall attempt to sharpen his conlusions by adducing additional evidence from the text of Hebrews itself, and to extend
them with an examination of the treatment of the oracle in the
LXX. Next some observations made by Aalen about the mutual
interpretation of the Nathan oracle and the oracle to Eli
will be examined in the LXX and related to the text of Hebrews,
and some conclusions drawn with regard to the Christology and
ecclesiology of Hebrews. Finally the comparison with Moses
must be re-examined on the basis of these conclusions.

The Nathan oracle in 3.1-6.

In recent years, the influence of the Nathan oracle on
Hebrews 3.1-6 has gained some scholarly recognition, but little
direct study. This is rather surprising, for a number of
features of the oracle recommend it as a significant background
for the passage, and Hebrews makes at least one explicit
citation from it (2 Sam. 7.14 in He. 1.5).[8] Three of the
Christological titles used in 3.1-6 could well derive from the
oracle. This *ex post facto* prophecy of Solomon recorded in
both 2 Samuel 7 and 1 Chronicles 17 was certainly regarded as a
prophecy of the messianic King, the son of David or Messiah.
In other words, it could well be in the background when the
title "Christ" is used in 3.6. Further, the passage explicitly
describes the son of David as also the son of God (2 Sam. 7.14,
1 Chr. 17.13) while the superiority of Jesus is based on his
status of "Christ as Son" in Hebrews (3.6). Finally, the
oracle promises that this son of David (Solomon) will be the

---

[7]"'Reign' and 'House' in the Kingdom of God. Supplement:
'Kingdom' and 'House' in Pre-Christian Judaism," *NTS* 8 (April,
1961), 215-240. Bruce (57, n. 15) makes reference to Aalen but
does not seem to have incorporated the insight into his
comments on the text in any systematic fashion. Aalen's study
was called to my attention by N. A. Dahl.

[8]Cf. Bruce, 57, n. 15.

builder of the house of God, the temple (2 Sam. 7.13, 1 Chr. 17.12) and Christ is also proclaimed the builder of the house in Hebrews (3.3).

Attention has been drawn to all of these points by Sverre Aalen[9] who also attempts to provide the basis for an explicit verbal link between the two passages. He remarks the verbal similarity between Hebrews 3.2 and the Targum on 1 Chr. 17.14 (RSV "I will confirm him in my house and in my kingdom for-ever"). The verse in question is the last verse of the Nathan oracle in the Chronicles version and already differs from the version of the same verse found in 2 Sam. 7.16 ("...Your house and your kingdom shall be made sure forever before me..."). The 2 Samuel 7 version of the verse speaks of David's lineage and their reign; the 1 Chronicles version seems to speak more clearly of the individual "son of David," the designated messianic descendent who will more than succeed to David's throne. Certainly the reading given to the verse by the Targumist suggests that it was so read by his time.[10] The single verb "confirm" (MT העמדתיהו, I will make him stand) is rendered by two words: a verb "I will raise him up" (ואקימיניה)[11] and the adjective "faithful" (מהימן). Thus the Targum reads: "I will raise him up faithful in...my house...." This expression seems equivalent or nearly equivalent to the phrase describing Christ in He. 3.2 "...being faithful to the one who appointed him...in his house" (πιστὸν ὄντα τῷ ποιήσαντι αὐτόν...ἐν τῷ οἴκῳ αὐτοῦ). As Aalen points out, the phrase in the Targum is applied to the messianic son of David, whom God calls his son (1 Chr. 17.13, cf. He. 3.5) and who is designated the builder of God's house (1 Chr. 17.12, cf. He. 3.3). Further, the Targumist gives to the word "house" a double interpretation similar to the one found in Hebrews: "I will raise him up *faithful* in my people (בעמי) and in my

---

[9]Aalen, 236.

[10]Aalen at least so asserts, 235.

[11]Citations from the Targums have been taken from Alexander Sperber, *The Bible in Aramaic II: The Former Prophets according to Targum Jonathan; IV: The Hagiographa* (Leiden: E. J. Brill, 1959).

sanctuary (בבת מקדשי) and in my kingdom." Aalen's comparison
of He. 3.1-6 and Tg. 1 Chr. 17.10-14 calls attention to: 1) the
phrase "faithful in my (his) house"; 2) "the...idea that both
Christ and God are builder of the house"; 3) "the motif of the
faithful son who is builder of God's house and is in God's
house" and 4) the interpretation of "'house'...as the people
or congregation of God."[12]

Because Aalen's comments on Hebrews are subsidiary to his
main point, he neither marshalls all the evidence in favor of
his observation nor draws out all its implications. Certain
pieces of the internal evidence in Hebrews 3.1-6 argue strongly
that 3.2 should be read as a citation of 1 Chr. 17.14.
Further implications can also be drawn with regard to the text
of Hebrews from the interpretation of the Nathan oracle in
Palestinian Judaism. Finally, Aalen does not treat the LXX or
the traditions of Hellenistic Judaism, and one must at least
test the possibility that these provide the immediate source
for any interpretation of the scriptures in the Letter to the
Hebrews.

1 Chr. 17.14 LXX in He. 3.2.

He. 3.1 ...Consider Jesus, the apostle and high priest
of our confession

.2 He was faithful to him who appointed him, just
as Moses also was faithful in (all) God's house.

3.1 ...κατανοήσατε τὸν ἀπόστολον καὶ ἀρχιερέα
τῆς ὁμολογίας ἡμῶν, Ἰησοῦν

.2 πιστὸν ὄντα τῷ ποιήσαντι αὐτὸν ὡς καὶ Μωϋσῆς
ἐν (ὅλῳ) τῷ οἴκῳ αὐτοῦ

1 Chr. 17.14 LXX
And I will make him firm/faithful in my house
and in his kingdom

καὶ πιστώσω αὐτὸν ἐν τῷ οἴκῳ μου καὶ ἐν τῇ
βασιλείᾳ αὐτοῦ

Even a surface comparison of He. 3.2 and 1 Chr. 17.14 LXX
suggests that Aalen's observations hold true even if (as is
probable) Hebrews is working from the LXX, for the verbal
similarity between the rather unusual πιστώσω of 1 Chr. 17.14

---

[12] 236-237.

and the πιστὸν ὄντα of He. 3.2 makes the dependence more clear, clear enough to suggest that the passage cited in 3.2 is not Nu. 12.7 but 1 Chr. 17.14. Two features of He. 3.2 which at first appear to tell against this observation actually bring us closer to asserting it.

The first objection is the presence of the word "all" which brings the wording of the verse closer to that of Nu. 12.7 than to the phrasing of 1 Chr. 17.14. However, although the word is included in the Nestle text, it is almost certainly not original. While the witnesses which include it are good, early and abundant,[13] the witnesses which omit it, if few, have at least an equal claim for their quality and antiquity,[14] and it is far easier to explain why the word would have been added than why it would have been deleted. Indeed the addition of ὅλῳ by so many correctors raises the question of why the author did not include the word, if the citation is Nu. 12.7.[15] Might not the omission argue that the citation is not Nu. 12.7, but 1 Chr. 17.14?

What, then of the second detail which relates the verse to Nu. 12.7, the phrase "...just as Moses also..."? This phrase should be read as a parenthetical allusion to Nu. 12.7,[16] a preview of the explicit citation in He. 3.5 which is

---

[13] ℵ A C D K P Ψ, the Koine tradition, the Latin texts, the Syriac, Armenian and Ethiopic versions, and Chrysostom and Cyril, among other Church Fathers (see Aland).

[14] $p^{13.46}$ vid$_B$, the Coptic versions, Ambrose and Cyril.

[15] Buchanan points out that the author seems to have omitted "all"; he, however, sees nothing strange in that omission. Yet if this is so, the author of Hebrews has described Christ as "faithful...in his house" and Moses as "faithful in *all God's* house"--a most peculiar contrast for a theologian attempting to establish the superiority of Christ (56). Spicq comments on the verse in a vein that highlights the significance of the word: "L'accent semble mis ici, pour servir de base de comparison entre Moïse et Jesus, sur l'ὅλῳ...." (66). But for a different estimate of the textual evidence, see Héring, 25, n. 6.

[16] Cf. Héring, 25. Michel notes that this verse allows for a misunderstanding which would make "his house," "Moses' house" and uses the tradition to correct the misunderstanding. The punctuation suggested here would avoid this (96).

a testimony to Moses, parallel to the testimony to Christ cited in 3.2. If "...just as Moses also..." (ὡς καὶ Μωϋσῆς) is treated as a parenthesis, the emphasis is shifted still more to the difficult phrase, "faithful to the one who made him..." (πιστὸν ὄντα τῷ ποιήσαντι αὐτόν): "Faithful to the one who made him in his house (as was Moses also)." While this reading confirms the RSV translation of ποιέω by "appoint," it also suggests that the phrase be seen as a unit, as a translation of the LXX πιστώσω αὐτὸν ἐν οἴκῳ μου.

Is it possible to explain the phrase "faithful to the one who made him" as a translation of the LXX πιστώσω? As a matter of fact, the simplest translation of πιστόω is "make πιστός." Liddell and Scott give the first meaning of the word as "to make trustworthy," and the first meaning of πιστός as "trusted."[17] While definitions of these words are best made in reference to the texts in which they are used, some preliminary observations can be made. First, πιστός has both an active and a passive meaning and the passive meaning is the first and dominant one. Further, the meanings of πιστόω relate directly to the meaning of the adjective. The passive meaning of πιστός is "trusted, trustworthy, reliable or genuine"; therefore also "entrusted or appointed." The (infrequent) active form of the verb corresponds to this meaning; it means "to make trust-worthy" e.g. by putting under oath, or perhaps, by appointing. The active meaning of πιστός, "faithful" or "believing," corresponds to the more frequent passive of πιστόω, which means either "be made trustworthy" or "be persuaded, believe or be confident."

If "faithful to the one who made him" is a translation of the LXX "I will establish," it appears that the author of Hebrews is dealing with the LXX in the same fashion that the Targumist treats the Hebrew text. "I will establish him" (πιστώσω αὐτόν) is rendered by two words: the verb "made him" (ποιήσαντι αὐτόν; actually a participle, but also the predi-cate of which αὐτόν is the direct object), and a participial adjective "being faithful" (πιστὸν ὄντα modifying αὐτόν). The form and sense of this construction are nearly equivalent to

---

[17]LSJ, s. v. πιστόω and πιστός.

that used by the Targumist to translate the Hebrew "I will
establish him" (העמדתיהו): "I will raise him up" (אקימינה, a
verb) "faithful" (מהימן). This rendering gives the interpreter
the fullest advantage of the double meaning of πιστώσω or
העמדתיהו. In the case of the expression in Hebrews, we see
the full force of that phrase only when it is read in the
double sense suggested by seeing the Nathan oracle as its
context: "faithful to the one who made him so, in his house;
faithful to the one who made him (appointed him) in his house."
Thus the difficulty of reading the word "created"--a contextual
as well as theological difficulty--is avoided without the
necessity of reaching back to "apostle and high priest" to give
the verb a predicate.[18] Jesus is the son of David/God made
sure (appointed)/faithful in the house which is the lineage to
which he belongs, and although "it is evident that our Lord
was descended from Judah" (7.14), the family of David, the
family in which he is the leader of many sons to glory is the
lineage of which he partakes through partaking of flesh and
blood (cf. 2.10,14).

It may be worth noting a case of still another translator
treating the word πιστόω in such a way as to elicit the
double meaning which most fully interprets the Nathan oracle.
Lactantius renders 2 Sam. 7.16 LXX: "et *fidem consequetur*
domus eius et regnum eius usque in saeculum (and his house will
pursue faith/attain firmness, as will his reign, forever)."
It appears that Lactantius is rendering the LXX πιστωθήσεται
by the words "fidem consequetur"[19] (Vulg. "et fidelis erit
domus eius"; cf. 1 Chr. 17.14 Vulg. "et statuam eum..."). More
will be said about the meaning of πιστόω and its relation to
the house; first it is necessary to summarize the advantages

---

[18] But see 1 Sam. 12.6: "Μάρτυς κύριος ὁ ποιήσας τὸν
Μωϋσῆν καὶ τὸν Ἀαρων ὁ ἀναγαγὼν τοὺς πατέρας ἡμῶν ἐξ Αἰγύπτου."
Here ποιήσας means both "created" or "raised up to his purpose"
and is synonymous with ἀπέστειλεν in 12.8. This usage is
particularly enlightening; cf. Michel (96, n. 4), who emphasizes creation, and Spicq (65-66), who emphasizes appointment.
Our reading allows both meanings but substitutes for the
offices "high priest" and "apostle" the office "in the house"
(cf. Bruce, 56, n. 10) or "πιστός in the house."

[19] Fletcher, 113, n. 7.

of the conclusion that 1 Chr. 17.14 is cited in He. 3.2.

Reading the citation in He. 3.2 as a citation of the Nathan oracle clarifies both the meaning of the verse and the structure of the passage. Jesus as the Messiah of David's house, the builder of the house of God, attested by the proof-text 1 Chr. 17.14 cited in He. 3.2, is compared to Moses the servant of God unique among God's people, so attested by the proof-text Nu. 12.7 cited in He. 3.5. The comparison is made upon points drawn from the Nathan oracle, and these points of the comparison are made in the order in which they occur in the Nathan oracle. In He. 3.2 the oracle is cited with 1 Chr. 17.14 providing the text. Then the superiority of Christ to Moses is declared: he is the builder of the house of God (3.3, 1 Chr. 17.12); he is God's son (3.5, 1 Chr. 17.13); he is "over God's house" (3.5 at least partially a reference to 1 Chr. 17.14). Further, the context of the Nathan oracle helps to explain the meaning of both the phrase πιστὸν ὄντα τῷ ποιήσαντι αὐτόν and of the house that we are. An examination of the career of the Nathan oracle in the tradition of interpretation further clarifies the meaning of these two words.

The Nathan Oracle in the LXX.

The Nathan oracle is of course not limited to 1 Chronicles 17 and 2 Samuel 7, but is a theme running through the account of the family of David. The heart of the oracle is the promise to establish a house, a lineage for David, to which the reign shall belong, corresponding to the house of the Lord that will be built by the scion of David. The LXX has chosen to empha-size the theme of stability by a consistent translation of a number of Hebrew words with the words πιστός and πιστόω.

In the Nathan oracle, God promises to David a sure house (2 Sam. 7.16: πιστωθήσεται ὁ οἶκος σου) or a descendent made secure in his (God's) house (1 Chr. 17.14: πιστώσω αὐτόν ἐν τῷ οἴκῳ μου), and David prays that God's promise will be secured, brought to pass (2 Sam. 7.26; 1 Chr. 17.23, 24). The LXX underlines this dialectic between God and David by the use of πιστόω to translate three different (although nearly synonymous) Hebrew words: נֶאְמַן, 2 Sam. 7.16, 1 Chr. 17.23,24;

קום, 2 Sam. 7.25; עמד, 1 Chr. 17.14.

This theme of God's firm/faithful promise of a firm/faithful house for David recurs. The progressive fulfillment of the oracle is described as God's affirmation (πιστώσω) of his word to David and his house, or of his divine name, because of that word (1 Kings 1.36, 1 Kings 8.26-27, 2 Chr. 1.9, 6.17). David is also described as faithful, trusted, secure (πιστός) and honorable in the house of Saul (1 Sam. 22.14). The epithet firm/faithful (πιστός) occurs in 2 Kings 11.2 and in 2 Sam. 23.1-2, both of which help to fill out the meaning of the word in regard to the fulfillment of the promise. In 2 Kings 11.2 Ahaz' contribution to the fall of Judah is prefaced with the declaration that he did not act faithfully (πιστῶς) as had David. 2 Sam. 23.1-7 is an oracle of David, his "last words." The LXX appears either to have had a text which differs from the MT or to have misread, perhaps deliberately, the Hebrew word נאם, oracle, as faithful. The RSV translates the difficult Hebrew:

    The oracle of David, son of Jesse
    The oracle of the man who was raised on high
    The annointed of the God of Jacob.

The LXX reads:

    πιστὸς Δαυειδ υἱὸς Ιεσσαί
    Faithful/firm is David, son of Jesse

    καὶ πιστὸς ἀνὴρ ὃν ἀνέστησεν κύριος
    faithful/firm also is the man whom the Lord has raised up

        ἐπὶ Χριστὸν θεοῦ Ιακώβ
        over (?) the Christ of the God of Jacob.

In this version the "man" or hero appears not to be David, but the seed which according to the Nathan oracle God would raise up (ἀναστήσω 2 Sam. 7.7-12; 1 Chr. 17.11). This is followed by a comparison between the sun, which is fixed and prominent in the heavens, and the house of David which is glorious and firm, because of the eternal covenant given to David (4-6).

The promise made to David is referred to as the promise of a house, in particular of a faithful or firm house, not only in the Nathan oracle and in the passage cited above but also elsewhere (1 Sam. 25.28, 1 Kings 1.36, οἶκον πιστόν). Psalm 88 LXX refers to the promise made to David with the same

vocabulary, calling it "mercy builded-as-a-house" (88.3 LXX:
ἔλεος οἰκοδομηθήσεται)[20] and "my covenant made firm with him"
(88.29 καὶ ἡ διαθήκη μου πιστὴ αὐτῷ) to which the sun is again
invoked as "the faithful witness, fixed in the heavens" (88.38
LXX: καὶ ὁ μάρτυς ἐν οὐρανῷ πιστός). Thus a double meaning for
the word πιστός emerges as a theme of the Nathan oracle in the
LXX. On the one hand, the word πιστός refers to the character
of God's promise, of his name with regard to the promise, of
the continuity of David's lineage, of the appointing of the
designated one of that lineage to the reign. The word "firm"
or "fixed" or "appointed" conveys this connotation of the
word. On the other hand, πιστός is also used to refer to the
deeds and conduct of David and his heirs. As the fixity of
the sun in the heavens requires its faithful appearance day by
day, so it is required that the seed of David act faithfully
before the Lord, doing what is right in his sight. Although
the promise does not become conditional on the faithfulness of
the scion of David, there is a reciprocity of faith: only the
faithful descendent is truly the appointed, designated son of
David. The role of this double meaning in the tradition helps
to explain why three translators concerned with the messianic
implications of the oracle would at once distinguish the two
meanings and emphasize both.

While the above discussion extends the context of both
words ("faithful" and "house") it by no means exhausts the
complexities of the theme, for yet another text, the oracle to
Eli the priest in 1 Sam. 2.35, is involved in the development
of the Nathan oracle in the tradition, and brings with it its
own set of elaborations and allusions.

The Nathan oracle and the oracle to Eli.

The relationship between these two texts has also been
remarked by Aalen, again on the basis of the Targums. He
suggests[21] that Tg. 1 Chr. 17.14, which translates the Hebrew
"I will confirm him" (העמדתיהו) by the circumlocution "I will

---

[20]Psalm 88 LXX is, of course, of particular interest
because we have already suspected its presence in 11.26.

[21]Aalen, 233-235.

raise him up faithful" (אקימיניה מהימן) was influenced by a
similar construction in Tg. 1 Sam. 2.35. In the MT, the text
reads "And I will raise up for myself a faithful priest (כהן
נאמן) who shall do according to what is in my heart and in my
mind; and I will build him a sure house (בית נאמן) and he shall
go in and out before my annointed forever" (RSV). In the
Targum, the first clause "*I will raise up* for myself a *faithful
priest*" is rendered ואקים קדמי כהין מהימן, a very literal
rendering of the Hebrew, and nearly identical with the expression used in Tg. 1 Chr. 17.14.

The interpenetration of the two oracles in the Targums is
more extensive than the rendering of והקמתי in 1 Sam. 2.35 and
העמדתיהו in 1 Chr. 17.14 by the interpretive translation
אקים...מהימן. It appears that the influence goes in both
directions: while in the case we have just examined the oracle
to Eli appears to have influenced the translation of the Nathan
oracle,[22] the translation of the oracle to Eli has also been
influenced by the Nathan oracle. In the Targums of the Nathan
oracle, 2 Sam. 7.11 and 1 Chr. 17.10, "...the Lord will make
you a house," appears as: "...the Lord will raise up for you
a reign" (kingdom: מלכו יקיים לך יוי). Although this is not
a literal translation, it certainly gives the sense. But Tg.
1 Sam. 2.35 also translates the word "house" (בית) as "kingdom
or reign" (מלכו) so that in the Targum the verse reads: "I
will raise up for myself a faithful priest...and I will raise
up for him a sure reign" (מלכו קימא). This translation of
"house" as "reign" is surprising; why is the faithful priest
promised not merely a lasting and faithful lineage, but also
a reign?

Unlike the Targums, the LXX produces no actual change of
meaning or wording in 1 Sam. 2.35. The oracle to Eli is
translated:

καὶ ἀναστήσω ἐμαυτῷ ἱερέα πιστὸν
and I will raise up for myself a faithful priest...
καὶ οἰκοδομήσω αὐτῷ οἶκὸν πιστὸν
and I will build for him a faithful house....

---

[22] Aalen, 235: "...its form (the participle) seems to
have its origin in 1 Sam. 2.35."

However there is a very obvious affinity between the vocabulary
in this text and that of the Nathan oracle:

1 Chr. 17.10 οἶκον οἰκοδομήσει σοι κύριος
the Lord shall build you a house

1 Chr. 17.11 καὶ <u>ἀναστήσω</u> τὸ σπέρμα σου μετὰ σέ
2 Sam. 7.12 And <u>I will raise up</u> your seed after you...
καὶ ἑτοιμήσω τὴν βασιλείαν αὐτοῦ
And I will prepare his kingdom

1 Chr. 17.14 καὶ πιστώσω αὐτὸν ἐν τῷ οἴκῳ μου
and I will affirm him in my house

2 Sam. 7.16 καὶ πιστωθήσεται ὁ οἶκος αὐτοῦ
and his house will be affirmed

Although the likeness is most striking when both versions of
of the Nathan oracle are read together, that is exactly what
the reader (if not the translator) would surely have done in
the first century, when differing versions of the oracle would
have been seen as amplifications rather than contradictions.
Thus also the promise made to David is referred to as the
promise of a faithful house (οἶκον πιστόν cf. esp. 1 Kings
11.38: οἰκοδομήσω σοι οἶκον πιστόν). It then appears that the
two oracles are being drawn together in the tradition, and that
their mutual interpretation antedates the translations. The
two points of contact in the oracles are the theme of the
leader or priest who is appointed (to be) faithful and the
promise of a faithful/sure house. What then are the implications of this mutual accommodation of the oracles?

This question requires a review of the function of the
oracle to Eli in the Old Testament and in the tradition of
interpretation. As is the case with the Nathan oracle, the
fulfillment of the oracle to Eli is a progressive theme in
the Old Testament. Samuel, the first of the succession, is
described by all Israel as faithful/appointed/accredited (LXX
πιστός) as a prophet (1 Sam. 3.20; cf. Si. 46.15). Zadok the
priest, intended by the Deuteronomic historian as the fulfillment of the oracle (1 Kings 2.27-35), is introduced to the
narrative immediately following the Nathan oracle: he is the
father of the legitimate priesthood, the faithful house, as
David also is father of the royal house. 1 Chr. 6.37-38
delineates his descent from Aaron through Eleazar and
Phineas, making it clear that the privileges given to

Aaron[23] are his and belong to his heirs. Sirach's treatment of
Phineas speaks of two covenants, one with David and his seed,
one with Aaron and his, asserting:

> The heritage of the king is from son to son only
> so the heritage of Aaron is for his descendents.
>
> (Sirach 45.26)

This passage emphasizes the distinctiveness of the two offices,
their inalienable attachment to the lineage of David and Aaron
respectively. The same attitude can be seen in the literature
of the Qumran community. The two offices are constitutive of
the community; the promise that they shall be filled by the
legitimate heir *forever* is understood not continuously but
eschatologically. In the end, they will be filled by the two
anointed designated heirs. Testimonies are collected to this
effect, which include the Nathan oracle, though not the oracle
to Eli.

Thus the oracle to Eli does have an inherent connection
with the Nathan oracle, which is then elaborated to fit
contemporary expectations by the LXX and the Targum. These
expectations might be similar to those of the Qumran community:
the Targum or the LXX might see the oracle to Eli as a testimony to the messianic priest, the counterpart of the witness
of the Nathan oracle to the royal son of David. There is,
however, another possibility. The degree to which the two
oracles are accommodated to one another in these translations
suggests the possibility that they were, or could at will be
read as applying to a single figure, a priestly messiah who is
appointed/faithful (1 Sam. 2.35; 1 Chr. 17.14) who is God's
son as well as David's (2 Sam. 7.14; 1 Chr. 17.13), who builds
the house of God (2 Sam. 7.13; 1 Chr. 17.12), who also heads
the house built by God (1 Sam. 2.35; 2 Sam. 7.11,12; 1 Chr.
17.10,11) or even, God's house (1 Chr. 17.14).

Zech. 6.11 ff. is another text which could provide a
warrant for the expectation of a priestly messiah to whom is
applied the promises of the Nathan oracle. The original text
appears to have spoken of two crowned figures, the scion of
David, the "branch," probably intended to refer to Zerubbabel,

---

[23]Buchanan, 57, on verse 3.

and the high priest, Joshua the son of Jehosedek. However, at some point before the LXX the name of the former disappeared from the Hebrew text, so that both LXX and MT can be read as referring to a single figure.[24] It will be useful to attempt a reading of the LXX for comparison with both the Nathan oracle and Hebrews.

Zech. 6.11 ...you will take silver and gold and make
...λήψη ἀργύριον καὶ χρύσιον καὶ ποιήσεις

crowns and set them on the head of Jesus
στεφάνους καὶ ἐπιθήσεις ἐπὶ τὴν κεφαλὴν Ἰησοῦ

son of Josedek, the great priest
τοῦ Ἰωσεδεκ τοῦ ἱερέως τοῦ μεγάλου

.12 and you will say to him, thus says the Lord,
καὶ ἐρεῖς πρὸς αὐτόν, ταδε λέγει κύριος

the ruler of all, "Behold a man, Sunrise
παντοκράτωρ   Ἰδοὺ ἀνήρ, Ἀνατολὴ

is his name, and from under
ὄνομα αὐτοῦ, καὶ ὑποκάτωθεν

him (he? there? it?) will rise up
αὐτοῦ   ἀνατελεῖ

and he will build the house of the Lord
καὶ οἰκοδομήσει τὸν οἶκον κυρίου

.13 and he will take power, and he will sit
καὶ αὐτὸς λήψεται ἀρετήν, καὶ καθιεῖται

and will rule upon his throne
καὶ κατάρξει ἐπὶ τοῦ θρονοῦ αὐτοῦ

and he will be a priest on his right hand...."
καὶ ἔσται ἱερεὺς ἐκ δεξίων αὐτοῦ

This translation of the LXX suggests the way in which this passage might have been read by a first century interpreter. It speaks of a "great priest" whose name is Jesus, to whom are given the promises made to the scion of David in the Nathan oracle; he will be the messianic shoot, the head of the household of David; he will build God's house; he will sit upon the throne and rule. The final verse can be read as referring to the right hand of God, recalling Ps. 110.1, which clearly celebrates the inauguration of a "royal priest":

the Lord said to my Lord: "Sit at my right hand..."
Εἶπεν κύριος τῷ κυρίῳ μου. καθοῦ ἐκ δεξιῶν μου...

---

[24]See notes *ad loc.* in *Oxford Annotated Bible* (1973).

"You are a priest forever"
Σὺ ἱερεὺς εἰς τὸν αἰῶνα...

Although Zech. 6.11 is sometimes cited as a source of the
expression "a great high priest over the house of God" (He.
10.21),[25] this suggestion is not entirely convincing. However,
the passage need not have inspired the Christology of Hebrews
directly in order to shed light on our investigation. For it
makes clear the ease with which the Nathan oracle is accommodated to a testimony to the royal priest, when the circumstances suggest the transfer to the commentator. Confirmation
is also found in the traditions of the earliest layer of the
Testament of the Twelve Patriarchs. If in Zechariah and
Psalm 110 the son of David appears to have become a priest, in
the *Testament*, kingship is bestowed on the priestly house, the
Tribe of Levi. The latter appears to reflect the Hasmonean
era when the claim for hegemony was made upon the basis of the
rulers' priestly descent. Both cases bring home the extent to
which history--or as these authors would see it, fulfillment--
acts upon expectation.[26]

The oracle of the royal priest and the Christology of Hebrews.

Frequently it has been remarked that in Christianity, the
expectation of the prophet like Moses, the Messiah (anointed
king), and the messianic high priest (the anointed priest)
have been brought together to explain the fulfillment that has
been found in the person of Jesus, in his death and resurrection. In Hebrews' Christology, the preeminence of the royal
priest in the explanation of Jesus' role cannot be disputed.
It appears then that the Christological model has brought the

---

[25] E.g. in the Nestle text.

[26] R. H. Charles, *The Apocrypha and Pseudepigrapha of the
Old Testament* II (Oxford: Clarendon Press, 1913), 294, cf. 290
and 312. On the process of the mutual interpretation of
history and the scriptures, see N. A. Dahl, "Eschatology and
History in Light of the Qumran Texts," *The Crucified Messiah*
(Minneapolis: Augsburg Publishing House, 1974), esp. 134-141.
Mr. Dahl's treatment of the messianic figures of the Qumran
community should also be read to supplement the rather shallow
treatment above. See Hans Kosmala, *Hebräer-Essener-Christen*
(Leiden: E. J. Brill, 1959), 80-83 and esp. 89.

author of Hebrews to find in the traditions relating the oracle
to Eli and the Nathan oracle an oracle of or testimony to the
royal priest, an oracle which is cited in 3.2, with the words
of 1 Chr. 17.14.

This observation gives us a new insight into the structure
and coherence of Hebrews. The greater theme of the letter's
Christology is enunciated in 2.17-18: "we have a merciful high
priest." The theme of Jesus as *faithful* (πιστός) high priest
is then developed in 3.1-6. Jesus is πιστός in fulfillment of
the promise: he is faithful (πιστός) to the one who made him
appointed (πιστός) as the Christ, as the builder of the house,
as the son, the priest over his faithful and elect house. If
He. 3.2 contains a citation evoking both the expectation of
the designated, anointed scion of David through 1 Chr. 17.14
and the promise of a faithful high priest through 1 Sam. 2.35,
the structural unity of Hebrews is vindicated. For the author
does not hold the theme of Jesus' priesthood in abeyance for
chapters 3 and 4, but broaches it immediately following its
introduction in 2.17-18.

1 Sam. 2.35 and the relationship of the house to the Christology in Hebrews 3 and 4.

The recognition that 1 Sam. 2.35 is also evoked by the
citation in He. 3.2 not only helps to explain the Christology,
but also sheds light upon the meaning of the "house" as
people in He. 3.1-6, for the context of 1 Sam. 2.35 offers
some elucidation both of the vocabulary of Hebrews and of the
function of the oracle.

First, an examination of the context of the oracle helps
to clear up the difficulty of applying to a single messianic
figure, the royal priest, the second half of 1 Sam. 2.35 LXX:
"...I will raise up for him a sure house, and he will go in
and out before my anointed for ever " (...οἰκοδομήσω αὐτῷ
οἶκον πιστὸν καὶ διελεύσεται ἐνώπιον τοῦ Χριστοῦ μου πάσας τὰς
ἡμέρας). So read, the verse speaks of a second figure, the
messiah, before whom the priest will serve in the house of the
Lord. However, it is also possible to read the verse: "...I
will build him a sure house and *it* shall go in and out before
my anointed always." Such a reading might easily be either

inspired by or justified from the immediate context: "Your house and your father's house will go in and out before me forever" (2.30). In both verses 30 and 35, διελεύσεται refers to the priestly service in the sanctuary. The house is the priestly line which serves in the sanctuary before the Lord and his Christ--by our reading, his anointed priest. Such a reading would of course admirably suit the purposes of the author of Hebrews. In He. 3.7-4.16, we, who are Christ's house if we stand firm, are exhorted to hear and to enter. This exhortation is summarized by the call to draw near after the example of our great high priest, Jesus who has "traversed" (διεληλυθότα) the heavens, entering through the veil into the eternal sanctuary (4.14-16; cf. 6.19-20, 10.20-22). The other biblical meaning of the word διελθεῖν, "to lead," also comes into play here: Christ traverses the heavens as "the captain of our salvation" (2.9), making for us the way by which we "with confidence draw near to the throne of grace, that we may receive mercy and find grace to help in time of need" (4.16).

Another characteristic and unusual feature of Hebrews' vocabulary of priesthood may also be related to 1 Sam. 2.30. In this verse of the oracle God rescinds the promise of priestly office once made to the house of Eli's father: "I promised that your house and the house of your father should go in and out before me forever; but now the Lord declares: far be it from me! For those that glorify me I will glorify and the one who despises me shall be *dishonored*" (τοὺς δὲ δοξάζοντάς με δοξάσω καὶ ὁ ἐξουθενῶν ἀτιμηθήσεται). That the bestowal of priesthood is *glory* and *honor* (δόξα καὶ τιμή) is clear in He. 5.4 and 5, but if we add 1 Sam. 2.30 to the list of Old Testament passages which form the background for this application of them,[27] the same context must attach to their use not only in the comparison with Moses in 3.3, but also in the citation from Psalm 8 and its exegesis in 2.5-11. In the

---

[27]Michel (96-97) remarks the close tie between "glory" and "honor" in 3.3 and discusses some of the biblical background of the word "glory." However, he appears to understand "honor" as a Hellenistic concept and therefore does not look for a biblical function of the pair, nor investigate their common function elsewhere in Hebrews. Cf. also below, chapter four, 158-164.

latter passage, the words are used in expressing the soteriological relation between Christ and the house: Christ the
"pioneer of their salvation," Christ "crowned with glory and
honor," leads his brothers, "many sons, to glory." Christ
the priest "who sanctifies and those who are sanctified have
all one origin." Thus it seems that for Hebrews Christ our
priest is the leader (ἀρχηγός) of a priestly house[28] whose
origin is the same as his: the passion by which he also was
"ordained" (τελειῶσαι).

The suggestion that the relation between Christ and the
house in Hebrews 3 and 4 is the relation between faithful
priest and faithful house is confirmed by the monitory function of the oracle to Eli in the tradition. According to
1 Samuel 2, the house of Eli is replaced by a faithful/sure
house because it has proved unfaithful, untrustworthy in its
guardianship of the service of the house of God. The house of
Zadok which replaces it is a house that is accounted faithful
because during the fall and captivity they held fast to the
service of the Lord (Ez. 44.15). Both of these stories as
well as the steadfast zeal of their ancestor Phineas contribute to the interpretation of the oracle as in some way
conditional upon the faith/fidelity of the house. The warning
appears with the use of the text not only in Hebrews but also
in the *Damascus Document*. *CD* 3.19 declares: "He built them
a *sure house* (בית נאמן) in Israel.... 20: Those who *hold
fast* (המחזיקים) to it are destined to live forever...."[29] The
likeness to He. 3.6 has been remarked by other commentators:
"And we are his house, if we *hold fast* (κατάσχωμεν) our
confidence and pride in our hope."[30]

---

[28]Cf. Buchanan, 54-55, on the priestly character of the
community; also Kosmala, passim, but esp. chapter 2: "Die
'Bruder,' die 'Heiligen,' die 'Gemeinde Gottes,'" 44-75.
Both authors concentrate on the epithets applied to the
community and both seek to establish that the recipients of
the letter are Essenes or "covenanters."

[29]The translation of the *Damascus Document* is that of
Geza Vermes, *The Dead Sea Scrolls in English* (Penguin Books,
1970), 99-101. The text used was that of Chaim Rabin, *The
Zadokite Documents* (Oxford: At the Clarendon Press, 1958),
11-15.

[30]Cf. Aalen, 236.

More impressive than these verbal similarities is the
functional parallel between the *contexts* of the two verses.
CD 3.7 presents the generation of the wilderness as "bad
example" because they refused to enter when God so commanded
them (Deut. 9.23). Hebrews also blames their example in this
matter although the texts cited are Psalm 95 and Numbers 14
rather than Deuteronomy (He. 3.7-11, 15-19). In the *Damascus
Document* they refuse to enter because they "chose their own
will and did not heed the voice of their Maker" (*CD* 3.7-8):
as Hebrews declares, out of disobedience, warning the reader
"Today if you hear his voice, do not harden your hearts" (He.
3.7, 15; 4.7). *CD* 3.12-14 relates that "with the remnant that
held fast," the prototype of the community, God made his
covenant, revealing that crown and testimony to his commandments, "His holy Sabbaths and his glorious feasts." So also
"there is a sabbath rest for the people of God" to which
Hebrews exhorts its readers (4.9-11, although its realization
may be entirely eschatological). The "sure house" of "those
who hold fast" is rewarded with "all the glory of Adam"
according to *CD* 3.19-20. According to He. 2.9, we who are
his house are led to glory by "the son of man crowned with
glory and honor" (cf. Ps. 8.5-7 in He. 2.6-10). The sin
against which the faithful/sure house must hold fast is
apostasy, for their good example is "The priests, the Levites
and the sons of Zadok who kept charge of my sanctuary when
the children of Israel strayed from me..." (*CD* 3.21-4.1;
citation is Ez. 44.15). In Hebrews also the sin is apostasy
(3.12-13, 18-19). Finally in both Hebrews and the *Damascus
Document*, there is a set term beyond which no one can enter
(He. 3.13; *CD* 4.10-12).

CD 3-4 and Hebrews 3-4 appear to be midrashic develop-
ments which mold nearly the same set of texts into a presentation of the community as the messianic "house of God,"
a priestly house which is not the exclusive heritage of the
line of Aaron through Eleazar, Phineas, and Zadok, but a
congregation which one joins by obedience. Functionally,
however, "presentation" is a misnomer when applied to these
two passages; they are in fact exhortations.

These and other similar points of contact between Hebrews

and the literature of the Qumran community have been remarked
by numerous commentators on Hebrews or the Scrolls. But it
is unnecessary to construe these likenesses as evidence that
the "Hebrews" were an Essene or Zadokite community, as is
sometimes done.[31] They point not to continuity between the
two communities, but to a similar (though far from identical)
self-understanding. Both the Zadokite sectaries and the
recipients of Hebrews understand themselves as a priestly
house. But the priestly service of the former consists in a
scrupulous (and idiosyncratic) practice of the "Torah of the
priests"; the function of the community is to serve spiritu-
ally, to "hold fast" by constantly holding itself in readiness
to restore the true worship in Jerusalem.[32] The priestly
service of the "Hebrews," on the other hand, is their confession; they serve by their affirmation that all service is
fulfilled in the once-for-all obedience of Jesus our high
priest.[33] It may be appropriate to note that we need not even
conclude that readers to whom the appeal of Hebrews 3-4 could
be addressed must be Jews as well as Christian believers. The
language of priesthood and the language of proselytism are
nearly the same in both Hebrew-speaking and Greek-speaking
Judaism.[34]

What conclusions have we then drawn in regard to the
function of 1 Sam. 2.35, the meaning of the house, and its
relationship to the Christology of He. 3.1-6? The comparison
of He. 3-4 and *CD* 3-4 has led us to conclude that the two
passages are functionally parallel, that they are both
exhortations to communities conceiving of themselves as
priestly communities, that each employs a set of traditional
texts in an allusive way, relying on what is apparently the
"obvious" meaning of these texts. The differences between
passages arise from their very divergent historical

---

[31]Buchanan, 58-59; Kosmala, esp. 68-70.

[32]Vermes, 42-47.

[33]See Hebrews 8-10 and the discussion below in chapter 5
on this.

[34]Both are based upon the multiple meanings of the Hebrew
word "to bring near." Cf. esp. *Siphre Bemidbar Beha'alothka*, 78.

circumstances and theological positions. In the case of
Hebrews, the theological conviction which creates the exhortation is the confession that Jesus is our Christ and true
high priest. The divergence between *CD* 3 and Hebrews 3 helps
to highlight the determinative role of the Christology in
Hebrews; the parallel helps affirm the integral connection
between the main Christological model in Hebrews, the model of
Christ the high priest and the cultic understanding of the
house. Indeed it suggests that the identification of the
house built by/for the son of David with the house that is the
faithful priesthood may be as important to the combination of
the oracles as is the theme of the faithful/appointed one.
Lactantius, who uses the two oracles in the same context (i.e.
in his discussion of prophecies of the office of Christ as son
of God) seems to bring them together on the grounds that the
faithful house and the true temple are one and the same.[35]

Summary: Function of the complex oracle in He. 3.1-6.

As this point it is useful to place these observations
within the setting of the other conclusions we have drawn
about Hebrews 3.1-6. First, 1 Chr. 17.14 is being cited in
Hebrews 3.2 with the words "being faithful to the one who
made him...in all his house," and this citation is intended
to introduce a testimony to Christ which then becomes the
structural basis of the passage. The testimony is an oracle
created (perhaps by Hebrews) from the Nathan oracle and the
oracle to Eli which are already related in the tradition.
It promises a high priest who is πιστός, *appointed* the Christ
as son of God, coming from the tribe of Judah and *entrusted*
with the messianic prerogatives of the son of David. He is
the builder of God's house and the son who is its head. This
house which he heads is the house which is, or replaces, the
house of David and the house of the faithful priest. It is
the house of Christ, to which he joins himself by partaking
in the flesh and blood which its children share--not the flesh
and blood of David alone, although he does share them, but
flesh and blood as such. Yet this does not mean that all who

---

[35]*Divine Institutes* IV.14; see citation above, p. 65.

partake of flesh and blood are automatically of the house of
Christ. This house is built by God through his perfecting of
Christ because it is also built by Christ through his leading
of many sons to glory, and both deeds are the single deed of
of Christ's passion. We only are his house who are bold to
hearken (3.7), to become partakers of a heavenly calling (3.1),
and to draw near on the way beyond the veil inaugurated for us
by Christ the high priest who goes before us (4.14-16; 10.
21-22).

One word of caution should be said in regard to the
Christological statements and their relation to the heritage
of Jewish interpretation of the Nathan oracle: it is necessary to underline the role of the event of Christ and the
theology or Christology of Hebrews in the letter's interpretation of the oracles. While the combined Nathan oracle/
oracle to Eli provides the structure of the argument in He.
3.1-6, the Christology of Hebrews could not have been produced
by combining those oracles. The process of interpretation
articulates rather than creates the Christology of the
interpreter.

This retrospect should also note that two of the questions
raised at the beginning of this chapter have been answered by
the examination of the Christological statements of He. 3.1-6.
First, the theme of Christ the high priest is not dropped
between 3.1 and 4.14, and the comparison in 3.1-6 is intimately related to the exhortation in 3.7-4.16.[36] The function
of the complex oracle of the royal priest and his faithful
house explains both the progress of the theme of the high
priest and the relation between these two sections. Second,
gains have also been made in the definition of the word
"faithful" (πιστός). Its use in the context of the complex
oracle corresponds both to the meaning of the word "by faith"
(πίστει) and to the function of the saints in chapter 11.
Christ is the faithful/firm/appointed high priest, apostle,

---

[36]Contra Michel, see n. 6 above, p. 68.

messianic son, as also the saints *by faith* and *as a pledge*
are the attested witnesses of the better things God has in
store for us.

With these insights in mind, we can now turn to the
questions which remain unanswered, all of which concern the
comparison with Moses, and most of which bear upon the function of the verse invoked as a testimony to him.

The comparison between Christ and Moses in He. 3.1-6.

The focus of He. 3.1-6 is on Christ; the degree to which
an examination of the Christology illumines the text more than
vindicates the assertion that the Christology controls the
progress of the argument and the picture of Moses. So far
the discussion of 3.1-6 has progressed without any attention
to Moses beyond the remark that He. 3.2 alludes to Nu. 12.7
and He. 3.5 cites that text as a testimony to Moses. It is
time now to ask how that testimony functions in He. 3.1-6 or
more precisely how it functions in the comparison with the
testimony to Christ, the oracle of the royal priest and his
faithful house.

The testimony to Moses is remarkable for its verbal
similarity to the texts used for the testimony to Christ, not
only in the Hebrew as represented by the MT but also in the
ancient translations, Tg. Onkelos and the LXX:

> Not so with my servant Moses; he is entrusted with
> (faithful in) all my house. RSV
>
> לא כן עבדי משה בכל ביתי נאמן הוא   MT
>
> לא כין עבדי משה בכל עמי מהימן הוא   Tg. Onk.
>
> (Not so my servant Moses; in all my people he is trusted)
>
> οὐχ οὕτως ὁ θεράπων μου Μωϋσῆς ἐν ὅλῳ τῷ οἴκῳ μου πιστός
> ἐστιν LXX

The two theme words of the Nathan oracle and the oracle to Eli
appear also in Nu. 12.7. Not only are they verbally identical
but their function in the original statement in later interpretation and in the context in Hebrews appears to be very
similar. The word translated by the RSV "entrusted" (MT נאמן,
Tg. מהימן, LXX πιστός) appears in fact to have the double
meaning appointed/faithful. Moses is appointed to/faithful
in his extraordinary role as prophet more than, uniquely

among, the house of God. "House" also appears to mean primarily the people of God in the Numbers passage; indeed, the Targum makes this explicit.

This verbal similarity makes it possible for the comparison to proceed count by count, more or less on the order of the Nathan oracle:

2.17	a faithful high priest	1 Sam. 2.35
3.1	Look to our high priest, faithful	1 Sam. 2.35
3.2	Jesus, faithful to the one who made him (faithful) in God's house	1 Chr. 17.14
	(as Moses also was faithful/ appointed in God's house)	Nu. 12.7
3.3	Jesus builder of God's house	1 Chr. 17.12 2 Sam. 7.13
	Moses (only) in God's house	Nu. 12.7
3.5	Moses appointed servant	Nu. 12.7
	(Jesus) Christ (anointed) son	1 Chr. 17.13 2 Sam. 7.12
	Moses in all his house	Nu. 12.7
	Jesus over his house	1 Chr. 17.14(?)
	whose house we are	1 Sam. 2.35 Tg. Nu. 12.7(?)

Evidently the Christological oracle provides the structure here and the testimony to Moses is fitted into it. But the way in which that testimony fits into the comparison is less evident. It seems that the comparison is being made on the basis of the respective roles of Moses and Jesus. Each is πιστός appointed/faithful as leader or head of the people, but the former as servant, the latter as son. Indeed, when the contrast is made between "in the house" and "over the house" it is difficult to follow the argument to its full implications. Is the author asserting that Jesus (unlike the scion of David) is *not* in the house? Does this mean that he is qualitatively different from the other sons? Conversely, when Moses is said to be *in* rather than *over* the people, is his leadership denied?

Still more puzzling is one of the questions with which this chapter began. Is Moses a member of the house which Christ has built, and over which he is head? On the basis of the treatment of Moses in 11, we would expect this author to

answer in the affirmative.[37] However, in 3.7-4.6, the example
of those whom Moses led out of Egypt is used as a warning,
implying that that was another house, with another leader,
which could have entered, but did not. To what house, then
did Moses belong? If he is in the house that is the house of
both God and Christ, how does he come to be a member of it?
How has he come to know and follow Christ? What is his role
as servant in that house? Does his witness to "the things that
would be spoken" refer to the law, and if so, why is Moses as
lawgiver compared to Christ as "son over the house"? Finally,
why is it necessary to prove Christ superior to Moses when his
superiority to the angels has already been asserted?

At the root of these questions and ambiguities lies the
problem of discovering the cutting edge of the comparison, and
resolving the comparison depends on clarifying the function of
Nu. 12.7 within it. The next chapter will attempt to do that
by examining the function of this verse in the tradition of
interpretation.

---

[37]Spicq II (67) and Bruce (58-59, n. 18) give that
affirmative answer: "Under Christ, as in the time of Moses,
there is but one continuous household of God; it goes back
beyond Moses and even Abraham to embrace Abel and Enoch
and Noah." Bruce, *ibid.*

CHAPTER THREE

MOSES THE MYSTIC:
NUMBERS 12.7 IN THE TRADITION OF INTERPRETATION.

Praised be Moses before all prophets
    for he first encountered God face to face
Not in dark visions
    but as by an image of flesh he beheld him.

Ineffably you passed under and into the divine darkness
    whence God called you, o Moses;
you received the table of the law written by his finger,
    for you were his great servant.

God established his obedience to his voice
    and manifested Moses the theopt before his people
that he might show his initiate
    fearsome with glory.

During the divine visions
    you became the divine scribe of ineffable mysteries;
with words you crafted the wise plan
    of the tabernacle,
but passed on its construction to the architect
    Beseleel.

Verses from the Orthros for the feast of Moses.[1]

Chapter two remarked the extent to which the Christological statements provide the structure of Hebrews 3.1-6 and
both extend and define the application of the words "faithful"
and "house." On the basis of the complex oracle which underlies the passage it has been possible to suggest that the
word "faithful" (πιστός) as applied to Jesus in 3.2 evokes
both appointment of the royal priest, his firm and sure election within the covenant or promise of God, and the fidelity
of his own deed, his own doing according to the will of God.
In addition, the oracle of the royal priest gives a dual context to the word "house": the priest is the builder of the
new house, the temple, as also the head of the new and

---

[1]From the *Menaion* for September 4, first verse from the
acrostic kanon, second two verses from sixth ode, fourth verse
from the seventh ode. Cf. the French of Jean Blanc in "La fête
de Moïse dans le rite Byzantine: Textes tirés de la fête de
Moïse du 4 Septembre," *Moïse, l'Homme de l'Alliance*, 349-351.

95

faithful household whose fidelity and indeed existence are
based upon the firm promise, the sure appointment of the God
who raises them up.

If then this is the context of Jesus' fidelity, how is
Jesus faithful like Moses? Moses' position as faithful/
appointed in the house of God must relate to that of Jesus;
they are being compared on the basis of their authority. But
the comparison is obscured by ambiguities which focus upon
Moses' qualifications: his faith, fidelity; his authority;
his entrustedness, appointment and the area of his authority
(the house). The resolution of these ambiguities is to be
found in the function of Nu. 12.7 in the tradition.

This chapter will make a series of observations about the
function of Nu. 12.7. This text has a highly significant
role in the biblical material which continues into the
interpretive tradition. It is a unique authorization of
Moses' prophecy on the basis of his uniquely intimate vision
of and discourse with God. In the earlier tradition (the
versions, the first-century interpreters and the Tannaitic
midrashim) this text and its context evoke a "high" picture of
Moses, authorizing him even above the angels and depicting him
as a mystic. His vision of God becomes the means for asking
a theological question: what of God can be seen? and a
soteriological one: what will be our vision in the future?
The later rabbinic tradition works out of this picture of
Moses but also attempts to specify the meaning of the text by
applying the words "my house" to 1) God's house/household, the
heavenly *familia*; 2) God's house/dwelling, the whole created
world; 3) God's house/dwelling, the house of the sanctuary;
4) God's house/household, his people, the house of Israel.
These applications can be made alternately or together, without contradicting each other, because the primary function of
the text depicts Moses as first in all these houses because
of his vision, his ascent to the place where God is, and his
having been entrusted with the Torah. This survey of the
tradition will contribute to our understanding of the details
and structure of 3.1-6 but will also make clear that questions
about the function of Moses in Hebrews can only be answered by
a careful examination of the argument of the text.

Numbers 12.7 as God's testimony to Moses.

Numbers 12.7 is the testimony to Moses *par excellence*, for it is God's own character witness to and authorization of Moses. Its overall function is parallel to that of the other classical text from the same passage, Nu. 12.3: "Now the man Moses was very meek, meeker than any man upon the face of the earth." These are nearly (if not absolutely) the only direct characterizations of Moses in the Torah, and as such, they become the basis of later exegetical traditions both as summary statements to be explored and expanded through the scriptures and as proof-texts to be used out of hand. Their common function is seen in the use that Sirach makes of them: "By faith and meekness he sanctified him" (πίστει καὶ πραΰτητι ἡγίασεν αὐτόν, Si. 45.4).

Its function as a proof-text or testimony is, as we have suggested, the over-arching function of the text, including also its more complex functions in extended exegeses. This function is of course most evident in exemplary lists such as *1 Clement* 17-19 and Philo's discussion of faith/belief in *Leg. All.* III.228. Philo also uses the text as evidence that faith/fidelity belongs to God and to his friends.[2] His most direct treatment of the passage is a defense of Moses' marriage to the Ethiopian, who is made the symbol of "the nature that has been tried by fire and cannot be changed."[3] Here Moses as πιστός is "firm, steadfast." In the rabbinic tradition the text is even more flexible of application. Nu. 12.7 is used over and over as a proof-text for Moses' fidelity and for his absolute authority[4] as well as for unspecified authorizations and even for his name being Heman (from the same consonants as the Hebrew נאמן).[5]

---

[2]*Leg. All.* III.204.

[3]*Leg. All.* II.67 (Loeb I, 267).

[4]Cf. Michel, 93, where he refers to the collection of Strack-Billerbeck, III, 683.

[5]*Mekilta Beshallaḥ* 4 (Lauterbach II, 221); *b.B.B.* 15a; *Gn. R.* 1.11, 99.5; *Ex. R.* 5.10, 18.5, 31.8, 33.5, 47.9, 51.6; *Nu. R.* 19.3.

Nu. 12.7 in the Moses traditions of the Hebrew scriptures.

If the numerous citations of Nu. 12.7 testify to its
centrality in later traditions about Moses, this is hardly
surprising, for it plays a nearly unique role in the Moses
traditions of the Hebrew scriptures. The function of this
verse in its context is determinative for later interpretation;
clarifying that function will provide a firm basis for the
explication of later uses of the text. At the same time it is
necessary to recognize that the text functions within a
complex of related texts and that these too will require
attention.

Numbers 11-12 is a literary creation (attributed to E)[6]
which asks and attempts to answer a series of theological
questions about the role of Moses as prophet, the meaning of
prophecy, and the character of Moses' prophetic authority.
The episodes of which it is composed are: the rebellion of
the people and the sending of the quails (11.1-23, 31-37); the
appointment and prophetic "ordination" of the seventy elders
(11.24-25); the incident of Eldad and Medad (11.26-27); and
finally the jealousy of Aaron and Miriam (12.1-16). Two
issues organize these legends into a narrative essay on Moses'
prophecy. The first issue is the meaning of Moses' role.
Chapter 11 explains Moses' role as a prophetic office, an
office that originates in Moses, but can and indeed must be
shared through God's gift of the prophetic spirit with others
who are thus authorized by God to help bear the burden of
this great and quarrelsome people. Thus the office is the
gift of God, the power of the spirit which is not qualitatively different from the spirit given to other prophets (i.e.
the elders) and to which Moses has no exclusive or even
determinative right (Eldad and Medad). Indeed, it would be
ideal if all the people of God could share, and as it were,
abolish the office.

The second issue is the uniqueness of Moses' prophetic
authority. In chapter 12, Miriam and Aaron, also prophets of
the Lord, challenge the unique authority of Moses, asking:
"Has the Lord spoken only through (to?) Moses? Has he not

_____

[6]See *Jerome Biblical Commentary* (1968), *ad loc.*

spoken through us also?" In response, God affirms the uniqueness of Moses' prophetic revelation, making it clear that he,
God, is jealous for the authority Moses is too meek to defend:

Nu. 12.6 If you have a prophet of the Lord
          in an apparition will I be known to him
          and in a dream will I speak with him.

    .7   Not so my servant Moses;
          in all my house he is trusted.

    .8   Mouth to mouth I speak with him and (in)
          sight and not with riddles (dark speech)
          and the image of the Lord he sees.
          And why did you not fear to speak against
          my servant, Moses?

Nu. 12.6   אם-יהיה נביאכם-יהוה
                         במראה אליו אתודע בחלום אדבר-בו

    .7   לא-כן עבדי משה בכל-ביתי נאמן הוא

    .8   פה אל-פה אדבר-בו ומראה ולא בחידת
                              ותמנת יהוה יביט
                         ומדוע לא יראתם לדבר בעבדי במשה

The Hebrew is difficult and the sense is made more
difficult by the fact that מראה is used both of the vision of
Moses (8) and of the vision of the prophets (6). The MT deals
with this problem by using differing vocalizations: מַרְאָה
for verse 6, meaning "mirror,"[7] and מַרְאֶה for verse 8, meaning
"vision" or "sight." Thus the uniqueness of Moses' vision is
protected and the distinction between Moses and all other
prophets is preserved and explained: his is a firsthand,
theirs is a refracted vision.

Thus according to Numbers 12 the authority of Moses as
the spokesman to whom God speaks is guaranteed by his uniquely
intimate vision. The question seems to be: "how does Moses
know what he knows about God?" and the answer: "More directly,
and therefore more, than any other prophet." Nu. 12.7, "He is
trusted in all my house," appears to be a shorthand version of
the passage, which covers both Moses' authority and his vision.

---

[7]BDB gives "vision, means of revelation" as the first
meaning and places the use of the word in Nu. 12.6 under this
category; Marcus Jastrow in *A Dictionary of the Targumin, the
Talmud Babli and Jerushalmi and the Midrashic Literature* (New
York: Pardes Publishing House, Inc., 1950), gives "mirror"
as the first meaning.

The tradition of interpretation: the LXX.

Nu. 12.6-8, then, is a guarantee of Moses' authority based upon his vision of God, and it remains so in the tradition. The LXX has already begun to interpret the text by translating with an increasing degree of definition:

.6 If you have a prophet of the Lord
 in a dream (or vision) I will be known to him
 and in sleep I will speak with him

.7 Not so my servant Moses: in all my house
 he is faithful/trusted

.8 Mouth to mouth will I speak with him
 in an image and not through riddles
 and the glory of the Lord he has seen.

 And why were you not afraid to speak against my
 servant Moses?

.6 ἐὰν γένηται προφήτης ὑμῶν κυρίῳ,
 ἐν ὁράματι αὐτῷ γνωσθήσομαι
 καὶ ἐν ὕπνῳ λαλήσω αὐτῷ·

.7 οὐχ οὕτως ὁ θεράπων μου Μωϋσῆς·
 ἐν ὅλῳ τῷ οἴκῳ μου πιστός ἐστιν·

.8 στόμα κατὰ στόμα λαλήσω αὐτῷ,
 ἐν εἴδει καὶ οὐ δι' αἰνιγμάτων,
 καὶ τὴν δόξαν τοῦ κυρίου εἶδεν·

 καὶ διὰ τί οὐκ ἐφοβήθητε καταλαλῆσαι
 κατὰ τοῦ θεράποντος μου Μωϋσῆς;

This version specifies the text not merely by translating נאמן with πιστός but also by translating "he sees" (יביט) with the aorist "he saw" (εἶδεν) and "image" (תמונה) with the word "glory" (δόξαν). The aorist suggests that the translation sees the oracle as referring to a definite past incident in God's communication with Moses, and the word "glory" (δόξαν) seems to indicate that the incident in question is the vision granted to Moses when he asked to be shown God's glory (cf. Ex. 33.17-23).

As was mentioned above, there are other texts related to Nu. 12.6-8 and these texts also show an increasingly specified mutual reference in the LXX. For instance, Dt. 34.5-10, the closing statement on the greatness of Moses, shows the effect of still another interpretive step. In the Hebrew the text seems to represent reflection on Nu. 12.7-8 and Ex. 33.11:

Ex. 33.11   Thus the Lord used to speak to Moses face to
             face as a man speaks to his friend.

Dt. 34.5   So Moses, the servant of the Lord (עבד יהוה)
             died there in the land of Moab....

   34.10   And there arose no prophet since in Israel
             like Moses, whom the Lord knew face to face.

The LXX version of these two verses relates them still
more closely to Nu. 12.7 than the Hebrew. By translating the
"servant of the Lord" (עבד יהוה) as the "household member" or
"household servant" of the Lord (οἰκέτης κυρίου), it condenses
Nu. 12.7: "My servant...in all my house" (θεράπων μου...ἐν
ὅλῳ τῷ οἴκῳ μου); by translating "face to face" (פנים אל פנים)
with πρόσωπον κατὰ πρόσωπον, it recalls Nu. 12.8, "mouth to
mouth" (στόμα κατὰ στόμα). At the same time it in effect
erases the relation to Ex. 33.11, of which the Hebrew text of
Ex. 34.10 is very nearly a literal quotation. For the LXX
renders the words "face to face" (פנים אל פנים) in Ex. 33.11
with the words ἐνώπιος τῷ ἐνωπίῳ.

Does this rendition intend to distinguish the text of
Ex. 33.11 from these others, and if so, why? It appears that
these translations may be an attempt on the part of the
translators to reconcile a difficulty which they find in the
course of Exodus 33. Ex. 33.11 says that God was accustomed
to speak with Moses face to face, but verses 19-20 say that
Moses cannot see God's face because a man cannot see God and
live. The translation of 33.11 therefore modifies that
statement with a more vague expression; thus Moses is said to
converse with God in the intimate presence of friend with
friend. It is possible to read the translation of Numbers
as consistent with that of Exodus by understanding "mouth to
mouth" as an expression of the intimate manner in which God
delivers his word to Moses and the form of the Lord that Moses
saw as the vision of God's glory, the vision of Kabod (δόξαν)
in which Moses saw God's *back* only. Likewise, the words of
Dt. 34.10 "whom the Lord knew face to face..." say nothing
about what Moses saw, and can be referred to the immediacy
with which Moses received God's word. The LXX, then, appears
to be concerned with translating Nu. 12.6-8 and the texts
related to it through their treatment of the prophecy or the
vision of Moses, in a fashion that is not so much verbally

homogeneous as theologically harmonious. Nor is the concern of the LXX simply to avoid anthropomorphism; rather, the care used to protect God's "face," if carried to its logical conclusion, suggests an acutely anthropomorphic view. Further, Ex. 33.12-17 LXX is far bolder than the MT on the same verses. The translation is influenced by, perhaps guided by, questions that are, properly speaking, theological: questions which seek to investigate the reality of God as transcendent and the problem of revelation.[8]

Numbers 12.6-8 and the vision of Moses in the Targums.

The Targums show a set of similar interpretive moves, also attempting to reconcile Ex. 33-34 with itself and to interpret Nu. 12.6-8 in light of the events described in those chapters. Nu. 12.8 is reconciled to Ex. 33-34 and the offense in both verses is removed by translating "mouth to mouth" (Nu. 12.8) and "face to face" (Ex. 33.11) with ממלל, "speech," instead of either "face" or "mouth".[9]

> Nu. 12.8 speech to speech (utterance for utterance?) will I speak with him
>
> Ex. 33.11 And the Lord spoke with Moses speech for speech as a man speaks with his comrade.[10]

In addition the Targums specify which "vision" Nu. 12.8 presents. Onkelos' version shows his interpretation to be

---

[8] For a similar view of Ex. 33.11-23 see Arthur Soffer, "Anthropomorphisms and Anthropopathisms in the Septuagint of Psalms," in Sidney Jellicoe, *Studies in the Septuagint: Origins, Recensions and Interpretations. Selected Essays with a Prolegomenon* (New York: KTAV Publishing House, 1974).

[9] Targums Onkelos, Jonathan ben Uzziel and Neofiti I (a representative of the Jerusalem Targum) appear to be at one on this particular point. The margins of Neofiti I also substitute the "Word of the Lord" (ממרא דייי) for "the Lord" (דייי) in Ex. 33.11. The editions used here are: Sperber, *The Bible in Aramaic I: The Pentateuch according to Targum Onkelos*; David Rieder, *Pseudo-Jonathan. Targum Jonathan ben 'Uziel on the Pentateuch* (Jerusalem: Rieder, 1974); Alejandro Diez-Macho, *Neofiti I*, 5 vols, English tr. by Martin McNamara and Michael Maher after the Spanish of Diez-Macho (Madrid-Barcelona, 1970).

[10] The translators of the Neofiti I versions of these

almost identical with that of LXX: "and he beholds the image of the glory of the Lord" (ובדמות יקרא דיו מסתכל). Targum Jonathan gives a more complex explanation of the vision: "in vision and not with mystery revealed I myself to him at the bush and he beheld the likeness of the back of My Shekinah" (ודמו דבתר שכינתי חזי). This translation distinguishes between "vision" (מראה, translated by חזי) which it refers to the incident at the bush in Ex. 3, and "image" (תמונח, translated by דמו) which it explains as what Moses saw in the revelation of Ex. 33-34: the back of God, or rather of his glory or his glorious Shekinah.[11]

Like the LXX, then, the Targums find the authorization of Moses on the basis of his vision particularly striking and even troublesome; they also correct it so as to harmonize with Exodus 33-34, in addition to harmonizing that passage with it-self. Most significantly, the LXX and the Targums agree in identifying the image of God which Moses saw with the glory, or the back (of the glory) in Ex. 33.23.

In both these versions of the Targum, the translation of Dt. 34.10 is also related to the texts of Ex. 33.11 and 18-23 and Nu. 12.6-8. In Onkelos, "whom the Lord knew face to face" is revised closer to the bolder statements of Numbers and Exodus: "unto whom the Lord revealed himself face to face." Jonathan is both more elaborate and more circumspect; it introduces into the prophecy a divine intermediary, the Word (ממרא) of the Lord, and revises the text to read: "speech for speech." In the context of Dt. 34.10, this change appears to mean that God's Word directed Moses by consultation at every step: "...because the Word of the Lord had known him to speak with him word for word, in all the

---

verses have chosen to render the phrase: "as one speaker to another speaker." However, the Aramaic is nearly identical with that of the other Targumim and the alternate translation "speech for speech" appears in the marginal notes.

[11]Neofiti I reads "and an image from *before* the Lord he used to contemplate." However this may well refer to the same occasion, for the expression "from before" may refer to this Targum's version of Ex. 33.23, where Moses is told: "...I will make the troops of angels pass by who stand and minister before me."

signs and wonders and manifestations which the Word of the
Lord sent him to perform...." In addition Jonathan adds to
the mighty deeds of Moses listed in Deuteronomy "all the
solemn things which Moses did when he received the two tables
of sapphire stone...."[12] Thus all the texts seem to be
increasingly concerned with the fact and manner of the
revelation of Moses.

In addition, the Targums give some special attention to
12.7, in particular to the phrase "trusted in all my house."
Onkelos substitutes for "my house" (ביתי), "my people" (עמי),
as we mentioned above. Jonathan explicates this phrase still
further: "in all the house of Israel, my people" (בכל בית
ישראל עמי). Possibly the explication refers to Dt. 34.10:
"...there did not rise up *in Israel* a prophet like Moses, whom
the Lord knew face to face." We shall return to the interpretation of the house;[13] for the moment, this observation
underlines the attempt of the interpreters to reconcile the
various explanations of Moses' prophecy and vision and to
reconcile them on a theological basis.

Early Midrashic interpretations of the visions of Moses:
Sirach, Philo and Paul.

The explication of the vision of Moses mentioned in Nu.
12.8 by the vision of Moses recounted in Exodus 33-34 appears
to be borne out by a variety of early interpretations of the
passage. Si. 45.4-6 appears to combine Nu. 12.7 with the
phrase from Ex. 33.11 as a description of Moses' role as
lawgiver, perhaps *via* Dt. 34.5-10.

---

[12]Tr. J. W. Etheridge, *The Targums of Onkelos and
Jonathan ben Uzziel on the Pentateuch, with the Fragments of
the Jerusalem Targum: From the Chaldee, vol. II, Leviticus,
Numbers and Deuteronomy* (London: Longman, Green, Longman and
Roberts, 1862-1865; reprint ed., New York: KTAV Publishing
House, 1968), 685.

[13]Neofiti I differs: "...in the whole world I have
created, he is faithful." This interpretation will be
discussed below.

Sirach 45.4-6

In faith and meekness he sanctified him; he chose him out from all flesh....	...faithful in all my house... Moses was very meek Nu. 12.7,3 ...in all my house/meeker than any man upon the face of the earth... Nu. 12.7,3
and made him hear his voice and led him into the darkness and gave him to his face the commandments.	...mouth to mouth I speak with him... Nu. 12.8 The Lord spoke to Moses face to face... Ex. 33.11 ...whom God knew face to face... Dt. 34.10

Thus it seems that Sirach has further defined the occasion when God spoke face to face with Moses as the revelation on Sinai when God gave Moses the commandments.

Two other very early interpretations of the text interest themselves in the extraordinary character of the revelation. Philo focuses on the mystical character of the prophecy of Moses as described by the distinction in Nu. 12.6 and 8. He combines this passage with Dt. 34.10 as the primary description of Moses' prophetic experience in order to deduce a prophetic office for Abraham based upon his night vision (which Philo understands as ecstatic).[14]

Paul also uses this text in combination with Dt. 34.10 to treat modes of the vision of God, but his concern is not with Moses at all. The distinction the old law makes between Moses and other prophets, Paul posits between our present vision and our future vision:

> Now we see in a mirror, dimly (δι' ἐσόπτρου, ἐν αἰνίγματι) but then, face to face (πρόσωπον πρὸς πρόσωπον).
>
> Now I know in part; then I shall understand as I have been understood (ἐπεγνώσθην; 1 Co. 13.12).

To "see face to face" is to share in the vision of Moses (Ex. 33.11, Nu. 12.8, Dt. 34.10); to "know as one has been known" is to exceed it (Dt. 34.10). Our present vision is that of the other prophets: it is through a mirror (or lens) and in a dark speech, or riddle. This description of the other prophets' vision seems to attest to Paul's knowledge of both the LXX and the Hebrew text, or some text or tradition which derives from it. The Hebrew text describes the other

---

[14]*Quis Rerum*, 262.

prophets' vision as "in a mirror" (במראה) in 6, and the Greek
text describes it as "through enigmas" (δι' αἰνιγμάτων) in 8
(for בחידות, darkly or in riddles).

This passage is also a witness to a very early choice to
translate the Hebrew word מראה in Nu. 12.6 by its second
meaning, "mirror," and for the possible antiquity of a similar
interpretation in *Lev. R.* 1.14:

> What difference is there between Moses and all the
> other prophets? R. Judah b. Il'ai and the rabbis
> [gave different explanations]. R. Judah said:
> Through nine *specularia* did the prophets behold
> [prophetic visions]. This is indicated by what is
> said: *And the appearance of the vision that I saw
> was like the vision that I saw when I came to
> destroy the city and the visions were like the
> vision that I saw by the river Chebar and I fell
> on my face* (Ezek. XLIII,3). But Moses beheld
> through one *specularium*, as it is said: *With him
> do I speak...in a vision and not in dark speeches*
> (Nu. XII,8). The rabbis said: All the prophets
> beheld through a blurred *specularium*, as it is said:
> *And I have multiplied visions and by the ministry
> of angels I have used similitudes* (Ho. XII,11).
> But Moses beheld prophetic visions through a
> polished *specularium*, as it is said: *The simili-
> tude of the Lord doth he behold* (*loc. cit.*).[15]

These interpretations (i.e. those of Rabbi Judah on the one
hand and of the rabbis on the other) differ from that of the
MT in that they make the distinction between Moses and the
prophets not by the use of differing vocalization, but by
adducing texts, and more significantly in that they place
a single *specularium* between Moses' vision and direct sight:
not even Moses' vision of God is immediate.[16]

Thus Sirach, Philo and Paul all show an interest in the
character of the revelation to Moses. In addition, the
interpretation of Paul demonstrates another function of the
passage. For Paul, the experience of Moses has served as a

---

[15]*Lev. R.* 1.14 (Soncino, 17; underlining mine). The
word ראה, meaning "see" appears eight times in differing forms
in the citation from Ezechiel, and one of these forms is
plural. The first form is מראה, hence 9 lenses.

[16]It should be pointed out that this interpretation does
not accept the MT solution of using differing vocalizations
for the use in 12.6 and that in 12.8, but solves the problem
by adducing texts.

means of posing and answering questions about our experience
of God, or more precisely about the possibilities of knowing
God.[17]

In summary, then, the versions and these early interpretations interpret Nu. 12.6-8 in combination with Exodus 33
and Dt. 34.5 and 10. Three aspects of the Numbers passage
continually gain in prominence within this complex of
interpretation:

1) the role of Moses as the servant in God's house
requires explication and illustration;

2) the text and its related texts are normally concerned
with establishing the uniqueness of Moses' prophecy in Israel;

3) the uniquely direct character of Moses' revelation,
i.e. the immediacy of God's communication with Moses, becomes
the subject of speculation.

These three functions of the text are handed on into the
rabbinic tradition. The major features of that interpretation
are best examined beginning from the discursive commentaries
of the Tannaitic Midrashim on Numbers, *Siphre Bemidbar* and its
smaller companion, *Siphre Zuta*. Since these texts are not
available in English,[18] it will be best to include first a
complete translation of the comments on Nu. 12.6-8 which are
pertinent to our discussion, then a brief commentary on the
commentary. *Siphre Zuta*, whose comments are more concise and
appear no less ancient, provides the better starting point.

---

[17]The passage from *Lev. R.* 1.14 cited above is followed
by a similar promise that our future vision shall equal and
even exceed the clarity of Moses' vision:

> R. Phineas said in the name of R. Hosha'iah: This may be
> compared to a king who allowed himself to be seen by
> his intimate friend [only] by means of his image. In
> this world the Shechinah manifests itself only to
> chosen individuals; in the Time to Come, however, *The
> glory of the Lord shall be revealed, and all the flesh
> shall see it together; for the mouth of the Lord hath
> spoken it* (Isa. XL.5).
>
> (Soncino, 17)

[18]But see note 28, below.

The Tannaitic Midrashim: *Siphre Zuta.*[19]

> IF YOU HAVE A PROPHET OF THE LORD, IN A VISION I WILL BE
> KNOWN TO HIM AND IN A DREAM I WILL SPEAK TO HIM.
> He says to them: "The prophets whom *you* call prophets,
> IN DREAMS and in visions I speak with them, as it is
> said:
>
>> In a dream-vision of the night
>> when deep sleep falls upon men
>>
>> [Dread came upon me and trembling
>> which made all my bones shake.
>>
>> A spirit glided past my face
>> the hair of my flesh stood up.
>>
>> It stood still;
>> but I could not discern its appearance (מראהו).
>>
>> A form (תמונה) was before my eyes;
>> there was silence (דממה) then I hear a voice:
>>
>> Can a mortal man be righteous before God?
>> Can a man be pure before his maker?
>>
>> Even in his servants he puts no trust
>> (הן בעבדיו לא יאמן)
>> and to his angels he imputes error.][20]
>
> NOT THUS have I dealt with MY SERVANT MOSES, but
> IN ALL MY HOUSE HE IS TRUSTED.
> All that is above and all that is below have I revealed
> to him, all that is in the sea and all that is in the
> dry land.
>
> Another interpretation: IN ALL MY HOUSE HE IS TRUSTED:
> even over (or more than)[21] the ministering angels and
> the sanctuary HE IS TRUSTED.
>
> MOUTH TO MOUTH I WILL SPEAK WITH HIM:
> This teaches that Moses' prophecy was not by the hands
> of an angel.[22]

---

[19]*Siphre Zuta Beha'alothka* 12.6-8 (Horowitz, 275-276).
The translation is my own. Much thanks is due to Alan Cooper
who kindly reviewed this translation and that of *Siphre
Bemidbar* below, 113-114.

[20]Only the first verse of the citation (Job 4.13) actually
appears in the text of *Siphre Zuta*. I have supplied the
bracketed verses (14-18) as the context seemed to require it.

[21]Alan Cooper has pointed out to me that על can be understood as "more than" as well as "over," and that Moses would
then be described here as honored more than the ministering
angels and the temple.

[22]"By the hands of an angel," i.e., through an angel.
This overly literal rendering is preserved in order to make
clear the likeness to Acts 7.35: "This man (Moses) God sent
as both leader and saviour with the hand of the angel who
appeared to him in the bush." See below, 111-112.

Perhaps the dread of the Shekinah was on Moses when he spoke with him? "And the Lord spoke with Moses face to face as a man speaks with his friend" (Ex. 33.11). As any one's friend speaks with him and he has no fear of him, so the dread of the Shekinah was not on Moses in the time when he was speaking with him.

AND THE IMAGE OF THE LORD HE SEES.
R. Simeon says that he would see the image directly.

AND WHY DID YOU NOT FEAR TO SPEAK AGAINST MY SERVANT MOSES? Why does scripture say, AGAINST *MY* SERVANT? Only because you have not made a stench to go up against him but rather against me, since there is no one worse than a thief except his fence.

Another interpretation: AGAINST MY SERVANT MOSES: *I* told him to separate from his wife.

Siphre Zuta is principally concerned with the uniqueness of Moses as prophet. It has elucidated 12.6, the description of the experience of the other prophets ("in an apparition" or mirror, במראה and "in a dream," בחלום) with a quotation from Job, a description of a vision which the interpreter (i.e., the author of the comments, or perhaps the compiler of *Siphre Zuta*) understands as a description of the way in which God normally deals with the prophets. Only a part of Job 4.13 actually appears in *Siphre Zuta*, and the first portion of that has been modified or follows a deviant text.[23] But a look at the context makes it clear that the whole of Job 4.13-18 is invoked to provide a warp upon which the fabric of interpretation is worked. The text of Job delineates precisely those features in which the prophecy of Moses, the revelation made to him, is unlike that of the other prophets. Their vision is חלום הזיון, a night vision, a dream which comes in sleep; it is accompanied by fear and trembling; there is a form (תמונה), but its appearance (מראה) is indistinct. Their vision is mediated, unclear, because God does not trust in his servants (the prophets)[24] and even deceives ("imputes error to"

---

[23]The MT reads here: "Amid thoughts from visions of the night" (בשעפים מחזיונות לילה); *Siphre Zuta* reads: "In a dream-vision of the night" (בחלום הזיון לילה). The first word, חלונו, is the word for "dream" in the text of Nu. 12.6. חזיון, "vision," appears in both the tannaitic Midrashim at this point, and the Aramaic forms which render מראה in the Targums are related to it.

[24]Cf. *Siphre on Deuteronomy*, #357.5, which declares that the title *servant* (עבד) is given to Moses (Dt. 34.5) in an

ובמלאכיו ישים תהלה, can also be understood "puts error in")
his angels.

Concerning precisely these details of the prophets'
vision, God says, "NOT THUS have I dealt with my servant Moses,
rather IN ALL MY HOUSE HE IS TRUSTED." There is nothing that
God hides from Moses, whether in the heavens or in the lower
regions, whether in the sea or in the dry land. This comment
extends the scope of Moses' vision and prophecy, at least in
appearance, to the natural world. It appears to be an interpretation similar to that of Neofiti I: "In all my world
which I have created, he is trusted." The two pairs of
opposites may be intended to be inclusive ("in the *whole*
world"), or the reference to the sea and the dry land may be
intended to particularize the context to the Exodus. Thus the
"above" would be the mountaintop of Moses' ascent and revelation, while "below" would be the wilderness where Moses
wrought mighty signs at the behest of God. The second interpretation, "even over the ministering angels and the heavenly
sanctuary," may simply be an extension of the first: "all
that is above and all that is below I have revealed to him,
even the ways of the angels and the heavenly sanctuary." It
is also possible to read the *dabar* '*aher* in close relation to
the course of the interpretation, as deriving from or at least
referring to Job 4.18, "...in his angels he puts error"; but
as for Moses, to him even more than to the ministering angels,
God reveals all things and himself plainly.

The comments on Nu. 12.8 which relate to Moses' vision
also appear to take the citation from Job into account. On
MOUTH TO MOUTH WILL I SPEAK WITH HIM the interpreter comments:
"This teaches that Moses' prophecy was not by the hand of an
angel," in whom, according to Job, God puts error. Further, in
the case of Moses, there is no fear; "no dread of the Shekinah
was upon Moses when he spoke with him." Rabbi Simeon's
comment may also be an attempt to read the two texts (Numbers
and Job) together; according to him the image (תמונה) which

---

honorific vein, because this title was applied to the prophets
of old. Amos 4.7 is adduced as evidence: "For the Lord God
does nothing without revealing his secret to his servants the
prophets."

Moses sees in Nu. 12.8 is the divine image (דמות) which Moses
sees "directly." His choice of דמות may be inspired by the
proximity of the words "form (תמונה, the same word as in Nu.
12.8), and "silence" (דממה, a word different from but not
unrelated to "image," דמות) in the text from Job. The choice
could have been suggested to him by reading Job 4.16 not "I
could not discern its appearance; a *form* (תמונה) was before my
eyes; *silence* (דממה) and I heard a voice,"; but "I could not
discern its appearance; a *form* was before my eyes, an *image*
(דממה) and I heard a voice." Thus for Rabbi Simeon the
difference between Moses' experience and that of the prophets
is the quality of the image they saw: Moses saw the image
(תמונה, דמות) directly, but the prophets "could not discern
its appearance" (מראהו), perhaps because they see in a mirror
or in a lens (במראה, Nu. 12.6).

Thus this commentator makes a very high estimation of the
intimacy and directness of Moses' vision and knowledge. Moses'
status as redeemer and lawgiver, as God's unique emissary,
must always place him in the problematic position of first
under God, his primacy at once a threat and an enhancement to
God's glory. By the assertion of God's direct dealing with
Moses, the commentator takes up a position on Moses in the
context of this debate. The declaration that Moses' prophecy
was "not by the hand of an angel" is particularly significant,
for there also exists a stream of the interpretive tradition
which places a high value on the immediacy of the message and
saving deed of God, and is characterized by the use of the
phrase, "not by the hands of a messenger."[25] This tradition
can cut either way with regard to the debate over the status
of Moses. Some of the statements in this form corroborate
the judgment of *Siphre Zuta* on Moses, the most striking of

---

[25]See on this phrase Judah Goldin, "Not by Means of an
Angel and Not by Means of a Messenger," *Religions in Antiquity*,
ed. Jacob Neusner (Leiden: E. J. Brill, 1968), 412-424. This
section of our discussion in particular was greatly influenced
by discussion which took place in and around Mr. Goldin's
class in Midrash and Talmud in 1973-1974 at Yale University.
On the phrase as implying a negative valuation of mediation,
see the dissertation of Terrance D. Callan, *The Law and the
Mediator; Ga. 3.19b-20* (Yale University, 1977), 177-183.

these being a passage from the opening of *ARNB*:

> Moses received Torah from Sinai--not from the *mouth*
> of an angel and not from the *mouth* of a seraph, but
> from the mouth of the king of kings over kings, the
> Holy One, blessed be He [i.e., MOUTH TO MOUTH I WILL
> SPEAK TO HIM] as it is said (Lev. 26.46), 'These are
> the statutes and ordinances and laws (which the Lord
> made between him and the children of Israel in Mount
> Sinai by the hand of Moses).'[26]

In contrast, the author of Luke-Acts takes a "low"
position insisting that Moses' prophecy was indeed by the hand
of an angel: God sent Moses to be leader and savior "with the
hand of the angel who appeared to him in the bush, (Acts
7.35)." Not only Moses' vision but also his prophetic signs
and his leadership of the people are accomplished through an
angel. The Passover Haggadah, on the other hand, seems to
desire to diminish or dispense with the prophecy of Moses in
the redemption, as lessening the immediacy of God's partici-
pation:

> And the Lord brought us forth out of Egypt, not by
> means of a seraph, not by means of a *messenger*
> (שליח). On the contrary, the Holy One, blessed be
> He, by His own glorious self [did it]....[27]

In the light of this debate, then, it is not surprising
that the commentator who glorifies Moses' prophecy for its
immediacy would take care to point out that it does not
diminish Israel's intimacy with God, for Moses as God's
emissary is as God himself. Perhaps for this reason, the last
comment of *Siphre Zuta* on Nu. 12.8 leaves the comparison with
the vision accorded to the other prophets and goes on to draw
the conclusion: Miriam and Aaron ought to have been afraid to
speak against Moses, who is God's representative; the startling
simile implies that God's position in the thing for which they
blame Moses is no better than Moses'. The second interpretation is only a more specific version of the same explication:

------

[26]The translation is Mr. Goldin's (419). The bracketed
phrase is my own addition, but see Mr. Goldin's comment on Nu.
12.6-8 (*ibid.*) as well as his explanation of the proof-text
from Leviticus (420).

[27]This translation is also that of Mr. Goldin (414);
Hebrew addition mine.

precisely in that matter for which they had criticized Moses,
he was carrying out the express command of God.

The Tannaitic Midrashim: *Siphre Bemidbar*.[28]

IF YOU HAVE A PROPHET OF THE LORD IN A VISION I AM KNOWN
TO HIM.
  Perhaps in the way that I speak with the prophets,
IN A DREAM
  and in an apparition thus I SPEAK WITH MOSES? Scripture
  says:
NOT THUS MY SERVANT MOSES.

IN ALL MY HOUSE HE IS TRUSTED.
  Except more than the ministering angels. R. Jose says,
  "Including more than the ministering angels."

MOUTH TO MOUTH I WILL SPEAK WITH HIM:
  MOUTH TO MOUTH I told him to separate from his wife.

IN A VISION.
  This is a vision of Dibbur. You say, "This is a vision
  of Dibbur? Rather, this is none other than a vision of
  Shekinah." Scripture says, "And he said, 'You shall
  not be able to see my face, for a man does not see me
  and live'" (Ex. 33.20).
  Rabbi Akiba says, "Man" literally and חי, these are the
  ministering angels.
  Rabbi Simeon the Temanite says, "God forbid that I
  should detract from the words of R. Akiba, but rather,
  I add to his words: "Man" literally and חי these are
  the *Hayoth haqodesh* and the ministering angels.
  Rabbi Eliezer be-Rabbi Jose says: "Not only do they
  not see, but they also do not know the place as it is
  said: 'Blessed be the glory of the Lord from his
  place'" (Ez. 3.12).

  And why does scripture say "...a man does not see me
  and live? While he lives he does not see, but he does
  see at the time of his death and thus it says: "*To his
  face* (לפניו) shall bend all who go down into the dust
  and whose soul does not live " (Ps. 22.30).

AND NOT IN RIDDLES.
  Why is this said? Because it says: "Son of man, riddle
  a riddle and compare a comparison" (Ez. 17.2). Perhaps as I speak with the prophets in riddles and com-
  parisons, thus I speak with Moses? Scripture says,
  AND NOT IN RIDDLES.

AND THE IMAGE OF THE LORD HE SEES.
  This is a vision of the back. You say, "This is a

---

[28]*Beha'alothka* 103 (Horowitz, 101-102). After this
translation was made, I discovered the translation of Paul
Levertoff, *Midrash Siphre on Numbers: Selections from Early
Rabbinic Interpretation* (London: SPCK, 1926) 84-86. However,
since Levertoff's translation is not based on the most recent
texts and is not complete, I have used by own.

vision of the back? Rather this is none other than
vision of the face." Scripture says "I shall take away
my hands, and you will see my back" (Ex. 33.23). This
speaks of a vision of the back. "But my face you shall
not see" (ibid.). [This speaks of a vision of the face.
But it says]29 "And he separated it before me and it was
written face and back (recto and verso)" (Ez. 2.10).
And do not even the barely learned and the ignorant do
that? Then why does scripture say "face and back"?
"Face"--in this world; "back"--for the world to come.
"Face"--the abundance of the wicked and the need of the
just in this world; and "back" meaning the reward of
the just and the retribution of the wicked for the world
to come. "And there was written upon it, 'lamentations,
and music and woe'" (ibid.). The lamentations of the
wicked, as it is said, "This is a lamentation which
shall be lamented, the daughters [of the nations shall
lament it, over Egypt and over all the multitudes shall
they lament it, says the Lord God]" (Ez. 32.16). And
the music of the righteous, as it is said, "The strains
of the lute and the strains of the harp, the strains of
the music upon the lyre. [For you make me glad by your
deeds, o Lord; at the works of your hand I sing for
joy]"30 (Ps. 92.4-5). And the woe of the wicked, as it
is said, "Disaster comes upon disaster" (Ez. 7.26).

AND WHY DID YOU NOT FEAR TO SPEAK AGAINST MY SERVANT?
Scripture says AGAINST MY SERVANT only that instead of
saying AGAINST MY SERVANT you should say, "Against me."
A comparison: To what is the matter like? Like a king
of flesh and blood, who had an *apotropos* (ἐπίτροπος,
administrator or viceroy) in a capitol city and the
citizens were speaking against him. The king said to
them, "Not against my servant have you spoken, but
against me have you spoken. And if you say, 'I do not
recognize his actions,' this is worse than the
former."31

Siphre's first comment on 6-7 is functionally parallel to
that of *Siphre Zuta*: it seeks to explicate the uniqueness of
Moses' prophecy by comparison with that of the other prophets.
As we noted above, the text poses a problem in that

29The textual tradition is disturbed here and the text
reads better without these verves.

30The bracketed verses of scripture are supplied to make
the significance of the citations more clear.

31Levertoff translated: "And if ye should say: 'The
king does not know of the steward's doings,' that is an
offence which is greater than the first." He explains: "i.e.
if they should say that the king is deceived about the character of his representative they would offend the king himself"
(86, n. 1). My translation suggests that the citizens refuse
to recognize the authority of the king in the steward.

the word מראה is used twice, once to describe the vision of
the prophets and once to describe that of Moses which is being
distinguished from the prophets' vision. *Siphre* has made the
distinction by replacing the word מראה in 12.6 with "apparition," חזיון, a word suggestive of the visions of the seer,
perhaps to be understood as ecstatic and hallucinatory, but
certainly reminiscent of the vision described in Job 4.13-18.
This same word is used by *Siphre Zuta* in the opening line of
the citation from Job, possibly placed there by the commentator.

The next comment also appears to relate to the interpretation of *Siphre Zuta*, although the relationship is less clearly
defined: "IN ALL MY HOUSE HE IS TRUSTED. Except more than the
ministering angels. Rabbi Jose says, 'Including more than the
ministering angels.'" The comment is not identical in meaning
with that of *Siphre Zuta*, which declares Moses trusted *over*
the ministering angels and the sanctuary. However, the two
may be related through the comment of *Zuta* on MOUTH TO MOUTH:
"Not through the hand of an angel" Moses' revelation came, for
he was more trusted than even the ministering angels.

Siphre's comments on 12.8 are less cohesive than those of
Siphre Zuta. The first of them, on MOUTH TO MOUTH, is reminiscent of the final comments on 12.8 in *Siphre Zuta* but here
authorizes the deed for which Aaron and Miriam criticize Moses
as a particular, perhaps private, revelation from God to Moses:
"MOUTH TO MOUTH did I speak with him that he separate from his
wife." The comment appears also in Targum Jonathan: "speech
for speech I spoke with him that he separate from sexual
intercourse."[32]

The words IN A VISION offer the occasion for a collection
of incompletely integrated comments on the vision of Moses, or
perhaps we should say, on the vision of God. The first of
these begins directly from the words IN A VISION, but seems to
have the whole of 12.7-8 in mind. The problem addressed is
the same problem which we remarked as influencing the LXX's

---

[32]This comment appears upon the lips of R. Judah b.
Bathyra in *ARNA* 2 (Goldin, *The Fathers*, 19), apparently in
opposition to the practice of building a fence around Torah.
R. Judah adduces Nu. 12.8 as a proof that Moses did not deduce
his own celibacy as a fence around Torah and by a *qal wehomer*,
but rather was given a direct command in a private revelation.

rendition of the biblical texts and that of the Targums: What was the character of Moses' "face to face" vision? What did he see? *Siphre* and an imaginary opponent put forward two possible answers to the first of these questions: 1) his vision was a vision of Dibbur, Word, and 2) his vision was a vision of the Shekinah. The first of these involves a revelation of the Word which is heard in the intimacy and directness of a face to face conversation, according to Ex. 33.11 as friend speaks to friend. He sees nothing, or at least, no form. The second involves a vision, seeing something. This is the point of the citation from Ex. 33.17: "you shall not see me, for a man cannot see me and live." In other words, it must have been a vision of Dibbur, which one cannot see, but hears. Since the vision was face to face, the mode of seeing is excluded. This deduction also appears in at least one version of the Targum Jonathan on Ex. 33.11 itself: "The Lord spoke to Moses speech for speech--the voice of the Word was heard, but the splendor of the face was not seen--as a man speaks with his friend."[33]

The exchange of opinions among the rabbis which follows is actually a set of comments upon Ex. 33.20, in which the vision of Moses becomes a means of inquiring after the possibilities of seeing God. Rabbi Akiba reads the second part of the verse as a substantive, חי "the living ones," and declares, "these are the ministering angels." Thus neither "a man" (Moses?) nor the ministering angels see God. Rabbi Simeon's comment, as he says, merely extends the reading of Rabbi Akiba, by drawing the more obvious conclusion: "the ones who live (חי - ḥay)"--These are the *ḥayoth haqodesh* (the holy living creatures) and the ministering angels." Thus the comment asserts that the knowledge of God's heavenly attendants is not greater than that of Moses; they also do not see in their vision of God.

The comment of Rabbi Eliezer extends this assertion: not only do they not see, but they even do not know the place. Despite textual difficulties with the scriptural citation, it is clear that his interpretation is made on the basis of

---

[33]Etheridge, I, *Genesis and Exodus*, 555.

Ez. 3.12-13: "The spirit lifted me up and I heard after me
the sound of a great earthquake: 'Blessed be the glory of the
Lord from his place.' And a sound of the wings of the ḥayoth
touching one another and a sound of the wheels beside them and
a sound of a great earthquake." His purpose in adducing the
text seems to be to establish that the creatures and the
angels can only praise the Lord on his departure from the
place; they cannot know the place.[34] Moses on the other hand
is said to have known the place, precisely on the basis of
Ex. 33.20-21, from which the debate began: "'But,' he said,
'you cannot see my face, for a man cannot see me and live.'
And the Lord said, 'Behold a place with me.'"

Midrash 'Agadah Wayyikra'[35] makes the comparison explicit:

> AND HE CALLED TO MOSES. The elevation of Moses is
> greater than the elevation of the angels, for the
> angels when they are praising him, do not know his
> place but answer and say: "Blessed be the name of
> the Lord from his place" and Moses is not so, but
> face to face he spoke with the Shekinah.

The continuation of this text is also of interest:

> And further, because the angels have six wings and with
> two they cover their faces, thereby they do not *see*
> (יבטו) the Shekinah, but Moses, peace be upon him,
> about him it is said: and when Moses went before the
> Lord to speak with him he took off the *covering* (מסוה)
> until he came out (Ex. 34.34) and not again (did he
> remove it) except when the Shekinah called to Moses.

Two features of this text from *Midrash 'Agadah* deserve
our notice. The first is that Nu. 12.7-8 seems to be playing
some inexplicit role in the text; the unidentified proof-text
that is cited is equally reminiscent of Ex. 33.11 and Nu. 12.
7-8:

---

[34]R. A. Greer has called my attention to the parallel
comment in *b. Ḥag.* 13b:

> Behold it is written: *Blessed be the glory of the Lord
> from His place*; accordingly, no one knows his place.

Israel Abrahams, the translator and editor, suggests that the
vagueness of "from his place" is the grounds for the conclusion. Soncino, 79, n. 3.

[35]1.1. Ed. Salomon Buber (Jerusalem, 1961).

Midrash 'Agadah: But Moses is not so, rather face to face he
speaks with the Shekinah.

ומשה אינו כן אל פנים עם פנים דבר עם השכינה

Nu. 12.7-8   Not so my servant Moses...mouth to mouth I
speak with him.

לא כן עבדי משה...פה אל פה אדבר בו

Ex. 33.11   And the Lord spoke with Moses face to face
as a man speaks with his friend.

ודבר יהוה אל משה פנים אל פנים כאשר איש אל רעהו

Midrash 'Agadah, then, seems to be another witness for the
phenomenon that Nu. 12.7-8 and Ex. 33.11 are being interpreted
together and in conjunction with Dt. 34.10.

The second notable feature is that the double comparison
between Moses and the angels in regard to speaking with God
and knowing his place may also point to a double comparison
behind the *Siphre* text; that is, Rabbi Akiba's interpretation
of Ex. 33.19 involves a comparison with Moses: the ministering angels and the Hayoth do not see, nor do they know his
place. So also, Moses is not permitted to see God's face,
but is granted a vision of Dibbur, a vision in which he hears
the voice of the Word, and knows his place. But God makes
two special allowances for Moses which grant him a rank of
privilege above that of the ministering angels: 1) the revelation in which he hears the Word is face to face (Ex. 33.11,
Nu. 12.8, Dt. 34.10); and 2) he is permitted to see God's
back (Ex. 33.18-23).

The third comment on IN A VISION appears to leave aside
the exchange among the rabbis and to return to the first
comment:

> Why does Scripture say, "...a man cannot see me and live?"
> while he lives he does not see, but at the time of his
> death he does see, and thus it says: "To his face shall
> bend down all who go down to dust and whose soul does
> not live." (Ps. 22.30).

Although the comment appears to be a generality, it may have a
specific reference to Moses. Compare the similar interpretation in *Siphre on Deuteronomy* on Dt. 34.10:

> WHOM THE LORD KNEW FACE TO FACE: why is it said?
> Because, as it is said: "And he said, 'make me please
> see your face,'" He said to him, "In this world you do
> not see,"--which is comparable to *face* as it is said:

"You will not be able to see my *face*--but you shall
see in the world to come."--which is comparable to
back as it is said: "And I will take away my hand and
you will see my back." When did he cause him to see?
At his death, to teach you that the dead see.[36]

There are then two possible ways of identifying this third
comment's function in *Siphre*. First, it may be an entirely
new and even contradictory interpretation denying that Moses
saw anything at all until the moment of his death. Second, as
seems more likely, it may extend the interpretation given in
the first comment still further: during his life, Moses spoke
with God face to face, hearing the voice of his Word; he also
saw a vision of God's glory, in which he actually saw the back
of God. At his death, Moses was further permitted to see the
face of God.

Thus all the comment on IN A VISION deal with the text on
two levels. They seek to explicate it both in terms of what
actually happened to Moses according to the account given by
the scriptures and in terms of what the experience of Moses
tells us about the possible modes of knowing God. The first
comment identifies the vision which Nu. 12.8 indicates by
these words as the face to face speaking and explains that
this was a vision of Dibbur, the Word, in which Moses heard,
but did not see. The exchange among the rabbis compares the
vision granted to Moses to that given to the living creatures
and the ministering angels, and declares it superior to theirs
on the ground that Moses knew the place and the angels and the
living creatures do not. The third comment explains that
Moses' vision and more is granted to the dead, as to Moses
also the greater vision was granted at the time of his death.

The running commentary on Nu. 12.8 continues with a
comment on AND NOT WITH RIDDLES, which also seems to bear on
the vision. It contrasts the vision (of the Word) which came
to Moses with that granted to the other prophets. Ezekiel's
experience as "Son of man" is the model for the experience
of most human messengers of God: "Riddle a riddle and compare
a comparison."

---

[36]*Siphre ad Deuteronomium*, 357, 10, ed. L. Finkelstein
(Berlin: Jüdischer Kulturbund, 1939) 431.

Up to this point, the comments on verse 8 seem to be traveling in a single functional stream, i.e. toward answering the question, "What is the מראה of Moses?" The answer is: it is the revelation of God's Word which was given to Moses in the tent of witness where he spoke with God face to face. This was God's customary way of speaking with Moses (Ex. 33.11, Dt. 34.10) and must not be thought to refer to the vision in which he *saw* an image, the vision of God's glory, which was *not* "face to face", at least not during Moses' lifetime. This revelation was, however, greater than that given to the angels, who do not know his place (and who cover their faces), and is not of the figurative (and therefore distorted) quality given to other human prophets.

Thus the interpreter or the compiler has made the first step in confronting the problem raised by Exodus 33 and Numbers 12. The next set of comments is intended to complete that solution:

> AND THE IMAGE (תמונת) OF THE LORD HE SEES.
> This is the vision (מראה) of the back. You say "This is the vision of the back? No, it is not, but this is a vision of the face." Scripture says, "I shall take away my hands and you will see my *back*." (Ex. 33.23)

The key to the interpretation is the commentator's reason for replacing "image," תמונת, in Nu. 12.8 by the word "vision," מראה. It is possible that the interpretation refers to the same vision as is discussed in the preceding comments, here interpreted with the aid of another verse from Exodus 33. In that case, the commentary is now offering an alternative, perhaps we should say contradictory, interpretation of this vision. But it is also possible that the commentator in fact intends to say: "THE IMAGE OF THE LORD HE SEES. This seeing of the image (תמונת) refers to another vision (מראה) than that spoken of above; this image was seen by Moses when he asked to see the glory of God and was permitted to see God's *back*." The opponent replies, "Nonsense, it's the same face-to-face vision as above." "But," replies the commentator, "Scripture says, 'I shall take away my hands and my face you shall not see.'" Therefore, the response implies, this second part of Nu. 12.8 must be speaking of a second vision, which was not

face-to-face, for it explicitly says that he saw an image.
Thus according to *Siphre*, Nu. 12.8 tells us that Moses had two
kinds of vision: God spoke with him face to face in a vision
of the Word (as Ex. 33.11 tells us), and God also showed him
his back in a vision of his glory (as is recounted in Ex.
33.17 ff.).

The same solution to the problem of Moses' vision is
proposed by the LXX. The first part of the verse is translated
in the future: "mouth to mouth will I speak with him, in a
vision and not with riddles," and thus refers to the series of
prophetic revelations made to Moses in the tent of witness.
The verb of the second part of the verse is translated in the
aorist: "And the glory of the Lord he saw." (καὶ τὴν δόξαν
τοῦ κυρίου εἶδεν). Thus it refers to the specific occasion on
which Moses was granted the unique revelation of the Kabod,
the vision of God's back. As we remarked above, the Targums
also make this distinction. Indeed, Targum Jonathan distinguishes still further: "MOUTH TO MOUTH is speaking (God *told*
Moses to separate from sexual intercourse); the VISION is the
imageless vision of the bush; the IMAGE is the vision of the
back of God."

In *Siphre* this distinction is followed by another complex
comment which offers an allegorical interpretation of the
words "face" and "back," by adducing a situation from the book
of Ezechiel. It differs from the similar comment from *Siphre
on Deuteronomy* in the passage cited above in that there *face*
applies to vision of God in the present and *back* to the vision
of God in the future, so that the words appear to have a
double meaning rather than an allegorical significance. In
this passage the revelation with which the passage appears to
be concerned is the revelation of the future of Israel or
perhaps of humanity: apparently Moses is shown the diverse
ends of the just and the wicked in his vision of God's back.
The idea also appears in Targum Jonathan's interpretation of
the vision in Ex. 33.12 ff. and 34.5-6. The allegorical
interpretation may be intended to deny that in fact Moses saw
anything of God; however, it is also possible, and somewhat
more likely, that it is intended to add to, rather than to
detract from the earlier interpretations.

Siphre's last comment on Nu. 12.8 is functionally identical with those of *Siphre Zuta*. MY SERVANT is my representative, says God, his authority is my authority and your treatment of him is equal to your treatment of me.[37]

In summary, then, the function of Nu. 12.6-8 is placed in two different perspectives by the two Tannaitic Midrashim. *Siphre Zuta* is concerned with the continuation of the function of these verses in Numbers, finding in them a distinction of Moses' prophecy from that of the other prophets. The interpreter sharpens this distinction by the introduction of a text from Job 4.13-18 which, as a (standard?) description of revelation to mortals, provides a foil for the extraordinary, direct way in which revelation comes to Moses.

Siphre is concerned with the same problem which the LXX and the Targums see in the series of statements which include Exodus 33, Nu. 12.6-8 and Dt. 34.10, all of which evoke the necessity of attempting to reconcile Exodus 33 with itself. *Siphre* distinguishes two kinds of vision which were granted to Moses:

1) A revelation of the Word: "this is the vision of Dibbur":

   Ex. 33.11　And God spoke with Moses face to face as a man speaks to his friend.

   Dt. 34.10　There did not arise another prophet in Israel like Moses whom the Lord knew face to face.

   Nu. 12.8　Mouth to mouth will I speak with him, in a vision and not with riddles.

2) A revelation in sight: "this is the vision of the back."

   Ex. 33.23　I shall take away my hands and you will see my back...

---

[37]Cf. the parallel from *Mekilta Beshallaḥ* adduced by Levertoff (85, n. 5) given here in the translation of Lauterbach (I.252):

AND THEY BELIEVED IN THE LORD AND IN HIS SERVANT MOSES (Ex. 14.31). If you say they believed in Moses, is it not implied by *Kal vehomer* that they believed in God? But this is to teach you that having faith in the shepherd of Israel is like having faith in him who spoke and the world came into being. In like manner you must interpret: "And the people spoke against God and against Moses" (Nu. 21.5). If you say they spoke against God, is it not implied by *Kal vehomer* that they spoke against Moses? But this comes to teach you that speaking against the shepherd of Israel is like speaking against Him who spoke and the world came into being.

Nu. 12.8   And the image of the Lord he sees.
The same problématique appears in the versions, and in Tg.
Jonathan a very nearly identical solution is proposed.

Both Tannaitic Midrashim, then, as well as the ancient
versions,are concerned with two large questions in their treatment of these verses. The first is the more obvious problem
of defining the uniqueness of Moses' prophecy on the basis of
this less than clear testimony. The second is the still
larger theological problem of discovering what one can know,
what can be seen, of God, and therefore of what our future
vision will be.

Moses appointed/faithful more than the angels.

Within these two larger functions the portion of the text
quoted by Hebrews has taken on another function still and one
which we find somewhat peculiar: it has entered into the
debate about Moses' superiority to the angels. In some way
the words "not so my servant Moses, over all my house he is
faithful/trusted" immediately inspire in the interpreter the
desire to clarify Moses' position with regard to the angels.
But why? One problem in giving an answer is that the two
texts of *Siphre* and *Siphre Zuta* seem to be answering different
questions: *Siphre Zuta*'s interpretation is a *dabar'aher* which
seems almost parenthetical to the course of the author's
thought. It has been interpreting the text in accordance
with the text of Job 4.13-18 and it is not unexpected that
the interpretation of this text should include a contrast with
Job 4.18:

> even in his servants (the prophets) he puts no trust
> (לֹא יַאֲמִן) and in his *angels* he puts error.

Thus the text of Nu. 12.7 could appear parallel to the author
of *Siphre Zuta*: God does not trust in his servants the
(other) prophets, except for his servant Moses, who is indeed
trusted in all his house and whom he does not deceive with
the angels, for he (God) speaks with him face to face, and not
by the hand of an angel. But the text does not say this; it
says "over the ministering angels and the house of the
sanctuary." While this comment could simply mean, "Moses is

more esteemed than even the ministering angels and the temple,"
it seems to be answering a specific question: "(how far does
the authority of Moses extend?) Even over the ministering
angels and the house of the sanctuary, HE IS TRUSTED."

Other (probably later) interpretations associate Nu. 12.7
with Moses' supervision of the work (especially the finances)
of the tabernacle. However, "house of the sanctuary" is
normally applied rather to the temple. Paired with the ministering angels, it seems to suggest that the house is the
heavenly temple and that Moses is the orchestrator (λειτουργός?) of the angelic liturgy conducted in it.

Siphre's comment on this verse seems to be more integrated into the course of the interpretation than does that of
Siphre Zuta. *Siphre* seems to be saying "Moses is more trusted
than the angels because of the vision in which God spoke with
him face to face" (which vision the angels do *not* have
according to the discussion added by R. Akiba, R. Simeon and
R. Eliezer).

But the form of the comment indicates a certain functional independence of the context in that it is formally and
functionally parallel to the comment on the similar text,
Nu. 12.3, in *Siphre* and functionally parallel to the tradition's handling of that text elsewhere.[38] As in Sirach 43.4
("by faith and meekness he sanctified him") the two texts
are seen to be proof-texts of Moses' superior virtue and R.
Jose delivers the more "pro-Moses" interpretation of each of
them, in the same form. The comment on Nu. 12.3 reads:

> (NOW THE MAN MOSES WAS VERY MEEK, MEEKER) THAN ANY MAN
> UPON THE FACE OF THE EARTH.
> And not than the fathers. R. Jose says: also than
> the Fathers. THAN EVERY MAN. And not than the
> ministering angels.[39]

It is not clear from the form of the passage whether R.
Jose concurs in the last opinion; it would seem that he does.
It is clear that R. Jose's opinion on the text is the

[38]*ARNA* 9; Judah Goldin, *The Fathers according to Rabbi
Nathan*, Yale Judaica Series X (New Haven: Yale University
Press, 1955) 56; *Siphre Zuta* 12.3 (Horowitz, 275).

[39]*Siphre Behaḥlothka* 101 (Horowitz, 100).

dissident opinion; *Siphre Zuta* and *ARNA* both stand over against him for the strictest possible interpretation of the verse: "than every man upon the face of the earth--that is than his own generation and not than the fathers, the future generations or the angels." This however does not mean that the opinion extends only as far back as R. Jose (2nd c.). The form at least suggests that the question of Moses' humility as opposed to that of the angels does not first arise with R. Jose but that his opinion is dissident from the majority decision on this question. This may be borne out by *Siphre Zuta* and *ARNA* neither of whom mention R. Jose although both treat the question.

The similar treatment of the text quoted in Hebrews suggests the existence of an independent debate about the status of Moses in which the interpreter asks: was he more humble, more trusted, greater,[40] stronger[41] than the angels, the patriarchs, the future generations? R. Jose's dissident opinion in *Siphre* witnesses in both cases that the question was a serious question, not merely a rhetorical one intended to play down the praise of Moses that stands in the Biblical text (as might indeed have been inferred from the version of the debate given in *ARNA*).[42]

The existence of such a debate explains for us a peculiarity of the structure of Hebrews: it tells us that it is by no means superfluous when Jesus has been proven superior to the angels to go on to demonstrate also his superiority to Moses. This is the more helpful in that Hebrews makes the comparison between Jesus and Moses precisely on this text which leads R. Jose to conclude that Moses is superior to the angels in

---

[40]Cf. *Midrash 'Agadah Wayyikra'* 1.

[41]*Midrash Tehillim* 103.18. See the translation of William G. Braude, *The Midrash on Psalms* II, Yale Judaica Series VI (New Haven: Yale University Press, 1959) 165.

[42]See *ARNA* 9 (Goldin, *The Fathers*, 56), also the discussion of this passage in Goldin's article "The First Chapter of Abot de Rabbi Nathan" in *Mordecai M. Kaplan: Jubilee Volume on the Occasion of his Seventieth Bithday* (New York: Jewish Theological Seminary of America, 1953) 263-280. See Appendix, 278.

regard to his trust.[43]

On the assumption that R. Jose reads 12.3 to mean that
Moses is more humble than the patriarchs and the future generations, but not than the ministering angels, we can also point
to the discrepancy between his two comments to attest to the
debate's serious concern with the text. Why does R. Jose
conclude that Moses is not more humble than the ministering
angels, but is more trusted (נאמן) than they? The first
answer seems to be that the close reading of the text informs
his answer as well as that of his opponents. Nu. 12.3 says
only that Moses is more humble than any man: "meeker than any
man on the face of the earth." Numbers 12.7 says: "in all my
house he is נאמן." Seemingly it is the word "house" which
permits the Rabbi to conclude that Moses is more נאמן even
than the angels. It may be construed as a vague statement
which simply admits of the inclusion of the angels, but two
features of the passage tell against that. First, "my house"
(ביתי), is not really more vague than "man" (איש), which can
in fact be read by the tradition to mean "angel".[44] Second, the
comment on Nu. 12.7 speaks *only* of the angels; it is not
interested in the patriarchs or the future generations. Thus
it would seem that the formulation of 12.7 positively suggests
the comparison with the angels and that it is the word "my
house" (ביתי), which in some way includes, suggests or even
is equivalent to the angels. And indeed, the tradition of
interpretation provides a meaning which will corraborate each
of these:

1) the tradition speaks of the *familia*, household, on high,
   which is the angels,
2) the tradition interprets "my house" (ביתי) as "creation"
   or the universe in which the angels are included and over
   which they have charge,

---

[43]Michel, 92-93, n. 1; Spicq II, 66; and Windisch, 29, all
make reference to the comment in *Siphre*. Michel alone seems to
apply it to the structure of Hebrews.

[44]The interchangeable use of the words "man" (איש) and
"angel" (מלאך) to describe God's messengers in the Hebrew
Scriptures make this a matter of course for the rabbinic
commentator. The most striking example might be "the *man*
Gabriel" (Dan. 9.21).

3) the tradition interprets "my house" as the tabernacle or temple, with which *Siphre Zuta* seems to link the angels.

It will be useful to examine the texts which provide each of these possibilities in the interest of answering two questions: 1) In what focus does the comparison between Moses and the angels place the use of this text in Hebrews? 2) What do these traditional interpretations tell us about the meaning of "house" in Hebrews 3.1-6?

My house/household, the *familia* on high.

The Latin word *familia* appears in transliteration (פמליא) in the rabbinic materials as a designation for the heavenly household,[45] that is, God's heavenly attendants and especially the ministering angels. One of the best examples of this use is a passage proclaiming the unique status of Moses. The passage is *Dt. R.* 11.10, Moses' response to the angel Sammael who is demanding of him his soul.

> I ascended heaven and trod out a path there and engaged in battle with the angels, and received the law of fire, and sojourned under [God's] throne of fire, and took shelter under the pillar of fire, and spoke with God face to face; and I prevailed over the heavenly *familia* and revealed unto the sons of men their secrets, and received the Law from the right hand of God and taught it to Israel,...[46]

The picture this passage intends to present is fairly clear; it is the traditional picture according to which Moses ascended to heaven when he ascended the mount to receive the law, and contended with the angels either to gain access to God or to get the Torah, got a tour of the heavenly environs and then returned to bestow the law on Israel. The notable feature of this particular passage is the repetition which expands upon "and engaged in battle with the angels and received the law of fire." Its formulation seems to have been influenced by Nu. 12.7-8: "and spoke with God face to face, and prevailed over the heavenly *familia*...."/"...in all my household he is

---

[45] See *Siphre Bemidbar Nissa* 42 (Horowitz, 47); *b. Hag.* 13 b; *Midrash Tehillim* 11.6 (Braude I, 163).

[46] *Dt. R.* 11.10 (Soncino, 185).

trusted: face to face do I speak with him...."

The legend of the contest between Moses and the angels for
Torah provides a very helpful focus for the traditions about
Moses and the angels. First of all it helps to further define
Siphre's commentary on the passage. According to *Siphre*, the
vision which Moses had was a vision of דבור in which he "spoke
to God face to face." So far I have simply suggested on the
basis of the future with which the LXX translates "I speak,"
that this face-to-face vision was the ordinary way in which
Moses received revelation from God. But the traditions offer
the possibility of being more precise than that. Two midrashic
texts, *Midrash Tehillim* 103.17-18 and *Midrash 'Agadah Wayyiqra'*
1 suggest that the vision of Dibbur is precisely or perhaps
preeminently the giving of Torah.

Three principal texts are involved in these two interpretations: Lev. 1.1, "And the Lord called to Moses from the tent"
which is cited explicitly; a parallel, Ex. 19.3, "And the Lord
called to Moses from the Mount and Moses ascended to God,"
which is not cited, but which has clearly been more significant in the formation of the tradition; and Ps. 103.20,
"...mighty in strength who do his Word, to hearken to the
voice of his Word." Although the treatment of the two midrashim differs in detail, the general lines of the interpretation are similar. Both decide (on the basis of the interpretation of Psalm 103) that the angels do not hear the voice
of God's Word; that "the mighty in strength who do God's Word
to hearken to the voice of His Word" are Israel at Sinai;
that the revelation at Sinai was precisely a vision of Dibbur.
In *Midrash 'Agadah* this means precisely the "ten words"[47] and
especially the first. The first commandment (דיבור הרשאון) is
seen as a theophany upon Israel. The conclusion of both
interpretations is best expressed by *Midrash Tehillim*:

> Who, then, can bear to hear God's voice? *He is mighty
> that executeth His word* (Joel 2.11), the *mighty* being
> the righteous man that executes His word and thereby
> is greater than the ministering angels. And who is
> this mighty man? Moses, who heard the sound (voice)
> of the word (הדיבור) of the Lord, as is said *And It
> called unto Moses* (Lev. 1.1). Hence it is said

---

[47] I.e. the ten commandments as they appear in Ex. 20.4-17.

*Ye mighty in strength that fulfill His word, hearkening
to the voice of His word.*[48]

It is noteworthy that the words, ויקרא אל משה, which in
both purport to be an interpretation of Lev. 1.1, in fact
interpret the verse according to the scene which follows the
same words in Ex. 19.3. The same phenomenon is apparent in
the parallel treatment in the *Midrash Rabbah* on Leviticus.[49]
What it suggests is not immediately obvious. There seem to be
at least two possibilities. Either the interpreter understood
the past tense, "And he (it) called" (ויקרא), in Lev. 1.1 as
referring to the giving of the law on Sinai, or he operated in
view of the relationship between the Word revealed to Moses on
the Mount and the Word speaking with Moses in the tent, as
bound together by the use of the word ויקרא, translated "and
it called." The vision in which God spoke face to face with
Moses, the vision of Dibbur, is then first and foremost the
encounter described in Ex. 19.3 ff.: the giving of the Law on
Sinai.

Sirach's praise of Moses is further evidence of the
relationship of this series of texts in the tradition, particularly of the characterization of the giving of the law as a
face to face vision:

> By faith and meekness he sanctified him
> and chose him from among all flesh
> He made him hear his voice
> and led him into the darkness
> and gave him face to face (κατὰ πρόσωπον) the
> commandments.[50]

In addition Nu. 12.7 explicitly enters the discussion of
the contest between Moses and the angels for Torah in combination with two other texts which appear to be central to the
development of that legend.

The first of these is Psalm 68, the whole of which is

---

[48]*Midrash Tehillim* 103.18 (Braude II, 165; Hebrew text,
Solomon Buber, Jerusalem, 1965). Cf. parallel treatments
which compare the strength of Moses to the sixty myriads of
Israel: e.g. *Lev. R.* 1.4 (Soncino, 8-9).

[49]*Lev. R.* 1.1 (Soncino, 2-3).

[50]Si. 45.4-6; cf. Nu. 12.3, 7, 8.

interpreted in reference to the event at Sinai, usually in some combination with Ex. 19.3 ff. Verse 19, "Thou hast ascended on high, thou hast led captivity captive," is usually referred to Moses' ascent (at Ex. 19.3) and his battle with the angels for Torah.[51] Verse 13 is referred to the actual giving of Torah; *Song of Songs Rabbah* demonstrates the two versions of this interpretation:

> What is meant by the words, 'And the fair one in the house divideth the spoil (Ps. *loc. cit.*)?' The fair one in the house is the Torah, 'and Thou' [protested the angels] 'givest it to him and he divides it as spoil!'[52]

Maurice Simon, the translator of the Soncino Midrash, puts the last part of the comment into the mouths of the angels as a protest over the bestowal of Torah upon Moses. Both the context and the parallels in *Deuteronomy Rabbah*,[53] *ARNA*, and *Midrash Tehillim* confirm this conjecture. In addition, the first part of verse 13 (MT) of the psalm is the verse so read as to indicate the presence of the angels at Sinai: Not *kings of armies* (מלכי צבאות) is read, but *hosts of angels* (מלאכי צבאות).[54] "The fair one in the house" is in this interpretation taken to be Torah in heaven, which God gives to *him*, Moses, as a spoil over the angels.

The second interpretation of the verse seems to be a direct response, an alternative to this comment:

> Another explanation: '*And the fair one in the house divideth the spoil*': O thou fairest in the house, thou dividest spoil below. 'The fairest in the house' is Moses, as it says, *He is trusted in all My house* (Nu. XII,7). Thou givest it to him and he

---

[51]Cf. *Midrash Tehillim* on 68 passim and *ARNA* 2; Goldin, *The Fathers*, 20.

[52]*S. of S. R.* VIII.11,2 (Soncino, 319). Cf. *Midrash Tehillim* 68.7 (Braude I, 541-542):

> ...after the children of Israel had been refreshed, at once they received Torah, as it is said: *The beauty of the house Thou didst divide as spoil* (Ps. 68.13).

[53]*Dt. R.* 7.9.

[54]Cf. *Midrash Tehillim* 68.7 (Braude I, 541-542), also the rather backhand evidence of *S. of S. R.* VII.11,2, which interprets the text as mentioning both kings and angels.

divides it as spoil among the dwellers on earth."[55]

The shift seems to consist chiefly in the correction of the
first interpretation by the use of Nu. 12.7: "The fair one in
the house" (נוה בבית) is not Torah, but Moses, who was "trusted
in all God's house" (נאמן בכל ביתי) i.e., who had access even
to the heavens, as the continuation of the psalm tells us in
verse 19.

Thus although the text does not actually interpret "my
house" as the *familia* on high, it interprets "house" as the
heavens and tells of the way in which Moses was trusted more
than and over the angels: he was given Torah, which they
could not have, and his word was taken over against theirs:

> Another explanation of WRITE THOU THESE WORDS:
> The angels began to say before the Holy One, Blessed
> be He, 'Dost thou grant permission to Moses to write
> down anything he wishes so that he may then say...to
> Israel, "*I* have given the Torah to you, and it was
> *I* who wrote and gave it to you?"' But God replied,
> 'Far be it from Moses to do such a thing; and in what-
> ever he does he can be fully trusted'. For it says;
> *My servant Moses is not so; he is trusted in all my
> house* (Nu. XII.7).[56]

The information that these texts offer on the meaning of
"house" does not seem consistent enough to identify the meaning of "house" in Hebrews. But we have already remarked the
light shed upon the structure of Hebrews by the place Nu. 12.7
holds in the debate over Moses' status in comparison with the
angels. It remains to be seen what focus is given to that
structure in the light of that comparison made on the basis of
the revelation or the giving of the law.

My house/dwelling, the whole created world.

This interpretation appears already in *Neofiti I*: "My
servant Moses is not like all the other prophets; in the whole
world which I have created he is faithful (trusted)." *Siphre
Zuta* is among the first witnesses to provide an elaboration
of it:

---

[55] *S. of S. R.* VIII.11,2 (Soncino, 319).

[56] *Ex. R.* 47.9 (Soncino, 545).

> NOT THUS have I dealt with MY SERVANT MOSES, but
> IN ALL MY HOUSE HE IS TRUSTED. All that is above
> and all that is below have I revealed to him, all
> that is in the sea and all that is in the dry land.[57]

Once again the immediate focus of the text is upon the
unique revelation given to Moses; it seems, however, that the
reference to sea and dry land functions not only to demonstrate
the all-encompassing character of the revelation by the
technique of inclusion by two opposites, but also to place the
statement in the context of the Exodus. Moses' prophecy is
pre-eminent not only by the all-encompassing revelation but
also by the all-encompassing authority that is given to him:

> R. Nathan in the name of Abba Joseph of Mahoz says,
> "Have I not long ago caused to be written: 'He is
> trusted in all My house' (Nu. 12.7)? You are under
> My authority and the sea is under My authority, and
> I have made you a commander over it."[58]

A more explicit connection between revelation and authorization lies behind the interpretation given in *Exodus Rabbah*[59]
in which Ex. 12.1 "and it came to pass at midnight" is referred
to God's accomplishment of Moses' word to Pharoah. "That
confirmeth the word of his servant" (Is. 44.26) is referred in
this context to Moses, the servant נאמן (apparently, "authorized") in all his house. What is accomplished is, of course,
Moses' prediction of the last plague, but Moses' authorization
as the unique servant and representative of God to know and to
foreknow and also to use the creation of God is illustrated
not only here and at the miracle of the sea, but also in the
accomplishment of all the plagues.

Yalkut Shimoni on *Esfah* seems to know and to have combined the two interpretations of *Siphre Zuta*, so that it sees
Moses' dominion over the creation of God as a facet of his
authorization over the angels.[60] This happens in two steps.

---

[57]*Siphre Zuta Beha'alothka* 12.7 (Horowitz, 275); cf.
above, 108.

[58]*Mekilta Beshallaḥ* 4 (Lauterbach I, 220-221); cf. parallel in *Ex. R.* 21.8, where the comment is ascribed to R. Simeon.

[59]*Ex. R.* 18.1.

[60]*Yalkut Shimoni* on *Esfah* (Strack-Billerbeck III, 683).

First, *Yalkut* extends the universality of Moses' revelation
by replacing "all that is in the sea and all that is in the
dry" with the pair "all that is in the past and all that is in
the future." Then two parables are added to explain the text.

In the first, God is likened to a king who has many
servants over specific storehouses--fire, hail, locusts--who
are the angels, but one servant over the all, who is Moses.
The picture this parable evokes is, of course, Moses' dominion
over the plagues. But two significant features of this passage
add a new context to that picture. First, the storehouse of
fire seems to belong not to the context of the plagues, but to
an eschatological context. Second, the change from "all that
is in the sea and all that is in the dry" to "all that is in
the past and all that is in the future" seems to be a deliberate shift from the context of the Exodus toward an eschatological picture: as Moses was put in charge over the vengeance
on Egypt in the past, so shall he also direct the eschatological retribution. Possibly the shift involves a theory of the
interpretation of scripture: as Moses was put in charge over
all that is in the past, and so was able to write in Torah
not only the story of the Exodus and the wandering but also
of the creation and of the careers of the patriarchs, so also
was he put in charge of the future. He was able to write not
only of his own death and of the future of Israel in the
land,[61] but also of the end of the righteous and the wicked,[62]
of the end of this world and the things of the world to come,
for the last things are like the first.[63] Another version of

---

[61]E.g. in Deuteronomy, cf. *Dt. R.* II.22.

[62]Cf. *Siphre Bemidbar*'s explication of Moses' vision of
the back (103, Horowitz, 102 with translation above, 114,
and the discussion above, 121).

[63]See esp. *Ec. R.* I.9,1, where R. Berekiah comments
upon the correspondence between the first redeemer (Moses)
and the latter redeemer (the messiah). Also significant
is the interpretation of "Declaring the end from the
beginning" (Is. 46.10), as an exegetical principle which
says that God caused creation and its description in Torah
to foretell the exodus and redemption: see *Gn. R.* 4.6,
16.16, 42.7; *Nu. R.* 6.6 and 16.16 and esp. *Dt. R.* 2.22
which applies the principle to the redemption as foretelling
the future of Israel and even the eschatological

this comment has been preserved by the Samaritan liturgy for
the feast of Tabernacles, which hails Moses: "The most
faithful/trusted in the house of God, in the seen and the
unseen, has come."[64] Though other applications are possible,
the inclusion by opposites recalls the comments from *Siphre*
and *Yalkut* so strongly that it also seems to speak of the
revelation made to Moses and in particular to his ascent to
the unseen world where God dwells amid the heavenly *familia*.
The tradition is of course convinced that Moses described
not only the creation of the world, but also the unseen world
in Torah.[65]

The second parable in *Yalkut* seems to confirm the
application of the first to Torah:

> (God is) like a rich man who bought lots and let the
> bill of sale be written in the name of another.
> Then they said, "Now will this man say they belong
> to him." But the rich man denies it: he is bewährt
> (נאמן). So had God also created the world by means
> of Torah, and named the latter by the name of Moses
> as it says: "Think on the Torah of Moses my servant
> (Mal. 3.23)." Then they say, "Now will this one
> say: 'I also am titleholder in his world.'" But
> God denies it: "In all my house he is bewährt
> (נאמן)."[66]

---

distress (see the opinion of R. Joḥanan). For a discussion
of these ideas, see N. A. Dahl, "Christ, Creation and the
Church," *Jesus in the Memory of the Early Church* (Minneapolis:
Augsburg Publishing House, 1976) 120-140, esp. 128-131, on
"protology" and eschatology. Also R. Le Déaut, *La Nuit
Pascale* (Rome: Institut Biblique Pontificale, 1963). The
thesis of this book is concerned with this idea, so it is
treated throughout, but see esp. 115-121 and the copious notes.

[64]This translation was taken from John MacDonald, *The
Theology of the Samaritans* (London: SCM Press Ltd., 1964),
193. The text is in Cowley, *The Samaritan Liturgy* II (Oxford:
Clarendon Press, 1901), 747. The translation seems to be
generally accepted (cf. Meeks, 220), and I am not really
competent to deal with the Samaritan materials. However, the
text seems to me closer to "in (with) what is revealed and
what is hidden" (בנגלאה ובסתרה). This statement might then
apply to an apocalyptic or esoteric interpretation of Torah.
At any rate, the picture given in this paragraph does not
really depend on this citation.

[65]See below, chapter five.

[66]The translation has been made from the German of
Strack-Billerbeck (III, 683).

It also assumes that Moses' relation to Torah gives him a role
of cosmic governance. Thus the interpretation "my house, the
created world" is closely related to "my house, the heavenly
household"; both explications seem to be connected with Moses'
ascent on high, his receiving of the law, his authority over
the angels and both give him a cosmic role. Nor is the third
major signification given to "my house" unrelated to these
two.

My house/dwelling, the tabernacle or the temple.

As the explication *familia* is an answer to the question
"what is 'my house/household'?" this explication is an answer
to the question "what is 'my house/dwelling'?" *Siphre Zuta*
gives an early explicit version of this interpretation: "IN
ALL MY HOUSE HE IS TRUSTED: even over the ministering angels
and *the house of the sanctuary* (בית המקדש). The comment is
difficult of interpretation on a number of points. The term
"house of the sanctuary" normally refers to the temple rather
than the tabernacle, though the distinction is not absolute.
The combination of the angels and the heavenly sanctuary may
be a pair of alternative interpretations, although it is more
likely to be a complementary pair. The comment in isolation
may declare that Moses was valued or favored above the angels
(the heavenly sanctuary?) and the (earthly?) sanctuary. In
the course of *Siphre Zuta*'s commentary, it seems more likely
that the word "over" is concerned with Moses' authority, and
the pair speak of the heavenly realities over which Moses is
entrusted; perhaps, as was suggested above, Moses is in
charge of the angelic liturgy in the heavenly temple. While
no single text can be cited to give exactly this picture,
there are a number of texts which give it a basic credibil-
ity.[67]

Although none of them articulate the role of Moses in
quite this way there are texts which disclose that Moses
ministered in heaven, not only upon his death, but also when
he ascended to speak with God face to face and see his image.

---

[67]*B. Ḥag.* 16b-17a; *b. Ḥull.* 12b; *Midrash Tehillim* on
Psalm 134. N. A. Dahl calls my attention to the *Angelic
Liturgy* of the Qumran Community (Vermes, 210-213).

> AND MOSES DIED THERE.... There are those who say:
> "Moses did not die, but he stands and ministers on
> high." It is said in this text "*there*" and it is
> said elsewhere "And he was *there* with the Lord"
> [forty days and forty nights; he neither ate bread
> nor drank water. And he wrote upon the tables the
> words of the covenant, the ten words. When Moses
> came down from Mount Sinai with the two tables of
> the testimony in his hands as he came down the
> mountain, Moses did not know that the skin of his
> face shone because he had been talking with God.][68]

Thus Moses' sojourn with God, when he ascended on high and
talked with God face to face, was transformed by his glory and
carried away the law of fire, is the paradigm of the ascent
at his death, and in both he is described as "ministering"
(משרת) on high with or over the heavenly *familia*, the ministering angels (מלאכי השרת).

Nu. 12.7 is also interpreted in a very mundane fashion
with regard to Moses' relationship to the tabernacle. *Exodus
Rabbah* records two stories which refer to Moses' fidelity/
entrustedness as the treasurer of the building of the tabernacle. *Ex. R.* 51.6 illustrates the way in which the double
meaning "appointed/faithful" functions in context. The text
is an interpretation of Ex. 38.1: "these are the accounts of
the tabernacle," and asks the question, "Why did Moses
have to render an account to Israel, when God had already
trusted him completely, as it is said: 'My servant Moses is
not so, he is trusted in all my house.'" Clearly the text is
being made to cut two ways: Moses is indeed faithful in all
God's house; and at the same time, Moses need not have proved
this, since God had already authorized him completely.

Ex. R. 51.1 belongs to a series of texts in which the
meaning "appointed" or "authorized" has come to the fore,
because נאמן has taken on the force of a title. Beginning
from Ex. 38.1 also R. Tanḥuma first assumes the comment made
in *Ex. R.* 51.6, then interprets the verse in terms of Pro.
28.20: "A faithful man abounds in blessings...."

---

[68]*Siphre on Deuteronomy* 357.5 (Finkelstein, 428). The
bracketed verses (Ex. 34.28-29) have been added for sense.
Cf. also the comments of W. A. Meeks (210) and the texts he
has collected.

You will find that God always brings blessings by the hand of one who is *faithful* (נאמן) but he that is not faithful (authorized, נאמן) and maketh haste to get rich shall not be unpunished. "A faithful man (איש אמונת)" is Moses who was *the faithful one* (or *the trusty*) of the Holy One, blessed be He (נאמנו של הקב"ה).[69]

There are numerous attempts to specify "the trusty of the Holy One, blessed be He (נאמנו של הקב"ה)." They are best illustrated by a story which is used to explain why Moses was entrusted with the building of the Tabernacle but Aaron given the high priesthood, and which translates the idea in one version into a Greek and the other into a Latin term. Moses is pictured as the intimate of a king who is made in one version *Catholicos* (קטליקוס)[70] and in another *Comes* (קומיס)[71] and told by the king that he was to appoint as *strategos* (in both versions) his brother; by implication this is both a disappointment and an honor for the friend. Aaron, the brother, is made *strategos*: the high priest. The meaning of *Catholicos* which best suits the application of the story is "supervisor of the accounts."[72] The same meaning can be given to *Comes*;[73] but the role of Moses in the story indicates that both terms are functioning also in a broader meaning, something like a viceroy, who is in charge in a general way, but also particularly in charge of disbursements for the palace ("the work of the sanctuary," מלאכת המשכן).[74]

---

[69]*Ex. R.* 51.1. Lehrman translates נאמנו "confidant of God"; this translation is my own but was guided by Lehrman's translation. The text is that printed in Jerusalem in 1956.

[70]*Ex. R.* 37.1.

[71]*Ex. R.* 37.2.

[72]See Samuel Krauss, *Griechische und Lateinische Lehnwörte im Talmud, Midrasch und Targum*, II (Hildesheim: Georg Olms Verlagsbuchhandlung, 1964) s.v. קתליקוס; also *Ex. R.* (Soncino, 443) where Lehrman translates "a controller of his finances."

[73]Krauss s.v. קומיס; also *Ex. R.* 37.2 (Soncino, 444) where Lehrman translates, "member of the imperial cabinet," but see n. 4.

[74]The text of the *Midrash Rabbah* consulted here was printed in Jerusalem in 1956.

The use of the phrase as a title for Moses which gives
him some status in regard to God analgous to a specific office
is broader than the application of the word "house" in this
verse to the tabernacle. Indeed, the story referred to above
need not apply only to Moses' role in the building of the
tabernacle but also to his whole role in the redemption of
Israel and the lawgiving. The broader possibilities of this
title are illustrated by a similar use of the text in a
comment upon the title of Psalm 90:

> Another reading: *A prayer of Moses, a man, the God....*
> Rabbi Eleazer said: Moses was God's *Magister Palatii*
> for God said of him: *My servant Moses is not so; he
> is trusted in all my house.*[75]

The title here seems to be the equivalent of *Comes* and of
the title *apotropos* (ἐπίτροπος) used in *Siphre*. Indeed, the
comment seems to be functionally the same as the final comments
of *Siphre* and *Siphre Zuta* on 12.8: "Why does it say AGAINST
MY SERVANT? Because it wants you to understand that against
Moses is the same as against me."[76] This conclusion is made
clearer still by the principle with which *Siphre Zuta* explains
the relationship of the spies who spied out the land to Israel
who sent them: "The ambassador of a man is in every place as
himself (שלוחו של אדם כמותו בכל מקום).[77]

My house/household, my people, the house of Israel.

This broader use of "trusty in the house" as a title for
Moses brings us back to the first application of "house" which
we remarked, the application of "house" to the people, which
appears in Targums Onkelos and Jonathan. Moses was stronger
than not only the angels, but also the myriads of Israel:

> R. Tanḥum bar Ḥanilai expounded: Have you ever in
> all your life seen a burden too heavy for ten men,

---

[75]*Midrash Tehillim* 90.5 (Braude II, 89). However the
translation of Braude reads *seneschal* instead of *Magister
Palatii*, the reading in the text. See Braude II, 494, n. 13.

[76]*Siphre* 103 (Horowitz, 102), above 114; cf. *Siphre Zuta*
12.8 (Horowitz, 296), above 109 and the discussion above 112
and 122.

[77]*Siphre Zuta Shalaḥ* 14.24 (Horowitz, 279).

but easy for one man? Yet after the children of
Israel had said: *If we hear the voice of the Lord
our God any more we shall die* (Dt. 5.22), it is
written, *Go thou near, and hear all that the Lord
our God may speak unto thee* (*ibid*. 5.24). --that
is, what sixty myriads could not bear to hear,
Moses heard by himself. Moreover, the very word
of the Lord called to Moses, as is said, *And It
called unto Moses* (Lev. 1.1), but Moses was not
harmed.[78]

Because he was able to bear this manifestation of the Word,
he speaks to them as the voice of God. In all that he does in
the redemption of Israel, and still more in all that he speaks
in the writing of Torah, it is God's own Word which is done
and said in Moses. This interpretation fits into stories and
comments in which some other application is also made, such
as the story of Moses who is made *Comes* or *Catholicos* to the
house of the king, the tabernacle. For where the tabernacle
is the house/dwelling of God, still Israel is his house/
household; where the whole created world is God's house/
dwelling, still Israel only is his house/household; where the
angels are the *familia*/household on high, still Israel is
the *familia*/household below:

> R. Alexandri said: He who studies the Torah for its
> own sake makes peace in the Upper Family and in the
> Lower Family [men][79] as it is written, *Or let him take
> hold of my strength* [i.e. the Torah] *that he may make
> peace with me; and he shall make peace with me.*[80]
> Rab said: It is as though he built the heavenly and
> the earthly Temples, as it is written, *And I have put
> my words in thy mouth and I have covered thee in the
> shadow of mine hand, that I may plant the heavens,
> and lay the foundations of the earth and say unto
> Zion, thou art my people.*[81] R. Joḥanan said: He
> also shields the whole world [from the consequences
> of its sins] for it is written *and I have covered*

---

[78]*Midrash Tehillim* 103.18 (Braude II, 165).

[79]The bracketed comments seem to be those of the general
editor, Isidore Epstein. In this particular case, I would
dispute his suggestion and suggest instead that the lower
familia are particularly "Israel who study Torah." Cf.
b. Ber. 17a.

[80]Is. 27.5.

[81]Is. 51.16.

[i.e., protected] thee in the shadow of mine hand.
Levi said: He also hastens the redemption, as it
is written, *And say unto Zion, Thou art my people.*[82]

This passage which does not cite our text or use the word
"house," yet relates the variety of differing applications in
such a way as to make clear that they have an intrinsic
relationship beyond their application to the word "my house."
Especially striking is the comment of Rab, for his proof-text
there seems to refer to the temple both as a place and as the
people (*and say to Zion, Thou art my people*).

A more obvious example of the double or multiple applications of our text can be found in *Midrash Tehillim*, in a
parable of a householder who tells his steward to measure the
wheat:

> Now, by the householder is meant the Holy One, blessed
> be He, for the fullness of the earth is His, as is said,
> *The earth is the Lord's and the fullness thereof* (Ps.
> 24.1); by the steward is meant Moses of whom God said:
> *He is trusted in all My house* (Nu. 12.7). What did the
> Holy One, blessed be He, say to Moses? Take no heed
> of the heathen for they are like stubble.... And what
> is done with stubble? It is floated off in the water
> as is said, *He shaked off Pharoah and his host in the
> Red Sea* (Ps. 136.15). ...Take heed of the children
> of Israel by counting them to make sure of how many
> they are, as is said *Take the sum of the children of
> Israel according to their number* (Ex. 30.12).[83]

Thus Moses is entrusted in all God's house, the creation, but
only for the sake of the children of Israel.

Although it is convenient to divide the rabbinic interpretation of Nu. 12.7 according to whether the "house" is
applied to the heavens, the creation, or the tabernacle, this
organization of the material breaks down. These applications
are never in fact tied to one function of the text in such a
way that that function and its application of the word "house"
excludes the other functions. This is especially clear with
regard to the first two applications which are of course very
close: Moses is trusted in all the house, i.e. the heavens--

---

[82]*B. San.* 99b (Soncino, 675), cf. *b. Ber.* 17a. For other
references see Krauss, s.v. פמליא.

[83]*Midrash Tehillim* 2.13 (Braude I, 44-45).

he is superior to the angels, he is allowed to know all things, he carried off Torah; Moses is trusted in all the house, i.e. creation--he is superior to the angels set over creation because he is allowed to know all things, because Torah is given to him and called by his name, and by Torah did God create the creation.

This seems less true of the interpretations which make "house" equal to tabernacle. These seem to evolve from a tendency to prescind totally from the context and to ask the meaning of a word or phrase in itself. Either the commentator asks: what is this, and answers something like, "ביתי, my house, is בית המקדש, the sanctuary." Or the question is "what is בבית נאמן?" and the answer "*apotropos*," or "*Comes*" or some title honoring Moses as God's viceroy or second. Yet even "house" as "tabernacle" and Moses as God's viceroy are not strictly connected interpretive moves. For Moses as the "trusty in all God's house" can also be the viceroy of God in creation. Further, *Siphre Zuta* connects Moses' superiority to the angels to his charge over the sanctuary, for the temple as God's dwellingplace is either the heavenly sanctuary to which Moses was admitted on his ascent, or the earthly sanctuary which Moses had built as a copy of that above, or the temple of Solomon, a copy of that earlier copy.

Thus the dominant function of the text in the rabbinic tradition seems to be the one which cuts across all the applications and makes it possible to apply the text to all of them without really contradicting any of them. Moses is trusted in all God's house. God called him on high into his house *the heavens*: there he trusted him more than the *angels*, speaking with him face to face; he revealed to him all that is in *creation*, giving him charge over the elements and their angels; he charged him with the work of the *tabernacle*, bidding him build according to what he saw; he made him his emissary to the house of *Israel*, in word and deed as himself. Thus the verse evokes not so much a single consistent inter-pretation, or a debate between alternative, mutually exclusive interpretations, as a picture of Moses; as it were a "high" picture of Moses as God's second in all creation, and as a mystic:

> Moses...prayed for forty days and forty nights.
> Accordingly the Holy One, blessed be He, said to the
> ministering angels: I liken Moses to you, as it is
> said, *Bless the Lord O mighty in strength...hearken-
> ing to the voice of His word* (Ps. 103.20).[84]

As a secondary function the text testifies also to the
faithfulness of Moses in regard to the work of the tabernacle
(i.e. his financial accountability), and indeed in regard to
his entrustedness with Torah and with the power of God in
creation, and in all with which God has charged him.

Application to Hebrews.

Paradoxically it is far easier to show how all of the
functions and applications attached to Nu. 12.7 by the rabbinic
tradition feed into the scheme of Hebrews than to give an
account of the precise function of the Numbers verse in He.
3.1-6.

Which meaning of "house" in the rabbinic tradition will
illuminate Hebrews' comparison of Jesus faithful/trusted in
God's house to Moses faithful/trusted in God's house? All of
the applications of "house" found in the rabbinic tradition
can be accommodated to the thought of Hebrews and will illuminate Hebrews' argument. Indeed, the reverse is also true:
Hebrews will also help us to illuminate the relationship
between the various meanings of "house" in the tradition.

This is especially true of the two related meanings
"heavens" or "heavenly *familia*" and "creation," and the way
in which Hebrews' use of the word *oikoumene* (οἰκουμένη) sub-
sumes them both.

1) Christ and Moses as appointed/faithful in the house/
oikoumene--the heavens or the heavenly *familia*.

The most striking contribution of the tradition of
interpretation to the understanding of Hebrews as a whole is
its vindication of the logical structure of the letter.
Commentators have long been troubled by the logic of Hebrews'
opening chapters: when the son has already been shown to be
superior to the angels in 1-2, why should it be necessary in

---

[84]*Midrash Tehillim* 90.6 (Braude II, 90).

3.1-6 to prove his superiority to Moses also?[85]

The tradition which makes Nu. 12.7 the testimony to
Moses' superiority to the angels reveals the cogency of
Hebrews' argument: the son superior to the angels--Moses also
superior to the angels (Nu. 12.7)--but the son as Christ also
superior to Moses the servant (1 Chr. 17.14). An examination
of the argument in Hebrews 1-2 which presents the son as
superior to the angels confirms that Hebrews is working in a
cosmology which will accomodate the rabbinic debate about the
status of Moses in relation to the angels. Chapter one is
laid out as a pre-cosmic, divine drama. God addresses his
testimony first to the son, then according to 1.6 he presents
the first-born to the *oikoumene*, and there follows a series of
testimonies addressed alternately to the son and to the
angels. It seems fairly clear that the *oikoumene* is not
"the inhabited world" but rather the cosmos, the audience of
this presentation--at this point, the angels.

In the tradition, the superiority of Moses to the angels
functions in particular in regard to the context of his
relationship to Torah. So also in Hebrews, the parenetic
point drawn from the superiority of the son to the angels is
that the new revelation which had its beginning through being
spoken by the Lord is superior to and more demanding than
the old. Thus one would expect the comparison between Jesus
and Moses to draw a similar parenetic conclusion: if the
revelation given through Moses the servant appointed/faithful
in the house incurred punishment for transgressions, how much
more so that given through Christ the son appointed/faithful
in the house? This conclusion is, however, not explicitly
drawn by 3.1-6.

2) Christ and Moses as faithful in the house/*oikoumene*,
creation.

In the tradition Nu. 12.7 also functions to establish the
superiority of Moses to the angels in his stewardship of
creation. This function of the text understands "house" to
apply to the whole creation, and also helps to explicate
Hebrews' comparison of Christ and the angels. The second

---

[85]See n. 43 above, 126.

point of that comparison is that it is not to the angels that
God has subjected the world (*oikoumene*) to come (τὴν
οἰκουμένην τὴν μέλλουσαν, He. 2.5). The assertion which
Hebrews seeks to contradict by this statement is illustrated
by *Yalkut* on *Esfah*, which tells how God has given an angel
charge over each of the eschatological elements and Moses
charge over all.[86]

For Hebrews the angels do not have charge over the coming
world, although presumably the letter's cosmology (like Paul's)
assumes that this world, its elements, rulers, countries, etc.,
are all subject to angelic powers, and quite possibly then that
Moses also has or had during his lifetime authority over them
all. On the basis of this assumption a comparison is implied:
to the angels is this world subject, but the coming world is
subject to the son. Can a similar comparison between Jesus
and Moses be implied in 3.1-6?

Whether or not this proves to be so, the relationship of
the meanings heavenly *familia*/created world for "house" in
Nu. 12.7 is laid out by the progression of meaning for
oikoumene in Hebrews 1-2. That Hebrews can use the word first
for the angels, God's ministers, and then for the creation
that is subject to them adds to the observations we made above
concerning the meaning of this word, and brings us to recall
our conclusion that it is Moses' ascent which makes sense of
the variety of applications of "my house."[87]

3) Moses appointed/faithful in the house--the tabernacle.

This application of "my house" is again one which suits
the milieu of Hebrews, which is a cultic milieu. The angels
are designated in 1.14 as ministering (λειτουργικά) spirits
and Christ is designated in 8.1 as "liturgist" (λειτουργός)
of the true tent. In fact the comparison drawn there is
precisely the one we would expect on the basis of Nu. 12.7:
Jesus, high priest of the true tent, as opposed to the high
priest who serves in the tent built by Moses. Commentators
have frequently suggested a liturgical import for "servant"

---

[86]Above, 132-133 and n. 60.

[87]Above, 141-142.

(θεράπων), the title given to Moses through Nu. 12.7. In fact, the comparison between Christ as son and Moses as servant is at least one of the points of the comparison made on the basis of the Nathan oracle and the text from Numbers. The high priest, Christ as son, is the builder of God's house/people, whereas Moses is only the servant in God's house, the tabernacle, which foreshadows that spiritual temple. If this is indeed the comparison, a more pointed comparison could have been made on the same texts: Christ the builder of the spiritual temple to Moses the builder of the tent in the wilderness.

4) Christ and Moses as appointed/faithful in God's house/the people.

There is still a fourth application possible from Hebrews: in the Numbers verse as well as in the Nathan oracle "house" can be understood as God's people. Although this meaning of the text is little represented in the rabbinic material, both Onkelos and Jonathan record it, and it is clearly suggested by the function of the Nathan oracle both in Hebrews and in the tradition represented by the Targumim on that passage. It is capable of absorbing the cultic references through the interpretation of the people as the spiritual temple.

Further, the designation of Moses as God's trusty (*Comes*, *Catholicos*, *apotropos*) over the house of the sanctuary and God's people, the house of Israel, helps to explain the use of the epithet *apostolos* and the participle "made" to Christ. A number of commentators have called attention to the use of the word "made" in 1 Sam. 12.6 LXX: "The Lord is my witness, who 'made' (ὁ ποιήσας) Moses and Aaron (and) who led our fathers out of Egypt." The full significance is seen only in relation to the synonymous expression in 12.8: "and the Lord sent (ἀπέστειλεν) Moses and Aaron and led our fathers out of Egypt." Textual criticism seems to have barred most commentators from adducing the version of Mk. 3.14 which introduces the word "apostles" as a parallel to the usage in 1 Sam. and in He. 3.1-2: "And he made twelve, and called them *apostles*."[88] Yet the meaning "made/sent for God's saving purpose"

---

[88]The text is in fact rather well attested in the

is attested by this version, whoever may have written it. Thus
the purpose for which God made/sent Moses and Aaron is the same
for which God made/sent and appointed/faithful as the one who
is sent (שליח), the ambassador or *apostolos* of the Lord, who
is everywhere as himself. "They have rejected not you but me,"
says God to Samuel. "AGAINST MY SERVANT is said only that you
should say 'against me,'" intimates *Siphre*.[89] This role as
the one who is made/sent for Israel's salvation is also the
role of the scion of David, who is appointed/faithful in the
house God builds for David.

There even exists a text which offers evidence for the
influence of the Nathan oracle upon the picture of Moses. The
Book of Enoch in its allegorical description of the Exodus
describes Moses as follows:

> And I saw in this vision till that sheep became a
> man and built a house for the Lord of the sheep and
> placed all the sheep in that house.... And I saw
> till the sheep came to a goodly place, and a pleas-
> ant and glorious land, and I saw till those sheep
> were satisfied and that house stood amongst them in
> a pleasant land.[90]

Moses, like the son of David, builds a house for God, the
tabernacle, that seems also to be a household of sheep and
possibly to be identical with the temple standing in the land.

But if Moses is being accommodated to the Davidic Messiah
in Hebrews, the application is clearly not the same. For the
Christ in Hebrews is Jesus, the builder of that house, nor
does it seem that his position in the comparison is that of
the builder of the household of God in the desert. Rather he
is the servant in the house and Jesus the son over the house.
If this is one house of God in both cases, then Moses is a
member of the house of which Jesus is builder. While Hebrews
does consider Moses a proleptic Christian, it is not clear
that this author is willing to allow the text to have no
historical application. Moses indeed bears the reproach of
Christ, but he did not inherit the promise; rather he is not

Alexandrian text type.

[89]See above, 114.

[90]*1 En.* 89.36,40 (Charles, *Pseudepigrapha*, 483).

perfected without us. Is Moses then a member of the house
over which Jesus is son? In what degree is Moses a proleptic
Christian? How did Moses become a Christian at all?

The first two applications of the word "house" seem to
suggest the likeness between Jesus and Moses: their superiority to the angels. The second two applications seem to bear
on the contrast implied in the comparison. No single one will
account for the argument presented in 3.1-6 in its entirety,
and indeed one suspects that all of them must in some way be
operative in it. If this is the case, it would seem that the
primary theme of Moses' vision must in some way be operative
in the argument.

Is the likening of Jesus, Christ as Son (i.e. the Davidic
Messiah) and Moses the servant being made upon the basis of
Moses' vision? The rabbis supply some texts which suggest
a comparison between Moses and David as prophets. For example,
Leviticus Rabbah points out the likeness between Moses and
David using testimonies taken from the Nathan oracle and
Nu. 12.8:

> Another interpretation: *Then thou spakest in a*
> *vision to Thy goodly ones* speaks of David with whom
> he communicated by both word and vision. This is
> indicated by what is said: *According to all these*
> *words and according to all this vision, so did*
> *Nathan speak to David* (II Sam. VII,17).[91]

> Another interpretation: *Then thou spakest in a*
> *vision to Thy goodly ones* speaks of Moses with whom
> He communicated by both word and vision, as it is
> said, *With him do I speak mouth to mouth in a*
> *vision and not in dark speeches.* (Nu. XII,8).[92]

Midrash Tehillim draws an explicit comparison between David
and Moses on the basis of the revelation granted to each:

> Another comment on *The earth is the Lord's and the*
> *fullness thereof*: R. Azariah, R. Nehemiah and R.
> Berechiah told the parable of a king who had two
> stewards, one in charge of the house and the other
> in charge of the fields. *The one in charge of the*
> *house* knew all that happened in the house and all
> that happened in the fields; but the one in charge
> of the field knew only what happened in the fields.

---

[91]*Lev. R.* 1.4 (Soncino, 8).

[92]Ibid.

> Even so, Moses, who had gone up to heaven, knew
> the upper as well as the nether worlds, and with
> the names of both praised the Holy One, blessed
> be He, as it is said: *Behold, the heaven and the*
> *heaven of heavens is the Lord's thy God's, the*
> *earth also and all that therein is* (Deut. 10.14);
> but David, who had not gone up to heaven, praised
> the Holy One, blessed be He, only with what he
> knew, as is said *The earth is the Lord's and the*
> *fullness thereof*.[93]

Moses as the house servant has the superior knowledge, and
Moses is the house servant with dominion over both heaven and
earth by reason of his having ascended into the house--heaven--
and there learned all that is above and all that is below.
David on the other hand is defined by comparison with Moses:
if Moses is the house servant, then David is the field servant.

Can it be that He. 3.6 is reversing the comparison of
Midrash Tehillim or rather superseding it? Moses greater than
David, but the Davidic Messiah greater than Moses. Clearly it
is as Davidic Messiah that Jesus is being compared to Moses in
this passage, but equally clearly he is not simply a Davidic
Messiah conformed to Moses. The Christology of the passage is
more complex than this. If Moses' vision is functioning in
the passage, it is not doing so by forming the Christology:
nothing is said of Jesus' vision or knowledge, nor in fact is
anything very explicit being said about Moses' vision or
knowledge.

Neither the action of the Nathan oracle on the story of
Moses (such as occurs in *l Enoch*) nor the action of Moses'
career upon the Nathan oracle or David as prophet (as in
Midrash Tehillim 24) explains the point at which they are
being compared in Hebrews. It is not that Jesus is appointed/
faithful like Moses in that Moses also was builder of a household, although Jesus was builder of the true house. Nor is it
that Jesus is appointed/faithful like Moses who was given
knowledge and so stewardship over this heaven and earth, while
Christ's superior knowledge gives him dominion over the next.

The history of interpretation of Nu. 12.7 has offered us
a wide variety of contexts for the meanings of the words
"faithful" and "house" and has shed some light on the

---

[93]*Midrash Tehillim* 24.5 (Braude I, 339-340).

structure of Hebrews by demonstrating the function of the text
as a proof-text for the superiority of Moses to the angels.
It has also uncovered a number of traditional points of contact with the Nathan oracle: it has made clear that the
double meanings "appointed/faithful" apply to Nu. 12.7 in much
the same way that they seem to apply to the Nathan oracle as
it is used in Hebrews, as well as that the double meaning of
house as "temple/people" also applies to the Numbers text.
Finally, it has shown that this text evokes a picture of Moses
as mystic or visionary which should relate to the visionary
theme of the life of Moses in He. 11.23-27.

However, this investigation has left us with two major
questions: How did Moses become a Christian? What is the
likeness between Jesus and Moses? The answer to the first
question should be found in Hebrews' explication of the vision
of Moses, whom God so trusted as to reveal to him "all that is
in the past and all that is in the future."[94] But we have not
yet discovered how Hebrews applies this understanding of Moses'
entrustedness. Nor are we ready to delineate the likeness
Hebrews sees between Jesus and Moses, for as was pointed out
in chapter two, the testimonies to the royal priest do not
explain the Christology of Hebrews. Thus it is not surprising
that the texts in themselves do not explain the point of likeness between Christ and Moses, or answer our questions about
the function of Moses in Hebrews. To do that it is necessary
to turn to the text and examine the point of comparison in the
argument of Hebrews 3.1-6.

---

[94]*Yalkut Schimoni* on *Esfah* (Strack-Billerbeck, III, 683).
See above, 132.

CHAPTER FOUR

MOSES LIKENED TO THE SON OF GOD ACCORDING TO GLORY:
THE THEOLOGICAL FUNCTION OF MOSES IN HEBREWS.

But tell us, prophet, how shall God shine upon the
dwellers on earth? From without humanity? Without
flesh? Impossible. Sight does not bear the beams
of divinity. The adversary will not come to the
lists; death shrinks from the creator, not daring
to swallow up a nature indestructible. Hades also
must tremble at the one on whom the cherubim do not
look. But divine nature needs a veil, not to hide
it but to conceal our hybris. Not Moses' veil, for
that is ignorance and mist; not the embroidered
curtain, for that bloom is from painted colours;
not the cherubim made by hands, for that marvel is
of art. But he needed the form of a sheep, to
deceive the man-eating wolf.[1]

In the foregoing two chapters, this study has reviewed the
history of interpretation of the texts used in He. 3.1-6.
Chapter two revealed that the structure of Hebrews' argument
in these verses seems to be guided by the Nathan oracle, or
rather by the complex oracle of the royal priest, and therefore that the Christological convictions of the author are
really in control of the interpretation of the passage.
Chapter three placed the function of Nu. 12.7 within a
traditionally "high" interpretation of Moses, suggesting that
the Moses of Hebrews is Moses the mystic, entrusted above all
God's house by his ascent and vision of God. Both chapters
have extended the context and application of the words
"faithful" and "house"; however, both chapters have also come
to the conclusion that the history of interpretation does not
finally explain Hebrews' use of the tradition and that only
an examination of the argument of Hebrews itself can do that.

At the end of chapter three we were left with two
questions: "What is the likeness between Jesus and Moses?"
and "How did Moses become a Christian?" Especially the first
of these questions can be applied to the text in the light of

---

[1]Proclus of Constantinople: *Oratio XIII In sanctam
Pascha* (PG 65.792-793).

the results of the last two chapters. What is the point of comparison between Christ and Moses? How are they alike and how is Christ greater than Moses?

A partial answer to the first question is to be found in our observations on the interpretation of Nu. 12.7 in relation to the structure of Hebrews. Jesus is appointed/faithful like Moses in that both Jesus and Moses are appointed/faithful above (or more than) the angels. According to Hebrews 1-2, Jesus is superior to the angels as son of God,[2] Davidic Messiah,[3] high priest seated at God's right hand;[4] according to the tradition, Moses is superior to the angels as the seer who ascended on high and "spoke with God with face unveiled."[5]

This likening raises a Christological problem, which the author attempts to resolve in 3.1-6. The question which inspires the comparison is one which could not have arisen in a non-Christian setting; it is not whether the prophet like Moses takes precedence over the Davidic Messiah (as it could well be in a setting like that of Qumran). Rather it is a question raised by Hebrews 2: How is Jesus' superiority to the angels different from that of Moses? If Jesus was "made for a little lower than the angels"[6] what of Moses who "ascended on high[7]...and prevailed over the heavenly *familia*?"[8] If Jesus "partook fully of the flesh and blood,"[9] what of Moses, of whom it is written, "*Moses, a man, the God*--when he ascended, he was as a man (before God), but when he descended, he was as God (before men)."[10] If of Jesus it was foretold

---

[2]He. 1.5 (2 Sam. 7.14; Ps. 2.7).

[3]He. 1.5, 8-9, 13 (2 Sam. 7.14; Ps. 45.7-8; Ps. 110.1).

[4]He. 1.13 (Ps. 110.1); He. 3.17.

[5]*Midrash 'Agada Wayyikra'* 1.1; cf. Nu. 12.8, Ex. 34.39 ff.

[6]He. 2.7 (Ps. 8.6).

[7]Ps. 68.17.

[8]*Dt. R.* 11.10 (Soncino, 185).

[9]He. 2.14.

[10]*Midrash Tehillim* 90.5 (Braude II, 88-89).

that he would be appointed/faithful in the house (of David as king, of God as priest),[11] what of Moses of whom it was written that on his ascent he was appointed/faithful with the whole house of creation?[12]

This is the Christological problem which occasioned the necessity of choosing texts nearly identical in wording, so that the comparison begins from the likeness between Jesus and Moses, rather than from the difference between them (as it is done in the case of the angels). Or perhaps I should say the urgency, the cogency of this move: for in fact, the comparison is not introduced out of necessity as a point of argument, but rather arises in a parenetic context, as a point from which exhortation can be made: "...look to Jesus our apostle and high priest...." The difference between Jesus and Moses is precisely that Jesus is the one who descended, while Moses is the one who ascended--the lowliness of the one is temporary, the exaltation of the other, not eternal. John also remarks this difference, but so radicalizes it as actually to deny the ascent of Moses: "No one has gone up to heaven except the one who has come down from heaven" (Jn. 3.13). Hebrews 3 is less extreme, but the implication is the same: in no way can Moses' ascent place him in the status of the son. The purpose of the comparison then is to spell out the relationship between the status of Moses and the status of Christ.

The author of Hebrews therefore extends the comparison, seeking to distinguish Moses and Jesus on the basis of glory. This extension of the comparison is often overlooked, because the word "glory" (δόξα) often means "reputation" or "opinion."[13] If this translation is used, no shift in the basis of the comparison occurs. The "glory" of Christ is the set of Christological texts; that of Moses is Nu. 12.7. The comparison is made between the titles of each: Jesus is the builder

---

[11]He. 3.1-6 (cf. 2 Sam. 7.12 ff., 1 Chr. 17.10 ff.).

[12]*Siphre Zuta* 12.7; Neofiti I on Nu. 12.7.

[13]Cf. however, Michel, 93, who remarks the relation between "glory" (δόξα) and "honor" (τιμή) as giving the former a "Hellenistic" meaning but does not overlook the more concrete biblical meaning of glory.

of the house, Moses a member of it; Jesus is Christ and son,
Moses, servant; Jesus is over the house, Moses in it. But
this solution has already proven unsatisfactory, for the
comparison cannot be consistently resolved in this fashion.
If Jesus is builder of the house as Messiah, then the house
is the people as spiritual temple. But Moses presumably can
be part of this house only proleptically. While Moses' proleptic Christianity presents no difficulty for Hebrews, it is
not true that this author makes no distinction between the
generations of the past and the present. If in 11.27 Moses
suffered the opprobrium of Christ, still, he did not receive
the promise, is not perfected without us. The oracle about
Moses "in the house" would lose its historical application
if the only meaning applied to it is that adduced from the
Christological oracles. In addition, the text would no longer
be dealing with the question of Moses' and Jesus' position
above the angels. But the greatest difficulty of all is He.
3.4: "For every house is built by someone, but the builder of
all things is God." In any case the statement is problematic;
the great majority of (recent) commentators have regarded it
as a parenthesis.[14] If we regard the glory of Moses and Jesus
as the estimation that is made of them, this verse occasions
not only an interruption in the progress of the argument, but
also a syntactical difficulty. In 3.5-6 the elements of the
two oracles are contrasted point by point:

> Μωϋσῆς μὲν...ὡς θεράπων ἐν τῷ οἴκῳ....
> Moses...as servant in the house....
>
> Χριστὸς δὲ ὡς υἱὸς ἐπὶ τὸν οἶκον αὐτοῦ.
> *But* Christ as son over the house.

He. 3.3 and 4 however, are introduced not by *but* (δὲ) but
rather by *for* (γάρ).[15] In some way, it would seem, the author
sees an inner cogency in the argument which leads from 2 to 3
to 4 by a logical progression rather than by contrast:

---

[14] See RSV; also Spicq II, 67; Héring, 25. Bruce, 57,
comments on the ambiguity of the second part of the verse.
Michel, 97, insists that the thought-structure is clear, but
in his insistence is forced to accuse the Fathers of a
deliberate misreading of the text.

[15] See Héring, 25.

Appointed/faithful...as was Moses.... *For* he
was accorded greater glory than Moses as the
builder has greater honor than the house.
For every house has a builder, but the builder
of all is God.

If there is an extension of the comparison in verse 3, then
the glory of Christ and the glory of Moses must be identified
with both their status over the angels and their relationship
to the house. What then is the glory of Moses?

This chapter will suggest that the glory of Moses in He.
3.3 is an idea familiar to the tradition but used in a unique
fashion. The glory of Moses is the glory of Christ, which
Moses caught when he saw the glory of God (the image of the
back of his glorious Shekinah) on the mount, the glory of God
which according to He. 1.3 is Christ the only son. This
relation of glory to glory explains the relation of house and
builder between Christ and Moses, as well as the way Moses
came to know Christ Jesus. It also makes sense of He. 3.4.
The Christological position of Hebrews, the concept of a made
maker in first-century Jewish theology and the theological
function of the vision of Moses will be explored to ground the
identification of Christ as the builder of all things, God.
The observations made in this survey will then be applied to
the theological function of Moses' vision in Hebrews, and some
questions raised with regard to the soteriological function
of Moses' vision in the letter.

The glory of Moses as the glory of Moses' face.

The resolution of the comparison between Christ and Moses
seems to require an identification of the glory of Moses and
the glory of Christ. Is there then some particular instance
in which "glory" is accorded to Moses, and which could form
the basis of this comparison? The tradition does indeed know
of one salient instance: when Moses descended from the
mountain after having seen the vision of God's glory and
received the commandments for the second time, "the skin of
his face shone" (Ex. 34.29):

In saying *And crownest him with glory and honor* (Ps.
8.6), they [the angels] were referring to Moses, of
whom it is said "Moses knew not that the skin of

his face sent forth beams by reason of His speaking with him (Ex. 34.29)."[16]

This comment is of course inspired by the strong visual image
conveyed by the text of Ex. 34.29: קרן--sent forth beams--
could also be translated "grew horns." The rays or horns of
light coming from Moses' face on his descent from the mount
are envisaged as a "crown of כבוד *glory* and הדר *honor* or
splendor." Although the comment is a very particular one,
rising directly from the text of Psalm 8, it offers three very
strong motives for our attention:

1) Psalm 8 is cited in Hebrews 2 and applied to Jesus in
a context similar to the one in which this comment arises. The
"they" of *Midrash Tehillim* is the angels, who are stating their
grievances against humanity to whom God has shown himself so
very overindulgent.

2) The application of Ex. 34.29 to these words of the
Psalm marks a stage in the interpretation of that passage of
particular interest to our investigation.

3) Most significantly, the comment shows the prominence
of the image inspired by Ex. 34.29. The commentator on Psalm
8, moving along the psalm and applying it verse by verse to
the spiritual heroes of biblical history, asks: "*Who* was
crowned with glory and honor?" and the answer is ready:
"Moses, on his descent from the mount."

The arresting quality of the image is attested by the
attention given to the word קרן by the Targumists as well as
by the commentators. All feel impelled to elaborate upon it
or to explain it. Onkelos develops the picture into a transfiguration: "great was the splendor (זיו brightness, bloom,
beauty) of the *glory* of his face" (סני זיו יקרא דאפוה).
Targum Jonathan uses a still more elaborate phrase: "the
glory of the form (εἰκόνιον) of his face was made bright"
(אתנהר זיו איקונין דאנפוי).

In the rabbinic tradition, the concrete picture conveyed
by קרן becomes more and more prominent, appearing in the
nominal formulation: "beams" or "horns of glory" קרני ההוד.[17]

---

[16] *Midrash Tehillim* 8.7 (Braude I, 128); brackets mine.

[17] Cf. Collection of Strack-Billerbeck on 2 Co. 3.7 (III,

An even more pictorial formulation arises from the explanation
of Moses' glory as a reward: "In reward of *and Moses hid his*
face (יסתר...פניו), he obtained the brightness of his face
(לקלסתר פניו)."[18] This brightness (קלסתר) is the Greek word
"*chrystallos*" (κρύσταλλος), used in rabbinic Hebrew as an
equivalent of זיו to mean either "brightness" or "beauty of
countenance."[19] The double meaning of these words suggests
the idea of transfiguration which is elaborated in the account
which pseudo-Philo gives of the incident in Ex. 34.29:

> And Moses came down: and whereas he was covered with
> invisible light—for he had gone down into the place
> where is the light of the sun and the moon—the light
> of his face overcame the brightness of the sun and the
> moon, and he knew it not. And it was so, when he came
> down to the children of Israel, they saw him and knew
> him not. But when he spoke, then they knew him. And
> this was like that which was done in Egypt when Joseph
> knew his brethren but they knew him not. And it came
> to pass that when Moses knew that his face was be-
> come glorious, he made him a veil to cover his face.[20]

These elaborations of the account lend credence to the con-
tention that the occasion is of sufficient significance that
"the glory of Moses" suggests to the commentator of antiquity
the glory which shone upon the face of Moses on his descent
from the Mount.

In the Greek tradition, the occasion become characterized chiefly by the single word "glory" (δόξα) in contrast
to the multiplication of graphic words which the Hebrew
commentaries produce. This is due chiefly to the LXX rendering of the passage, "that the appearance of the skin of his
face was become glorious while he was speaking with him"
(ὅτι δεδόξασται ἡ ὄψις τοῦ χρώματος τοῦ προσώπου αὐτοῦ ἐν τῷ

514, esp. #2a.

[18]*B. Ber.* 7a (*The Hebrew-English Talmud*, London: The
Soncino Press, 1960).

[19]Jastrow, s.v. But Krauss (s.v.), who credits this
opinion to Rabbi Hillel ben Eliakim, suggests in its stead
εἰκονάστηρ, or some word related to εἰκών. He gives the
meaning as "visage" or "image."

[20]M. R. James, *The Biblical Antiquities of Philo* (London:
SPCK and New York: Macmillan, 1917; reprint ed., New York:
KTAV Publishing House, 1971), 110.

λαλεῖν αὐτὸν αὐτῷ). The elaboration is reminiscent of Targum
Jonathan, but the image of the rays so prominent in the
Rabbinic tradition does not appear in the Greek at all.

Paul's interpretation of Ex. 34.29 ff. in 2 Co. 3.7 ff.
demonstrates both the prominence of the word "glory" (δόξα),
which can seemingly be credited to the influence of the LXX,
and the persistence of the imagery of the rays of light. Paul
speaks of "the glory (δόξα) of the face of Moses" (3.7) and
even uses both participle and indicative of the perfect of
"glorify" (δοξάζω): "that which was glorified...was glorified"
(δεδόξασται τὸ δεδοξασμένον) 3.10; as does the LXX at 34.29,
"the appearance was become glorious" (δεδόξασται ἡ ὄψις, cf.
30: δεδοξασμένη ἡ ὄψις). At this point, the LXX rendering
is so idiosyncratic that it is almost impossible to believe
that Paul arrived at his construction in 3.10 independently,
or indeed as anything less than a conscious midrash on the
text of the LXX. In 4.4 however he seems to be making use of
the picture given by the Hebrew text: "so that the enlightenment of the gospel of the glory of Christ not shine out
(αὐγάσαι)." The most natural translation of קרן and the one
which would occur to a reader picturing the rays about Moses'
face would be ηὔγασε (beamed out).

Thus the tradition demonstrates a particular interest in
the "beaming" or "shining" of Moses' face and an inclination
especially in the Greek tradition to characterize it as
"glory." Latent in this tendency is an explanation of the
source of that light in Moses' face.

The glory of Moses' face explained.

> MOSES KNEW NOT THAT THE SKIN OF HIS FACE SENT FORTH
> BEAMS. [Ex. 34.29]
> Whence did Moses derive those beams of glory? The
> Sages said; From the cleft of the rock, as it says,
> *And it shall come to pass while My glory passeth by,*
> *that I will put thee in a cleft of the rock and I*
> *will cover thee with My hand until I have passed*
> *by* [ibid., XXXIII.22].[21]

The biblical text has already begun the explanation of
the source of Moses' glory: the skin of his face shone

---

[21]*Ex. R.* 47.6 (Soncino, 541). Brackets mine.

because he had been talking with God (בדברו איתו--literally,
"in his talking with him" 34.29). Seemingly Moses "caught" the
glory which he saw during the revelation made to him in Exodus
34. The versions make this explanation of the phenomenon
increasingly explicit. The LXX rendering of the passage by
the use of the word "glorify" (δοξάζω), recalls the use of the
word "glory" (δόξα) in Moses' prayer and vision. Moses' face
is glorified by the glory which he prayed to see, which passed
by him, and the back of which he did see (Ex. 33.18, 22). In
fact, the LXX presents a more homogeneous picture of the
theophany as a revelation of God's glory than does the MT;
where the letter reads "I will make all my goodness pass
before you," the former has "I will make all my glory pass
before you" (33.19).

The Targums also explain the brightness of Moses' face
as the reflection of the glory. Onkelos' elaboration of "his
face shone" is "great was the brightness of the *glory* (יקרא),"
the same word as that which the Targum uses to translate
כבוד in 33.18 and 22. Even more striking is the Targum's
interpretation of "hand" in 33.23: "And I will remove the
word of My glory (דברת יקרי) Hebrew כפי) and you will see my
back (דבתרי)." Targum Jonathan gives the same explanation of
the glory, but quite explicitly: "...the visage of his face
shone with the splendour which had come upon him *from the
glory of the Lord's Shekinah* (מין זיו איקר שכינא דיוי) in the
time of his speaking with him." Thus the commentators seem to
be asking, "What shone in Moses' face because he had spoken
with the Lord?" and the answer is: "the glory, כבוד, which
he had seen." This interpretive move must be one step in the
interpretation of Psalm 8 which we remarked above: "What
human being partook of the כבוד, glory?"--"Moses, whose face
shone by reason of his speaking with him."[22]

The rabbinic tradition attempts to be more specific still
about the moment and the mode in which the rays were communicated to Moses' face. The story from *Exodus Rabbah* cited
above[23] seems to place the moment at the passing of God's

---

[22]*Midrash Tehillim* 8.7 (above, 155-156).

[23]47.6, see n. 21.

glory. There is a parallel in Tanchuma B[24] which combines
Ex. 33.22 with Hab. 3.3-4 which speaks of the *splendor*
(הוד) of God and of *rays* (קרנין) coming forth from his hand.
It may be that both versions of the story actually intend to
suggest that the rays of glory (קרני ההוד) came to Moses
(i.e. rubbed off on him) from the touch of God's hand.

Other rabbinic texts attach the communication of the rays
to the lawgiving rather than to the vision of glory: the rays
came from the mouth of the Shekinah when Moses learned the
law; they came from the light beaming out from the partially
uncovered (or unrolled) tablets; they came from the ink with
which Moses wrote the commandments when he dried the pen in
his hair. A slightly less literal-minded explanation sees the
glory of Moses' face as fire deriving from the fire of the
law (Dt. 33.2) in the theophany.[25]

Thus the tradition envisages two possible sources of the
glory of Moses' face: 1) it was the glory of the vision, or
of the passage of the Lord; 2) it came from Torah, when God
gave Moses the commandments. These two possible occasions of
the communication of the glory roughly correspond to the two
"visions" distinguished by *Siphre Bemidbar* in its discussion
of Nu. 12.8: a vision which is the vision of God's image
(תמונת), when God set Moses on the rock and all his glory
passed by and he saw his *back* (Ex. 33.22-23; 34.5-9); and the
vision of the *Word* (דיבור), with which he speaks to him mouth
to mouth--i.e. at the giving of the commandments (34.19-28).[26]

It should be noted however that these texts are not
making the distinction which *Siphre* makes. Rather, one group
of texts take the words בדברו איתו "when he was speaking with
him" very literally and understands it to mean that the
speaking of God, or the *Shekinah*, or the *Word* of God, i.e.
Torah, produced the rays of glory. The other set of texts
concentrates on the vision of glory. Probably, however, both

---

[24]כי-תשא 121a; for text and parallels, see Strack-
Billerbeck III, 514, on 2 Co. 3.7.

[25]Cf. *Ex. R.* 47.6; Strack-Billerbeck on 2 Co. 3.7 (III,
513-516).

[26]See above, 122-123.

interpretations, like the OT text itself, envisage the whole
scene as a single incident; Pseudo-Philo certainly does, for
that author joins the incident of Moses' glorified face to his
first ascent and forty-day sojourn.[27] Even the distinction
made by *Siphre Bemidbar* is to be thought of as a distinction
between modes rather than moments of revelation. The difference in the texts is a matter of emphasis: one version
accounts for the glory in terms of "the presence" or "emanation of glory" (שכינה) of which Moses saw (no more than) the
back; the other suggests that the communication of Torah
communicated the glory to Moses' face. But in fact one
involves the other; Paul's commentary on the incident reveals
this understanding of the text: "if then the dispensation of
death was with glory..." (2 Co. 3.7). The glory of Moses'
face is the result of the glory that accompanied the giving
of Torah.[28]

The glory of Moses and the glory of the son.

If Hebrews' comparison of Jesus and Moses is based upon
the glory accorded to Moses through the vision of God's glory
and the giving of Torah, an entirely new light is shed upon
the working of the comparison.

For he (Jesus) is accounted worthy of greater glory than
Moses as the one who has built a house has greater honor than
the house. "For every house is built by someone...."

That "every house is built by someone" is a version of
the "divine artificer" argument: no artifact without an
artisan--from the work one deduces (the existence of) the
worker, from the house, the builder; from Moses (crowned) with
glory and honor, as in the house, Jesus, crowned with glory
(2.9) and honored as the builder of the house.[29]

Thus, while it is said of both Moses and Jesus "faithful/

---

[27]Pseudo-Philo XII.1.

[28]See on this Isaac I. Friesen, *The Glory of the Ministry
of Jesus Christ, Illustrated by a Study of 2 Co. 2.14-3.18*
(Basel: Friedrich Reinhardt Kommissionsverlag, 1971) 47-53.

[29]The divine artificer argument is treated further below,
163-164, 180.

trusted in God's house, even above the angels" the difference
between them is the difference between the glory with which
Moses was glorified, and the glory of God which he saw.[30]

Startling as this suggestion at first appears, the
Christology of Hebrews does allow an identification of the
glory of Christ with the glory that Moses saw. The exordium
of the letter proclaims the son "the refulgence of his glory"
(ἀπαύγμασμα τῆς δόξης). As we shall see, it is not the glory
of the son that is identified with the glory of God, but the
son himself. If this identification is applied to 3.3, the
comparison is further clarified: Jesus' glory is greater
than Moses', for Moses' glory was the reflection, or remnant,
of the glory that he saw, but the glory that he saw was the
son, the glory of God.

At the first reading then, 3.2 suggests that Nu. 12.7 is
governing the interpretation of the Nathan oracle: that Jesus
as Christ and son is faithful/trusted like (on the same basis
that) Moses is faithful/trusted in the house: in his superiority to, his ascent over, the angels. On closer inspection
however, the direction of the likening is precisely the
opposite direction: not from Moses to Jesus, not Jesus like
Moses, but Moses likened to the son of God, transformed by his
ascent, conformed to the one he beheld, according to his glory:

---

[30]This was first suggested to me by the commentary of
Aquinas *ad loc*:

> ...Christus autem fabricavit domum. Ps. LXXXIII.16:
> "Tu fabricatus es aurorem et solem." Prov. IX.1:
> "Sapientia aedificavit sibi domum, id est, Ecclesiam."
> Ipse enim Christus, per quem gratia et veritas facta
> est, tamquam legislator aedificavit Ecclesiam. Moyses
> autem tamquam legis pronuntiator; et ideo solum ut
> pronuntiatori debetur gloria Moysi: unde et
> resplenduit facies eius,de qua Ex. XXXIV.29 et II
> Co. III.7: "Ita ut non possunt filii Israel
> intendere in faciem Moysi propter gloriam vultus
> eius."

(Ad Hebraeos 161)

A. T. Hanson has also suggested that He. 3.1-6 is based upon
the author's conviction that Moses saw Christ and spoke with
him in the lawgiving ("Christ in the Old Testament according
to Hebrews," *St. Ev.* II, 1964, 394-397). His conclusions are
all based upon the LXX and he does not dwell upon the glory
of Moses' face or discuss the divine artificer argument.

Another reading: *A prayer of Moses, a man, the God*
(Ps. 90.1). If man, how *God*? If God, how *man*? ...
Another comment: When Moses went up on high, he
was a man. *How bright is a candle in the presence
of Moses?* When a mortal goes up to the Holy One,
blessed be He, He who is pure fire and his ministers
are fire--and Moses did go up to Him--he is a man.
But after he comes down, he is called "God."[31]

On the basis of this conforming of Moses to the Son, the
comparison in 3.2 can be followed out in two alternative ways
to two alternative conclusions represented in 3.4.

The simpler of these two ways of reading the text does
not attempt to discern any identity between the meaning of
"house" in 3.2, that is, the "house" which the two OT oracles
place under the sway of Moses and of Jesus, and "house" in
3.3-4:

...Jesus, appointed/faithful to the one who made him
(faithful) like Moses, (by his ascent) in the house,
the heavens.

For this one (Jesus) is accounted of greater glory
than Moses (on his descent)

As much as the one who has built a house has greater
honor (or a greater price) than the house.

For every house is built by someone--from the house,
deduce the builder, from the glory of Moses, the
glory of Jesus--

But the builder of all is God--who is the source of
the glory of both Moses and Jesus.

The second possibility leads toward a continuity of meaning
in the uses of the word "house." This possibility arises from
understanding the builder to house comparison to apply not
merely analogously to the difference between the glory of
Jesus and the glory of Moses but also literally to the
difference between Jesus and Moses in themselves. It leans
more heavily than the former interpretation on the explanation
of the glory of Jesus as the glory of God that the son is:
not merely is Jesus' glory the light or fire that Moses saw,

---

[31]*Midrash Tehillim* 90.5 (Braude II, 88-89 and n. 12, 494).
I have taken the liberty of restoring the words within the
asterisks from Braude's note. They are from Buber's edition,
which is Braude's norm in the rest of the translation. His
reading from the (uncritical) Printed Edition, is: "In the
presence of God, how bright is a candle? How bright is even
a torch in the presence of God?"

and Moses' glory reflection of it, but even Jesus *is* light, Moses, reflection; Jesus *is* builder, Moses, house; Jesus *is* creator, Moses created.

> ...Jesus, appointed/faithful to the one who made him (faithful) like Moses (by his ascent) in his house, the heavens.

> For this one (Jesus) is accounted of greater glory than Moses (on his descent)

> As much as the one who built the house (Jesus) has more honor than the house (Moses as creature).

> For every house is built by someone--from house deduce builder, from glorified Moses, glory of God, the son --but the one who built the all (the house of creation, heaven and earth and Moses) is God.

This interpretation has the advantage of providing continuity for the meanings of "house" throughout the passage: Jesus as trusted in the created heavens has authority over the created universe, including over Moses as builder over house. Further, the operation of the Nathan oracle suggests that "builder" ought to be applied literally to Jesus. However, it also has distinct disadvantages. It does not explain how we can be only conditionally his house as 3.6 seems to envisage the matter; it seems to exclude any meaning such as "created" or "made" from ποιήσαντι in 3.2; it requires the introduction of what appears to be an extra step in the argument: "the builder of Moses is the builder of (the) all." Most striking of all it imputes to the text a theological decision both bold and rare in the New Testament: the naming of Jesus "creator" and God.

No matter of interpretation can ever be settled with absolute certainty; however, there are three areas of investigation which can assist us in assessing the probability of this second interpretation. The first of these is the Christology of Hebrews: does the letter admit of a view of Christ as God and creator? The second is the source of such a Christology: from what theological milieu does a Christology of glory come, and does it make such a Christological decision possible? The third is the function of the vision of Moses in the contemporary theological tradition: what theological questions are being worked out through the use of this text?

"God" and "creator" in the Christology of Hebrews.

Does Hebrews admit of a view of Christ as creator and God? An examination of Hebrews 1 suggests that the letter not only admits of such a Christology but even consciously ascribes it to the messianic oracles cited in that chapter: in other words, to the oracles about the son of David, precisely the oracles involved in the argument in 3 by the citation of 1 Chr. 17.14.

The full significance of the oracles in 1.5-13 is only apparent if the formal character of that passage is recognized. The first chapter of Hebrews is intended to present itself as a divine, precosmic drama similar in intent and content to the prologue of the gospel of John. The scriptural citations are intended to be understood as oracles in the strict sense, i.e. pronouncements of God, and the πρός which introduces them should be read as "(addressed) to" (as in πρὸς Ἑβραίους, "to the Hebrews") rather than "(spoken) of"--"to the angels he says" (1.7)..."but to the son" (1.8).

In the beginning (1.5 "today?" eternally?)[32] the father calls the son: "today have I begotten you" (Ps. 2.7)..."I will be to him a father, and he will be to me a son" (2 Sam. 7.14/1 Chr. 17.13). These oracles to the anointed king and scion of David are given a precosmic setting.

Then the father leads the son to the created world (οἰκουμένη, 1.6) and proclaims: "Let all *God's* angels worship him" (Dt. 32.43; Ps. 97.7). While the command to worship is sufficient warrant for the superiority over the angels Hebrews claims for the son, it is quite possible that the author intends not only "Him" but also its antecedent, "God's" to refer to the son.

The next oracle, Ps. 104.4 is addressed *to* the angels, but appears to be *about* the son: (look) the one who makes his angels spirits, and his ministers a flame of fire.

This proclamation of the son as God and creator becomes more prominent in the progression of oracles as long as they

---

[32] On the temporal problem here see Héring, 9, on 1.6; also Bruce, 16-17. The ascription of this dialogue to a pre-cosmic eternity seems to me to obviate the problem.

are consistently read as addressed *to* the son:

> Your throne, O God, is forever and ever...
> Therefore, O God, your God has anointed you[33]
> You before the ages, O Lord, founded the earth
> and the works of your hands are the heavens.[34]

Finally, the author cites Ps. 110.1:

> Sit at my right hand, until I set your enemies as a
> footstool under your feet.

The interpretation of this verse in Mark is the best attestation for an early Christian application of the verse to the Christ so as consciously to reinterpret the Davidic Messiah as the divine son:[35]

> David himself, inspired by the Holy Spirit, declared:
> The Lord said to my Lord,
> Sit at my right hand
> till I put thy enemies under thy feet.
> David himself calls him Lord; so how is he his son?[36]

This Lord who is not merely the son of David is still the Davidic Messiah. The same appears to be true of Hebrews' interpretation, and most probably of interpreters who precede Hebrews. "O God your God has anointed you" must be a traditional text about the Christ at least for early Christianity. So also it seems that the Nathan oracle promise, "His throne shall be established forever," has determined the interpretation not only of the traditionally messianic Ps. 45.7, "your throne, O God, is forever and ever," but also of Ps. 102.26-28 whose declaration of eternity once applied to God:

> They perish, but you remain;
> you are the same and your years do not fail.[37]

---

[33]Ps. 45.7-8 in He. 1.8-9. On the vocative in these verses, see Héring, 10; Bruce, 19; and Spicq II, 19-20.

[34]Ps. 102.26 in He. 1.10. On these citations as addressed to Christ, see Michel, 57-58.

[35]On this argument see David M. Hay, *Glory at the Right Hand: Psalm 110 in Early Christianity* (Nashville and New York: Abingdon Press, 1973).

[36]Mk. 12.35-36.

[37]Cf. n. 34 above. For an opposing view, see Buchanan, 19-23, but esp. 20.

The 1 Chr. 17.14 version of the Nathan oracle sets the promise of a perpetual throne in the following context:

> I will be to him a father and he will be to me a son,
> and I will maintain him faithful (make him sure) in
> my house and in my kingdom, and his throne will be
> established forever (LXX).

The LXX reads "his throne" where the MT reads "your throne"; thus in the Greek tradition the oracle which originally promised a perpetual succession to David comes to prophesy an eternal throne to his descendant. This interpretation of the Nathan oracle undergirds not only Hebrews' ascription of eternity to the son as Christ, (which indeed invokes the LXX version of the oracles) but also John's dictum: "We heard from the Law that the Christ remains forever" (8.35, cf. 12.34: "The slave does not remain in the house forever, but the son remains forever").[38] John, however, is unlikely to be dependent on the LXX; the interpretation of the Nathan oracle to apply to the eternal messianic king may well have caused the difference in the LXX text rather than resulted from it.

Thus it seems that it is not merely a possibility for Hebrews to name the son creator and God, but that this is in fact the intent of the first chapter, and that this intent is carried out through the promises about the Davidic Messiah (Christ as son) which also provide the text which serves as the testimony for Jesus in 3. Once again, it is not possible to establish this interpretation of Hebrews 1 with absolute certainty. The single greatest argument in its favor is the consistency with which the chapter can be read, so as to absorb and even to make prominent the startling declarations of Ps. 45.7 and Ps. 102.26, which seem unequivocally to address the son as God and creator.[39]

Although the oracles about the son of David are capable of bearing this interpretation, that they have produced the comparison in 3.1-6 seems less likely. It is necessary to look for the source of this Christological decision elsewhere

---

[38] Cf. Aalen, 237-238.

[39] Cf. Michel, 97, and Spicq, 67.

as well. What kind of Christology names Jesus the "glory of God" or "the reflection of his glory"?

Sources for the Christological decision of 3.2-4.

The peculiar phrase, "refulgence of his glory" seems to belong to the same context as the comparison of the glory of Moses to the glory of Christ. Whatever philosophical origin the phrase might have had, it is extremely likely that the author, whether or not espousing the philosophical import of the Greek phrase, applies the phrase itself to the glory which Moses both saw and wore. The same phenomenon, which the rabbis name the beams of glory (קרני ההוד) and the Targums name splendor of the glory (זיו יקרא), could be described in Greek as the beams of glory (αὐγαι τῆς δόξης) or even brilliance or refulgence of the glory (ἀπαύγασμα τῆς δόξης).

In fact, one possible source of Hebrews' phrase, and seemingly of the letter's Christology, is the description of wisdom given in the Wisdom of Solomon 7.25-26:

ἀτμὶς γάρ ἐστιν τῆς τοῦ θεοῦ δυνάμεως
She is a breath of the power of God

καὶ ἀπόρροια τῆς τοῦ παντοκράτορος δόξης εἰλικρινής·
and a pure emanation of the glory of the almighty;

διὰ τοῦτο οὐδὲν μεμιαμμένον εἰς αὐτὴν παρεμπίπτει.
hence nothing impure can find a way into her.

ἀπαύγασμα γάρ ἐστιν φωτὸς ἀιδίου
She is a reflection of the eternal brightness

καὶ ἐσόπτρον ἀκηλίδωτον τῆς τοῦ θεοῦ ἐνεργείας
untarnished mirror of God's active power,

καὶ εἰκὼν τῆς ἀγαθότητος αὐτοῦ.
image of his goodness.

If Hebrews knows Wisdom the phrase in 1.3 could be a condensation of "emanation of glory" and "reflection of eternal light," but this possibility by no means weakens the possibility that the phrase refers also to the glory that Moses saw/wore in Exodus 34. For Wisdom seems to be identifying wisdom as the glory which Moses saw. The "emanation of glory" might well envisage the vision of glory (כבוד), which in the tradition of interpretation tends to become the Shekinah. "The reflection" or "refulgence" of light would be readily suggested by "beam" (קרן) or more directly by one of its

translations or elaborations. In addition, the source of
"mirror" (ἔσοπτρον) and "image" (εἰκών) can even be said to be
strikingly clear: the choice of these two words suggests that
wisdom is the subject or perhaps the medium of that extraordinary vision of Moses described in Nu. 12.8:

...מראה, in a mirror (ἔσοπτρον) and not in riddles,
and the תמונת, image (εἰκών) of the Lord he sees.[40]

The qualification of "image" as the "image of his goodness" reflects another traditional step in the interpretation
of Nu. 12.8: the explication of Nu. 12.8 by the vision of
Moses as it is described in Ex. 33.18-23. The LXX attaches
these verses to Nu. 12.8 by interpreting "image" as glory,
thus focusing on Ex. 33.21, as does Onkelos, which explicates
it as "the image of the glory of the Lord." Targum Jonathan
and *Siphre Bemidbar* interpret the "image" as referring to the
same vision by suggesting that the image is the "back" as it
says in Ex. 33.23.[41] Thus it would seem that at least
Wisdom 7.26 and probably also 25 is depicting wisdom precisely
as that which Moses saw in his vision. While we cannot be
sure that Hebrews would have read the description with that
understanding, to posit that the writer did so helps to explain the phrase "refulgence of his glory" (ἀπαύγασμα τῆς
δόξης) which gives a picture still closer to the text and
versions of Ex. 34.29 ff. than the images given in Wisdom.
In addition if Hebrews is relying on a traditional interpretation of Exodus whose activity in Wisdom passages would be
obvious, its author can rely on the intelligibility of the
slight reference to the "glory of Moses and the glory of
Christ" in the comparison.

The phrase "refulgence of his glory" has a functional
implication which is of particular interest in the interpretation of the Hebrews passage. Since it seems to derive
from "beam" (קרן) in Ex. 34.29 and from such interpretations

---

[40]This formulation presupposes that the interpretation
is not made exclusively upon the LXX reading, but is either
made from the Hebrew text or supplemented by the tradition.

[41]Above, 120-121.

of it as are found in the Targums, it focuses in particular
on the glory of God as the *source* of Moses' glory, the glory
of God as transforming, as communicating itself. The
continuation of the description of wisdom in Wis. 7.25-26 may
well be an explanation of this transforming role of wisdom.
In 7.27 it is said of wisdom:

> By generations passing into holy souls
> Friends of God and prophets she builds (κατασκευάζει).

While the description intends to emphasize the providence
which bestows saints on every generation, *the* "friend of God
and prophet" par excellence is clearly Moses, *the* prophet:
"The Lord spoke with Moses face to face as a man speaks with
his friend" (Ex. 33.11, cf. Dt. 34.10). Thus wisdom builds
(furnishes, fashions) Moses as prophet: Moses in his generation is the manifestation of wisdom.

Wisdom, however, is not only the source of Moses'
prophecy, but also the means of the creation of humanity:

> God of the fathers and Lord of mercies
> Who have made the universe by your word
> And by your wisdom have built the human being
> (ὁ...κατασκευάσας; Wis. 9.1-2).[42]

Thus for Wisdom, the wisdom of God is both builder of Moses
as prophet and the agent of his creation as a human being.
Further, "wisdom" and "Word" seem to be synonymous, so that
wisdom is also the agent of the creation of the universe; cf.
7.21: "the artisan of the universe, wisdom." This ascription of the creation to the agency of the Word or the wisdom
of God derives from the interpretation of the creation account
in light of Pro. 8.25-27 and at Ps. 33.6: "By the Word of
the Lord the heavens were made." Neofiti I provides a
similar interpretation of the creation account and reverses
the roles of the agents of God as they are described in Wis.
9.1:

> From the beginning by Wisdom the Lord created the
> heavens and the earth [43]

---

[42]On the meaning of this word, see Hanson, 395-396, and
Spicq, 67.

[43]Neofiti I. This reading is given by Diez-Macho, et.

And the Word of the Lord created the son of man in
his (own) image, in a resemblance from before the
Lord he created him. [44]

Thus one problematic aspect of the interpretation we are
investigating can be resolved by the theological function of
wisdom. The "extra step" of saying that the builder of Moses
is the builder of the all is a matter of course within the
same tradition which supplies an intermediary for the creation.

Further, the wisdom tradition provides us with a source
for other aspects of the Christology of Hebrews. Elsewhere
in the letter the son is described with traits ascribed to
wisdom in the other sapiential works. Particularly noteworthy
are some resonances between Hebrews and Sirach. The son
appointed heir of all (He. 1.2) recalls Si. 24.7-8 and 13.
Si. 24.10, "in the holy tent I ministered before him," could
well lie behind the formulation of He. 8.2: "...minister of
the true tent...." Of course the theme of preexistence always
evokes the wisdom speculation, but Si. 24.9 appears to be a
midrash on the same verses of Psalm 102 which Hebrews chooses
to describe the eternity of the son:

Before the ages, from the beginning, he
created me and forever I shall not fail.   (Si. 24.9)

You at the beginning Lord founded the earth....

You are the same and your years do not   (Ps. 102.26,28)
fail.

This stream of speculation about the preexistence of
wisdom and its origin provides a theological milieu in which
it is possible both to sustain the application of 3.4 to
Jesus and to retain some of the meaning of "made" for

---

al., in the margins. The text actually reads: "in the
beginning by wisdom the son of the Lord perfected the heavens
and the earth." מלקדמין בהכמה ברא דיי שכלל ית שמיא וית ארעא
The ambiguity of the text is evident; Diez-Macho discusses
the problems in I, 497, n. 1.

[44]Translation is that of Diez-Macho, et. al., I, 499. On
the relation of glory and image in the creation of Adam and
the glorification of Moses, see J. Jervell, *Imago Dei. Gen.
1.26 f. im Spätjudentum, in der Gnosis und in den Paulinischen
Briefen* (Göttingen: Vandenhoeck and Ruprecht, 1960), 100-101.
The problem is very complex and invites further investigation
of the relation of Nu. 12.6-8 to the image and glory themes
in creation, salvation and Christology.

ποιήσαντι in 3.2. For within the wisdom tradition the notion
of a "made maker" becomes intelligible. If 3.1-6 is interpreted within the context of the wisdom literature, Pro. 8.22 ff.
and Si. 1.6, 8 and 24.9 may well lie behind the meaning of
ποιήσαντι. Although the LXX of these verses states unequivocally that wisdom is created (κτίζω), Hebrews never uses the
more explicit verb,[45] but uses ποιέω instead. As a result,
the meaning "make" can be combined with the meaning "appoint"
or "make sure" (πιστόν ποιῆσαι-πιστῶσαι) so that the "creation"
of wisdom can be combined with the appointment of the son of
David and of God. The result of this combination is something
very close to the primitive attempt to evolve the theory we
call the generation of the son.

Finally wisdom also provides us with a pattern for naming
Jesus builder of the house as people/temple as well as heavens/
creation. For one thing, the tradition takes up the interpretation of the Nathan oracle; wisdom as the consort of Solomon
assists him to build the temple and rule the people in
fulfillment of the promise to David his father (Wis. 9.1-10).
More significant still, however, is the function of Wisdom as
transformer. The people, who all are of the creation, the
house that wisdom built,[46] are only of that house conditionally, by their pursuit of wisdom. Thus wisdom is not only the
builder of the creation and of the created man, but of the
saints who chose to serve her (cf. Wis. 9.18-10.21; Sirach
44-47), of the wise man as long as he will be wise.

This role of wisdom as the fashioner of saints finds
significant thematic development in the LXX version of Si.
42.15-47. In this version the section becomes a treatise on
the glory of God, which can be contemplated in creation
(42.15-43), which is the source of men's fame, but which also
transforms--or forms--"glorious men." "Glorious men" need
not be famous (44.9), but as men of favor, they partake of the
glory of God. So also with Christ, the glory of God and

---

[45]The noun κτίσις is used for "creature" (as subject to
the Word's omniscience, 4.13) and "creation" ("of this
creation," 9.11).

[46]Cf. Aquinas' comment above, n. 30.

builder of the house. As we are builded by him in creation, so we too, like Moses glorified, are his house, builded by our holding fast to the hope--of the glory to which we are being led as sons (2.10).

These features of the wisdom theology extend and explain the role of the oracle of the royal priest in explaining how the house can at once be the house of David's descent, the temple and the congregation joined by faith and/or obedience. In chapter two the discussion of the relation of the royal high priest and the faithful house[47] included a passage from the *Damascus Document* in which the relationship of creation and the sure house was also brought to light:

> ...he built them a sure house in Israel whose like has never existed from former times until now. Those who hold fast to it are destined to live forever and all the glory of Adam shall be theirs....[48]

The *Damascus Document* clearly perceives the life of the community as a pursuit of wisdom[49] and the house to which the congregants cling is the house of the Law.[50] Elsewhere the sectarian texts speak clearly of the role of wisdom as creator of the universe, of the individual human being, and of the new sanctity of the sectarian.[51] By their adherence to the law and to wisdom (that is to the community) the sectarians become the priestly house, the spiritual temple of the promise, and are transformed to the former glory of creation. In this community then we discover that the wisdom theology supplements or informs the explanation of the community as the faithful house of the faithful priest. It seems that a similar use of the wisdom theology can have taken place in the community of Hebrews, with the singular difference that in Hebrews the faithful priest is not the

---

[47]Above, 86-89.

[48]*CD* III.19-20 (Vermes, 100).

[49]*CD* II.1-4, III.14-16 (Vermes, 98, 100-101).

[50]*CD* VIII.10-13 (Vermes, 106-107).

[51]See esp. Hymn I (Vermes, 150-154).

disciple or even the master of wisdom, but the wisdom of God and emanation of his glory.

Thus the operation of the wisdom speculation in He. 3.1-6 makes it possible to give a consistent though shifting significance to the word "house" not merely within the comparison (2-4), but even in the whole of the passage. It solves the major difficulties which we noted in the equation of Jesus with "the one who built all, God":

1) It allows a very full sense to "made."
2) It explains the relationship between the building of Moses and the building of the all.
3) It explains how we as created can be still only conditionally "his house."
4) Finally, it provides a medium through which arises the possibility of naming the son creator and God.

However, it is not quite clear *how* this theological medium enters the comparison. The gospel of John has made a direct application of this sort of interpretation in its explanation of Jesus: the creative Word of God is God, is his son, is Jesus.[52] Hebrews certainly knows and approves an application at least similar to John's; He. 11.2 credits the creation of the ages to "a word of the Lord," while 1.2 relates that God made the ages through the agency of his son. Can we then say that Hebrews has made the same direct identification that John has made? Is the Christology of 3.1-6 being formed or directed in some degree by a "wisdom Christology" which has filled out the collection of messianic oracles and organized them into a single picture?

Two significant qualifications of this question contravene a direct answer. The first of these arises from the viewpoint of Hebrews, the second from that of the tradition, in particular the traditional interpretation of Exodus 33-34.

At no point does the letter to the Hebrews explicitly identify Jesus as the son with the wisdom of God. Rather traditional language and notions elsewhere applied to wisdom (e.g. the reflection of his glory, through whom he made the

---

[52]Esp. 1.1, 14, 16; see also Martin McNamara, *Targum and Testament* (Grand Rapids: William B. Eerdmans Publishing Co., 1972), 101-106.

ages, who sustains the universe) or the Word are applied
to the son of God in Hebrews. Furthermore, that application
is not made at the same direct level at which it appears to
be made in the prologue of John. If Hebrews 1.2 and 11.2
testify to the identification of the son and God's word,
utterance, or speaking, they also testify to the incompleteness
of that identification. As it turns out, a divine, powerful
word can also be attributed to the son: "...sustaining the
universe by the word of his power" (1.3). This variety of
formulation seems to suggest very strongly that Hebrews has
not simply identified the son with wisdom as an "hypostasis"
of God fully distinguished from God by a pre-Christian
tradition.

That 3.1-6 can be explained by an identification of the
son with wisdom is further qualified by the treatment of
Exodus 33-34 in the tradition. Wisdom explains Moses' vision
as a vision of wisdom. The Targums similarly propose an
intermediary only in part distinguished from God as the
subject of Moses' vision. Or rather, they propose intermediaries. In Tg. Onkelos, the glory seems to equal the
Shekinah, for it is the Shekinah which passed by in 34.6; God
covered Moses with his Word (Memra) and then took away his
Word (Dibbur) and Moses saw his back--possibly, Moses saw
his Dibbur, which is the back of the Memra (the text reads:
"I will take away my word (דברתי) and you will see my back
(דבתרי)"; the two words are equivalent by the identity of
their consonants. Tg. Jonathan and the Palestinian Tg.
represented by Neofiti I give an increasing role to the Memra.
In Tg. Jonathan, the name to be proclaimed in the oracle is
the name of the Memra (19); God covers Moses with the Memra
as in Onkelos, but the words "I will take away my hand" are
omitted completely. The vision is accompanied by a passage
of the ministering angels who stand before God's face (to
hide the face of the Shekinah?) and Moses is allowed to see
"the handborder to the tephila of my glorious Shekinah." In
Neofiti I none of these substitutes appears, but the vision
seems to be a vision of Dibbur:

> And I will make the troops of angels pass by who
> stand and minister before me and you will see the

> Word of the glory of my Shekinah but it is not
> possible that you see the face of the glory of my
> Shekinah.[53]

It is difficult to glean a very clear picture of what these
translators actually think Moses saw. That the name of the
Memra is proclaimed according to Jonathan suggests that that
version believes him to have seen the Memra. Had Ex. 33.23
been rendered as it is in Neofiti, Jonathan would present a
consistent view that Moses saw the Memra which is the back of
the Shekinah. It may be that Jonathan intends us to understand that the Memra which Moses is allowed to see is (only
so much as) the handborder of the tephila of the Shekinah.

The interpretation of Exodus 33-34 seems to require of the
ancient interpreter some sort of intermediary. In the Targums,
the interpreter appears to equate glory with the Shekinah,
while Moses' vision seems to have been a vision of the Word as
Siphre Bemidbar also decides. But Shekinah and Dibbur are
not as clearly distinguished in these texts as they appear to
be in *Siphre*, at least they are not mutually exclusive.
Indeed, Shekinah, Memra and Dibbur although they can be
distinguished in the abstract are not very clearly distinguished one from the other in this passage, because they are
not fully distinct from God. Calling any one of them an
hypostasis of God would very clearly be an overstatement.
Rather they are protections of God's transcendence, attempts
to make intelligible a passage which demands that God be and
be not seen.

While the same function will not completely explain the
role of wisdom, the Word and the Shekinah in the creation
accounts, the same problem may well explain at least the
interpretation of Gen. 1.27 Palestinian Targum: God's
transcendence requires that visible man be made by the Word
in the image of the Shekinah.[54] In general Memra, Shekinah,
Word, and wisdom are used without great consistency precisely
because they are only partially distinguished from God, are
as much his attributes as his agents, so that they can be

---

[53]Diez-Macho II, *Exodo*.

[54]See Etheridge I, 170.

overlooked or interchanged when some other focus is more important.[55] Even in the book of Wisdom, which appears to treat wisdom as a personal being, "she" is not fully distinguished either from God or from the Word. Not only 9.1-3 but also 7.15-21 show that wisdom is still an attribute of God which can be shared by men. Apparently then, the sort of interpretation which requires them ought to be regarded as the source of both wisdom speculation and the Christology of Hebrews. The seeker of wisdom and the Christian theologian both look back over the passages which invite the intervention of intermediaries and say: "Here was wisdom!" "Here was the son!" Thus Jesus is not so much cast in the pattern already formed (e.g. wisdom as found in the sapiential literature) as he is himself the new fact which ferrets out the hints in the story and makes of them an intelligible pattern. Thus for Hebrews: the glory of God which Moses saw, the divine Word by which were created heaven and earth, this is the son of God, Jesus.

At this point, then, Hebrews does seem to allow for a Christology which acclaims Jesus as God and Creator. Further, the Christological notion on the basis of which he seems to be so acclaimed (the son, God, God's glory) appears to belong to a stream of interpretation (including wisdom speculation) which is theological in the strict sense--i.e. asks questions about God as God, questions about God's transcendence and the way in which revelation and perhaps also creation might compromise it. The next step in our attempt to ascertain the probability of 3.4 being applied to Jesus is to look at the function of the theological question about God's transcendence in two other interpretations of Exodus 33-34: that of Philo and that of John.

---

[55]On the problem of distinguishing the intermediate from God, see J. Abelson, *The Immanence of God in Rabbinical Literature* (London: Macmillan and Co., Limited, 1912) 58. For a brief view of the distinction and function, see Chapter III entitled: "Some Post-Biblical Views of Divine Immanence (outside Rabbinic Literature)," 55-56.

178

The function of Moses' vision in 1st century theology: Philo
and the Gospel of John.   •

The theological question which underlies the treatment of
Exodus 33-34 in the tradition originates in the theological
problem addressed by the text in Exodus itself. To explain
and extol the unique intimacy with God which validates Moses'
prophecy, and therefore the law which is its product, Exodus
relates that in the tent of witness, "The Lord spoke with
Moses face to face as a man speaks with his friend" (Ex.
33.11). Then to explain this extraordinary communication he
describes its origin and that of the law in an encounter in
which it is made clear that Moses cannot see the Lord's face
(33.18-34.28). This is followed up with another description
of the habitual communication in the tent which makes it clear
that the revelation given in the tent was the equal of that
given on the mount, and which adds yet another protection to
God's transcendence. Moses speaks with God with his face
uncovered, so that the communication is indeed face to face
(as it is not in Ex. 3.6, where Moses covered his face) but
now Moses face must be covered, for the sake of the people,
so great is his small share in the glory he saw (34.29 ff).
The problem is clear: faith and theology require at once
that God must be most intimately known and that God be beyond
our knowing. It is equally clear that the problem is not
solved in Exodus. Indeed, the "solution" only produces a new
problem, a contradiction in the text.

The treatment which Philo and John give to Exodus 33-34
is an example of the axiom that the problematic text becomes
the locus of explication. The theological question which
underlies their interpretation appears to be "What of God
can be seen?" and the only answer which they find acceptable
involves a monotheistic compromise of precisely the sort
which Hebrews seems to have made.

The exegetical question which corresponds to this
theological question is "what did Moses see?" The exegetical
question appears a number of times in Philo's work and his
interpretation is fairly consistent, but the theological
function of the question is perhaps best seen in *De*

Specialibus Legibus.[56] There Philo undertakes a direct
exegesis of the text under the topic *De Monarchia*, "On Monotheism" or rather "on the unique rule." There it becomes
apparent why the theological question is so easily delineated
in Philo's treatment of the passage. His philosophy on the
one hand and his text (i.e. the LXX) on the other have carried
to extremes the statement of the two horns of the dilemma:
God cannot be seen-known/God must be seen-known.

This radicalizing of the demands takes place at a level
more sophisticated than statements about the utter greatness
of God or the preeminence of sight as evidence, although
such statements abound in Philo. Philo's argument for
monotheism attempts to identify the unique government of the
universe (over against such manifold influences as the
planets), with an unseen mind which rules it as our invisible
minds rule our visible persons. In some way, the guarantee
of God's unique rule has become his invisibility:

> Therefore carrying our thoughts beyond all the realm
> of visible existence let us proceed to give honour
> to the Immaterial, the Invisible, the Apprehended by
> the understanding alone, who is not only God of gods,
> whether perceived by sense or by mind, but also the
> Maker of all.[57]

In fact, the issue of this section becomes not so much the
oneness of God as his invisibility, which distinguishes him
from other "gods" as their ruler.

On the other hand, Philo's text of Exodus, the LXX,
makes the boldness of Moses' request far clearer than does
the MT, for where the latter reads: "Show me Thy way (33.12)
...Show me Thy glory" (33.18), the LXX reads: "Show me
Thyself, that I may see Thee with knowledge (ἐμφάνισόν με
σεαυτὸν, γνώστως ἴδω σε, 33.12)...Show me Thy glory" (33.18).

After disposing of the gods of the nations and the
idolization of lesser desires, Philo delineates the two kinds
of knowledge about God which can be sought: whether God
exists (κατὰ τὸ εἶναι) and what God is according to His own

---

[56]*De Spec. Leg.* I.40 ff.

[57]I.20 (Loeb VII, 109-111).

being (κατὰ τὴν οὐσίαν).[58] The first he dismisses with a
brief résumé of the "divine artificer" argument, a version in
which the world is paralleled with artifact, ship, house, but
especially with a well-ruled city.[59] The problem of knowing
God (κατὰ τὴν οὐσίαν) requires considerably more exertion of
Philo's intellectual energies. To demonstrate the difficulties of the search for knowledge of God's being he gives an
account of Ex. 33.12-23 as the description of Moses' mystic-
philosophical search.

Moses, who has already discovered what he can of God from
the world as of artisan from work or of father from son, goes
on as "one seeking only to serve (θεραπεύειν) you" and asks:
SHOW ME YOURSELF (Ex. 33.13). This request God refuses, although he approves the desire which prompted it and grants
Moses another request. Moses then asks: "'SHOW ME THY GLORY'
(Ex. 33.18), by which I understand the attendant powers,"
i.e. ideas. This request also God refuses, but with a
qualification rather than a denial. The powers also are
unseeable (ἀόρατοι) as God Himself is unseeable (ἀόρατος).
However, Moses will be able to behold, with the eyes of his
mind, their operation (ἐνέργεια) in the world, the τύποι,
impressions, they produce in the world as seals do in wax.

This solution is inspired in part by the tradition of
interpretation and in part by the philosophy of Philo. From
the tradition Philo takes the skeletal solution of the text
which distinguishes God's glory from himself and the seeable
of that glory from the unseeable. The "glory" is then
defined by his philosophy: the "glory" is the powers of God
which are the ideas, the forms. Of these Moses will be able
to see the operation, their impressions in the world *with the
eyes of his mind*.[60]

Philo's solution then is not that the unseeable of God

---

[58]*De Spec. Leg.* I.32.

[59]*Ibid.*, 33-35. Williamson contrasts Philo's references to the universe as house and to the divine artificer
argument with the similar expressions in Hebrews on philosophical grounds (462-464) but recognizes no similarity of
function.

[60]*Ibid.*, 41-50.

becomes somehow seeable for Moses, but that Moses is somehow
modified by his search, so as to be able to see that which is
appropriate to his nature--what is indeed already seeable
of the "unseeable things of God" (cf. Ro. 1.20). Wherever
Philo treats the passage elsewhere, this much of the solution
is the same: Moses' desire to see God in himself, not "to
see your reflection in any other thing"[61] is laudable, but
his request is impossible. Moses cannot see God with the
eyes of his body, although he will come to contemplate with
the "unsleeping eyes" of his mind (τοῖς διανοίας ἀκοιμήτοις
ὄμμασι)[62] the operations of the ideas in the world.[63] However,
the character of the knowledge he obtains is very nearly a
denial of knowledge received:

> And out of this quest there accrues to him a vast
> boon, namely to apprehend that the God of real Being
> is apprehensible by no one, and to see precisely
> this, that He is incapable of being seen (καὶ αὐτὸ
> τοῦτο ἰδεῖν ὅτι ἐστιν ἀόρατος).[64]

In other words, Philo denies precisely what the Targums
and the rabbis--and after the text--always affirm: that Moses
saw something of God with the eyes of his body. Perhaps
because of this decision he never takes up the interpretation
of Ex. 34.5-9 where the vision actually takes place. He also
appears to diminish the significance of Ex. 34.29 ff. In the
only explicit citation of the latter passage, the splendor
of Moses' face has the sole function of increasing the
miraculous character of Moses' forty-day fast.[65] Elsewhere,

---

[61]*Leg. All.* III.101. The structure and the questions in
this passage are almost identical with those of our passage
and it will be discussed in another connection. The other
passages which employ or refer to Ex. 33.11-23 are: *De
Posteritate Caini*, 13-16 and 167-169; *De Mutatione Nominum*,
6-10; *De Fuga et Inventione*, 165; and *Quaestiones in Exodum*,
unidentified fragment 1 (Loeb Supp. II, 258).

[62]*De Spec. Leg.* I.47.

[63]ἐκμαγεῖόν τι καὶ ἀπεικόνισμα τῆς ἑαυτῶν ἐνεργείας
ibid.

[64]*De Post. Caini*, 15 (Loeb II,337).

[65]*Vita* II.70.

however, Philo may have provided a complete sublimation of
Moses' glory:

> ...he prays Him to reveal clearly his own nature,
> most difficult of perception, so that by partaking
> of an unlying glory (δόξης--opinion) he might change
> over from uncertain doubt to most sure trust (πίστιν
> --certainty, authority).[66]

Thus the vision that gave Moses glory (δόξαν) and authority
(πίστιν) for the less philosophical interpreters, becomes for
Philo a search for knowledge, in which true opinion will yield
certainty. Further, Ex. 33.11 is invoked by Philo only in
reference to Moses as God's friend, and Nu. 12.8 also seems
to be robbed of its force.

Although Philo's interpretation only fulfills the
exigencies of both demands laid upon it at the cost of denying
that Moses had in fact *seen* anything, it also demonstrates a
solution to which he has been forced by the exigencies of
theology and the text in much the same way as the other
interpreters we have seen. Although Philo will not admit
Moses to have *seen* anything, he, like Wisdom and the Targums,
has been forced into what we might call a monotheistic
compromise in order to protect the unseeability (τὰ ἀόρατα,
cf. Ro. 1.20) of God. Moses is allowed to see the glory of
God which is an emanation of God in some way distinguished
from himself: for Wisdom, the glory of God is his wisdom,
for the Targums, it is his Shekinah and/or Memra; for Philo,
the powers, equal to the ideas. Of this "second" of God, he
saw only the back: for Onkelos, perhaps the Word (דבתרי=
דברתי); Tg. Jonathan, "the knot of the tephila of the
Shekinah";[67] for Philo, the impressions, τύποι, of the ideas
as of seals.[68]

It is possible to suggest that the transition from God
to Shekinah to Memra to Dibbur represents a transition from
transcendence to revelation. However, only in Philo's
treatment of the text does the operation of the theological

---

[66]*De Post Caini*, 13.

[67]Above, 127-129.

[68]Cf. *De Spec. Leg.* 1.47.

difficulty become explicit. This "second" of God must be unseeable (ἀόρατος) even as God himself is unseeable, in order to reveal him as himself. Indeed the ideas are unseeable in almost the sense in which the absolute use of the adjective is understood in He. 11.27: as a synonym for "God."[69] They partake in that aspect of God's nature which Moses is able to know: that He is the Unseeable. Yet they are able to manifest themselves in some way--in their operation--which is also seeable, accessible to the mind of the man Moses. It is worth noting again that in fact there is no question of any literal "seeing" in Philo's treatment at all. What is being resolved in Philo is not a contradiction in the text between "face to face" and "My face you cannot see," nor even the primitive theological problem which produced that contradiction, but a highly sophisticated theological problem which attempts to resolve the problem of seeing the unseeable of God.

The same theological problem underlies the treatment of this text (Exodus 33-34) in the Gospel of John. Two radical shifts in viewpoint bring out the intellectual distance between these two first-century authors. Both affect the way in which the vision of Moses functions in John's thought. First of all, John is completely removed from the world of philosophical discourse in which Philo travels. By this I do not mean that John espouses a different philosophical stance from Philo's; I mean rather that he has no philosophical currency at all, neither vocabulary, nor notions nor system, beyond his popular theological notions. The word ἀόρατος never occurs in the Gospel, nor as far as I can recall does any approximation of the "divine artificer" argument appear in it. In the second place, a still more radical shift has occurred in the author's religious viewpoint; as a Christian he asks a concrete question about what of God is seeable: "What did *we* see?"--"How is the revelation in Jesus to be explained?" His answer is explicated in terms of Moses' vision by reason of the process described above: the Christian theologian looks back on the history and its interpretations for hints which help explain the new fact, the

---

[69]Michel, 275.

new event, so that it is the appearance of Jesus which
arranges and explains the hints: "The divine Word by which
were made heaven and earth (Jn. 1.3-5), the glory of God
which Moses saw (1.14-18),[70] this is the one whom we have
seen, of whom John told us that he was before him: Jesus
Christ."

Perhaps I ought to have said rather "his question is
asked in terms of Moses' vision" for in fact John is concerned
with what Moses saw as well. Indeed, the process by which he
has explained our vision (or perhaps his own vision as eyewitness) has placed Moses' vision and that of the Christian
(eyewitness?) on the same level. John never says "Prophets
and kings have yearned to see what you see, and did not";
instead he says "Abraham yearned to see my day; he saw it
and was glad" (8.58).

So, too, with Moses: "We have seen his glory," i.e. what
Moses saw on the mount, "his glory...full of grace and truth"
(Ex. 34.7),[71] when the Lord passed by. It was not God whom
Moses saw, nor whom we saw (nor anyone else ever); rather it
was the only (one of) God (1.18) who became flesh and dwelt-
in-a-tent among us, as also he dwelt-in-a-tent outside the
camp, where Moses went to speak with him face to face. Thus
we and Moses have seen, not God, but his glory, the offspring,
refulgence who is God the only one/son , whom we see only in
the flesh (the back?).[72]

At least the skeleton of the traditional solution remains here. In particular one is reminded of Tg. Jonathan,
as that interpreter declares that the oracle is "the name

---

[70]On Jn. 1.13-18 as an interpretation of Moses' vision,
see N. A. Dahl, "The Johannine Church and History," *Memory*,
99-119, Raymond Brown, *The Gospel according to John*, 2 vols.
AB, 29 (Garden City, New York: Doubleday and Company, 1966),
I.25-27 and 30-36. Augustine applies these verses of John 1
to Moses' vision also (*Tract. in Ioh.* III.18), as does
Chrysostom (*Hom. in Ev. S. Ioh.* XV.1).

[71]Πλήρης χάριτος καὶ ἀληθείας. The Hebrew of Ex. 34.6
reads: רב חסד ואמת (RSV: "abounding in steadfast love and
faithfulness").

[72]Cf. Augustine: "*Facies* autem eius illa *dei forma* in
qua *non rapinam arbitratus esse aequalis deo patri* quod *nemo
potest videre et vivere....* posteriora Christi hoc est
carnem...." (*De Trin.* II.17; CCL 50, 117, 119).

of the Memra of the Lord," John also understands the verses of
the oracle as a description of the one whom Moses saw, the
glory of the only (one/son)of God, full of grace and truth.
John's solution also contains at least the rudiments of the
later Christian solution: Moses saw not God but his glory,
that is his son, not the face of his glory, that is the divine
eternal son, but the back, that is the incarnate Lord.[73]
While this formulation is certainly not explicit in John, he
has decidedly indentified the glory of God as his son, and
the visions of that glory granted to the prophets seem to be
visions of the incarnate Lord. In 12.42 for instance, Isaiah
is said to have seen the glory of the son and prophesied about
him. The prophecy, "Lord, who has believed our hearing, or
to whom has the arm of the Lord been revealed?" applies to the
rejection, but in particular to the cross of the Lord. Indeed,
"glory" like "hour" is a theme directly connected with the
cross throughout John. Abraham also is granted a vision of
Jesus' day, which would seem to be the time of his incarnation
if not his "hour."[74]

Still more significant for our investigation is the
resemblance that John's solution bears to the solution of
Philo, or rather the resemblance of John's theological
problem to Philo's. In attempting to say what we have seen,
John also is forced to ask what of God is seeable. Nor is
this question a minor force in the prologue, for its answer
is the climax, perhaps we should say the decision of the prologue: "No one has at any time seen God; the only
God, who is in the bosom of the Father, he has made the
report."[75] For John as for Philo, God is unseeable, yet only
God reveals God. For John as for Philo the revelation is
accomplished in a "second" of God, who must like God be

---

[73]Augustine denies that Moses actually saw the incarnate
Christ and therefore that he actually saw God. He interprets
Jn. 1.18 to mean that "an angel, bearing the type of the
Lord, spoke with Moses and all those things which were done
through the angel promised that grace and truth." (*Tract.
in Ioh*. III.18; CCL 36.28).

[74]Dahl, "The Johannine Church," 107-108, 110.

[75]For survey of the readings of this verse, see Brown, 17.

unseen God in order to reveal him as himself, and yet who becomes seen in the world: the only (one/son of) God becomes flesh. Thus John also has resolved the probem by a monotheistic compromise, not because he or any one between him and Philo has replaced the powers/ideas with the Word or the Word as son, but because of the theological exigencies of his question. As in Philo Moses' vision functions to help the philosopher ask what can be seen of the unseen God (i.e. what can *we* see of the unseen God), in John it functions to assist the Christian theologian to say what we have seen of the unseen God. The theological function of Moses' vision continues, but it operates within the Christology. By asking what we have seen through Moses' vision, John is able to answer that we have seen the unseen God made seeable in Jesus.

The distance between these two first-century authors is so great as to make clear that the question is not a philosophical but a religious question, and that the two authors are driven to their conclusions by the exigencies of the question with its theological givens: only as unseeable is God himself, and only as himself is he truly known.

These three areas of investigation, then, give us grounds for concluding that Hebrews probably intends to identify Jesus as "the one who has built all, God." Hebrews' Christology, in particular its handling of the oracles about the Davidic Messiah, allows for, indeed suggests, such an identification. Further the "glory"-Christology which forms the hinge of the comparison in 3.2-4 arises from the theological stream which we are accustomed to call "wisdom-speculation" and which provides us with a source for just such a Christological decision. Finally the function of Moses' vision of God's glory is a theological function, and even when in John it is transferred to the Christology, it remains a theological function; the only questions it can answer about Christ are questions about Christ as God. We would, then, expect the vision of Moses to have a theological function also within the Christology of Hebrews.

The theological function of the vision of Moses in Hebrews.

In the beginning of this chapter I suggested that the argument in Hebrews 1-2 implies a Christological problem which is then addressed in 3.1-6: how is the son, superior to the angels but made for a little lower than they, different from Moses, who ascended and was entrusted in all his house, even over the angels? The answer is that the son differs from Moses as he is greater than the angels: as "the one who makes his angels spirits" he is also more glorious than Moses as "the one who has built him (Moses)," as "the one who has built the whole, God." The function of Moses for the Christian author is a theological function with the Christology. John very rightly pairs Moses' testimony with that of the Baptist in his prologue, for their testimony is mutually corroborating: both testify to the preexistence of the one who was "first" of both (1.5).

This theological function of Moses within the Christology makes it possible to answer another of our major questions about the function of Moses in Hebrews: how did Moses become a Christian? If for Hebrews as for John, Moses' vision of the unseen God is the parallel of ours, the answer to this question is given in 11 where it is raised: "as seeing the Unseen, he endured." The possibility arises that "the Unseen" refers to Jesus whom "we do not yet see crowned with glory and honor." The objection to this identification is that Jesus ought not to be described as the Unseen (ἀόρατον, unseeable) as he is in 11, but as "not yet seen" (μηδέπω βλεπόμενον, cf. 2.9, also 11.7, where the flood is so described in relation to Noah building the ark). The theological function of Moses' vision shows that this objection will not hold; the seeing is only significant if the one he sees is the Unseen in precisely the sense which the commentaries say that appellation must be understood: as a synonym for God.[76] Moses' vision is a vision of God the Unseeable

---

[76] *TDNT*, vol. v, 368-371, sub ὁράω. Cf. Col. 1.15, "He is the image of the unseen God (ὅς ἐστιν εἰκὼν τοῦ θεοῦ τοῦ ἀοράτου)." Jacob Jervell (*Imago Dei*, 219 and n. 187) appears to suggest that the word "image" derives from one theological context and "unseen" (ἀόρατος), from another. I do not fully

in so far as God is seeable, that is in Jesus the divine son
to whom he has fitted a body. Jesus is the visible of God,
not as *visibilis filius invisibilis patris* but as *visibilis
invisibilis filii*: the seeable of the Unseen (God), the son.[77]

There are of course difficulties involved in the application of this function of the vision to 11.27, for it would
seem to fix the reference of that verse to a point of Moses'
life far removed from his departure from Egypt.[78] It is of
course possible to point to later Christian interpretation of
the event of the burning bush as a manifestation of Christ,
but the designation of Jesus as the Unseen (ἀόρατος) ought in
some way be related to Exodus 33-34. There are two ways of
approaching this difficulty; the first is through the avenue
of the tradition, the second is through the Hebrews' handling
of the tradition.

The tradition connects Ex. 3.2 ff. and Exodus 33-34
through the medium of Nu. 12.8. The simplest level at which
this is done we have already remarked in the rendering of
Nu. 12.8 given by Tg. Jonathan "speech for speech do I speak
with him, who has separated himself from sexual intercourse;
in vision and not with mystery at the bush, and the image of

---

follow his argument, but in view of our discussion above, I
suggest that the two words belong to the common context of
the theological reflection upon the vision of Moses.

[77]Cf. Chrysostom, *Hom. in Ev. S. Ioh.* XV.1 on 1.18
(NPNF 14, 52):

> It (invisibility) belongs also to the Son; and to
> show that it does so, hear Paul declaring this
> point, and saying that He is the Image of the
> Invisible. He must be invisible himself for other-
> wise He would not be an "image."

> ...ἀλλὰ καὶ τῷ Υἱῷ. Ὅτι δὲ καὶ αὐτῷ ἄκουε Παύλου
> τοῦτο δηλοῦντος καὶ λέγοντος. Ὅς ἐστιν εἰκὼν
> τοῦ θεοῦ τοῦ ἀοράτου. Ὁ δὲ τοῦ ἀοράτου εἰκὼν ὢν
> καὶ αὐτὸς ἀόρατος. ἐπεὶ οὐκ ἂν εἴη εἰκών.
>   (PG 59.97)

Also Aug. *Tract. in Ioh.* III.17-19 (CCL 36, p. 28):

> Sapientia Dei videre oculis non potest. Fratres si
> Christus Sapientia Dei et Virtus Dei, si Christus
> Verbum Dei: verbum hominis oculis non videtur,
> Verbum Dei videre sic potest?

[78]I.e., to his vision of God in Exodus 33-34.

the back of the Shekinah did he see." Some distinction is
clearly being preserved here between the two visions: at the
bush there was a clear but imageless vision, at the lawgiving (even) the image of God's back. The whole of Nu. 12.8
however is still meant as a characterization of the way in
which God communicates with Moses and in fact, the text of
Exodus 33-34 is intended also as an explanation of the
character, as of the inauguration, of Moses' extraordinary
prophetic vision. It may well be that Tg. Jonathan sees
Exodus 3 as its inauguration (after which Moses ceased con-
jugal intercourse) and Exodus 33-34 as the explanation of it.

The Talmud seems to relate Exodus 3 and Exodus 33-34 as
cause and effect in such a way as to explain Moses' revelation
as growing progressively more intimate. At the beginning
Moses shielded his face from the apparition in the bush:
"And Moses hid his face, for he feared to look upon God."
For his piety, God awarded to him what he himself did not
presume to seize.

> R. Samuel b. Nahmani said in the name of R. [79]
> Jonathan: As a reward of three [pious acts]
> Moses was privileged to obtain three [favours].
> In reward of *And Moses hid his face* (Ex. 3.6) he
> obtained the brightness of his face.[80] In
> reward of *For he was afraid* (Ex. 3.6) he obtained
> the privilege that *They were afraid to come nigh
> him* (Ex. 34.30). In reward of *To look upon God*
> (Ex. 3.6) he obtained *The similitude of the Lord
> doth he behold* (Nu. 12.8).[81]

There are two ways of understanding this story; the first
is that as a reward for the piety which Moses showed when God
first appeared to him he received a more extraordinary
revelation, the vision of Ex. 33.13-34.28, of which Ex. 34.29
is the result and which Nu. 12.8 describes. The second
possibility makes the chronology of lesser importance, and

---

[79]See n. 2 of translator, Maurice Simon: "Mentioned in
Ex. III.6: (i) *And Moses hid his face*, (ii) *for he was
afraid*, (iii) *to look upon God*."

[80]לקלסתר פנים‎, cf. Ex. 34.29; cf. *Ex. R.* III.1, above,
157.

[81]*B. Ber.* 7a (Soncino 34; also the Soncino Hebrew-English
Talmud; parentheses mine).

sees Ex. 3.6 as recording the piety which made Moses pre-
eminent as seer, and the "reward" verses as description of
his preeminence. In either case, there is some tendency to
make the visions of Moses explain each other and his prophecy
in an increasingly homogeneous way.

Hebrews' handling of the tradition in 11 also shows this
tendency to homogenize like events to emphasize their
significance, in particular their exemplary significance.
The first chapter of this dissertation has already remarked
the difficulty of delineating the exact events to which these
verses, in particular 11.27, refer. Moses' departure from
Egypt is especially difficult. Is this departure, the
example of his endurance, his flight before Pharoah or is it
his departure at the head of Israel in the Exodus? The
answer seems to be that the two are being interpreted together,
as the unfolding of a single virtuous decision on Moses'
part.[82] Thus it is not at all unlikely that the two salient
examples of Moses' prophetic preeminence should combine their
separate circumstances to give the meaning of his role as
prophet--and as believer.

A similar move has taken place in the passage on Moses
from Sirach's treatise on glory:

...Moses of blessed memory.	
He made him the equal of the holy ones in glory,	Ex. 34.29
and made him strong to the terror of his enemies.	11.3
At the word of Moses he made the miracles stop;	8.3
he raised him high in the respect of kings.	7.1
He gave him commandments for his people,	19.1? 3.13f?
and showed him something of his glory.	33.20
For his faith and meekness he sanctified him,	Nu. 12.3-8
choosing him alone out of all mankind.	
He allowed him to hear his voice	Ex. 19.19f
and led him into the darkness;	20.21
he gave him the commandments face to face,	24.18
the law of life and knowledge,	34.
to teach Jacob his ordinances	Dt. 4.6-8,
and Israel his decrees.[83]	32.47

In this passage Moses' glorification, which suits Sirach's

_____

[82]Above, chapter one, 58-59.

[83]Si. 45.1-5.

theme, is placed first as a summary of his greatness and then the description is climactically arranged so that Moses' greatest honor, his role in the lawgiving, is placed last and has really become the point of the whole story. The rest leads up to it, and the chronology of the lawgiving has disappeared.

Hebrews also has arranged the recounting of Moses' exemplary faith in such a way as to lead to the ground on which he is appointed/faithful in all the house: in his vision of the unseen God.

The new function of Moses' vision in Christianity: explaining the status of the law.

The function of Moses' vision is then primarily theological: it assists the interpreter to articulate the possibilities of knowing God, to explain what is seeable of the unseen God by deciding what Moses saw. It should be noted that a theological decision about what Moses could have seen is really prior to and informs the interpreter's reading of the text: Philo interprets the text in the light of his foregone conclusion that the *ousia* of God is unseeable and indeed unseeability; John reads the text under the conviction that the one we have seen is God unseeable. Their convictions help to raise questions with regard to the text; the text and the traditions which interpret it assist in the articulation of these convictions.

John's decision is emblematic of the decision of Christian theology in that in Christianity, the ground of the theological reflection raised by the passage has been transferred to the realm of Christology, so that what Moses saw is now examined to help the Christian say what we have seen of God in *Christ*. It should be emphasized that the Christological decision has been made prior to and apart from its articulation through the interpretation of the text; indeed it seems that the vision of Moses as it is described in Exodus 33-34 plays no role at all in the reflection of authors with a low Christology. For instance, the vision of Moses plays no role in the Christology of Luke-Acts; for this

author, Moses' prophecy *was* by the hand of an angel,[84] and
Luke seems also to have misunderstood the account of the
transfiguration in which the vision of Moses must otherwise
have come into question.[85]

Once this decision is made, however, a new question is
raised about the vision of Moses: what is the significance of
Moses' vision now that John can write, "we have seen his
glory"? Why was Moses trusted in all his house? Why was he
permitted to enter the house, the heavens, and take charge
over the ministering angels and write down the law of fire?
If God was one day to speak through the builder of the house
and his son, why should he so have entrusted the servant
Moses? According to Hebrews, Moses was "trusted as servant
for the witnessing of the things which would be said" (3.5).
Moses' prophecy is a *witnessing*, a corroboration of the
"salvation that had its beginning through being spoken by the
Lord."

There lies behind this function of Moses as witness an
exegetical principle grounded in a Christian explanation of
Moses' vision. It says that the law is read according to
Christ ("Christ is the end of the law," Ro. 10.4) because
Moses saw him and wrote about him. Thus in John, Christ
supplants the law: "The law came through Moses, grace and
truth through Jesus Christ," not because the revelation given
to Christ was greater, but because he is "the Lord, the Lord...

---

[84] Acts 7.35, see chapter three above, 112.

[85] Luke seems to interpret the offer of "three tents" as
a clumsy attempt on the part of Peter to keep the two prophets
from departing. In the simpler account of Mark, the question
appears to refer to the tent of Moses, which is a meeting
place of Moses and God, where they speak face to face (Ex.
33.7-11). Jesus' glory tells Peter that his vision is the
same as Moses' (Exodus 33-34) or Elijah's (1 Ki. 19.9-18),
and so he foresees three prophetic tents, and three prophets
in constant communion with God on Israel's behalf. But he is
mistaken: Jesus is not a third great seer, with whom God
will speak in the witness tent; he is the one who was seen on
the mount by Moses and Elijah. Commenting on Nu. 12.7 Origen
contends that Moses saw the glory of the Lord when he was
present with Elijah at the transfiguration (*Hom. in. Nu.*
VII.2; GCS 7, 40).

full of grace and truth" (רב חֶסֶד וֶאֱמֶת RSV, "abounding in
steadfast love and faithfulness")[86] whom Moses saw upon the
mount. And concerning this grace and truth, as a witness to
him, Moses wrote, although he was only able to communicate
the law (Jn. 5.46-47). Thus, although the expression "grace
and truth" is intended by John to refer to the covenantal
love, "the abundance of steadfast love and fidelity," of which
the oracle speaks,[87] the relation of his phrase to the Old
Testament (covenant) is not fully expressed by the translation
"enduring love" (NAB).[88] For John does not intend the
expression to convey the covenantal law bestowed on upon
Israel, but rather its fulfillment--new covenant indeed, but
also "true covenant." Although "grace" (χάρις) occurs only in
the prologue of John and may well be understood as "covenant"
or "covenantal love," "truth" (ἀλήθεια) is a favored Johannine
theme and a key to one of the modes in which he speaks of
Jesus. For John, Jesus fulfills the Old Testament and the old
covenant as reality does shadow: "I am the true vine" (15.1);
"I am the good shepherd" (10.11); "My flesh is true bread and
my blood true drink" (6.55); "God is spirit, and those who
worship him must worship in spirit and in truth" (4.24). Thus
the "grace and truth" in Jesus is indeed the covenant which
endures, but because it is the truth, the reality of which the
law as grace is only the temporary reflection. When Moses
wrote it, not only did he write "full of grace and truth" of
him, but also of him he wrote the accounts of the manna (6),
the brazen serpent (3) and the well of Jacob (4), as well as
the prescriptions for sacrificing the pasch (19). Not only
are the writings of Moses prophetic, but also the events of

---

[86]See above, pp. 183-184 and notes 70-72.

[87]See Dahl, "The Johannine Church," 132-133. See also
Brown's treatment of the relation between χάρις καὶ ἀλήθεια
and חסד וֶאֱמֶת (I,14). Note particularly that he cites Ex. 34.6,
although he fails to note that πλήρης is a translation of
רב (I,14).

[88]Contra Brown, who uses this translation, although he
refers the reader to his longer discussion of ἀλήθεια in
App. I,2 (I, 499-501).

194

which he writes are the shadow of things to come.

The relationship which John expresses as law/grace and truth, Paul expresses as letter/spirit,[89] or covenant written with ink upon tablets of stone/covenant written with the spirit upon fleshly hearts.[90] Because Paul's sole concern in the discussion of Ex. 34.29 ff. is the superiority of the new covenant to the old, the theological function of the vision of Moses has been eclipsed by the newer concern and his treatment of the law is more pointed than John's, directed at showing how the prescriptive character of the letter is swallowed up in the spirit so that only its predictive character remains.[91] Like John he places in parallel positions Moses' prophecy and the apostolic witness, and the difference between the two makes the second the interpreter of the first.

In 2 Co. 3.12-18, Paul grounds his argument for the superiority of the new with an explication of how the old is to be read. He has already remarked that the glory Moses received on his ministration of the letter was so great that the Israelites were not able to look upon it and he was forced to veil his face. Now he goes to discuss the results of that veiling: they were not able to perceive the end of that which was passing away--i.e. the letter, or the covenant of death written with letters.[92] But it is written of Moses

---

[89]2 Co. 3.6-7.

[90]2 Co. 3.3. The ancients apparently found the rather miraculous aspects of the first process appropriate to the lawgiving: the Rabbis also are convinced that the stone tablets were written with pen and ink (and rolled up like a scroll, in fact); see *Ex. R.* 47.6 and Strack-Billerbeck III, 513-516.

[91]Cf. Jean Héring, *The Second Epistle of Saint Paul to the Corinthians* (London: The Epworth Press, 1967), 23. However, Paul's use of the dichotomy "letter" and "spirit" should not be applied to our dichotomy literal/allegorical (although Paul does consciously employ allegorical interpretation) but to prescriptive versus predictive function of the law: "literal"="to be done"; "spiritual"="to be believed."

[92]On the passing character of the teaching of Moses, the mediator of flesh and blood, see Callan, 183, and Introduction, n. 4, above, 6-7.

"Whenever he turns to the Lord" entering the tent of witness,
"he removes the veil" (Ex. 34.35; 2 Co. 3.16) so that with
face unveiled he gazes upon the glory of the Lord (Ex. 33.18
ff), that is the image (Nu. 12.8), Christ (cf. 2 Co. 4.4),
and he is transformed from the glory he sees into a reflection
of that glory (2 Co. 3.18). Thus also now, when Moses turns
to the Lord, that is when he is read by Jews (as by Christians)
as referring to Christ (3.15), the Lord and life-giving spirit
("the Lord" is "the spirit" 3.17), "he removes the veil," i.e.,
"it is unveiled that by Christ, the letter of the law is
being destroyed (3.14)...because where is the spirit of the
Lord, there is freedom (from the letter)" (3.17).

This is of course how Christians read the law--from the
same side of the veil as Moses. "For we all with unveiled
faces looking through the mirror like Moses who saw not with
a reflective mirror (ἔσοπτρον) but through a straight lens,
onto the true image,[93] are transformed from glory (as from
the Lord, the spirit) to glory." The principle which Paul
elsewhere expresses "Christ is the end of the law," he explains
here.[94] Christ is the law's end because it is written about
him, as John also believes. Christ is also the end of the law
because he brings it to its end. The difference between the
exegetical principle of Paul and that of John is in the way
in which they are applied. For John, the signs of Moses and
of the law are prefigurative shadows, of which the signs of
Jesus are the truth. For Paul, the application of the
principle means that the Word of God in the law is no longer
to be done, but rather to be believed. This does not mean
that it is only or predominantly the prescriptive portion of
the law which can and must apply to and come to end in Christ;
the concern of the spirit is not simply justification by faith
rather than by works; rather the ministry of the spirit is a
ministry of reconciliation. Moses must be made to witness

---

[93]See above, Introduction, 8, n. 7.

[94]Cf. Origen on Nu. 12.8 (*Hom. In Nu.* VII.2, GCS 7). He
interprets "in a riddle" (in aenigmate) in conjunction with
1 Co. 10.1 ff. to apply to the law, the events and the sacraments of the old covenant, "in sight, appearance, or face"
(in specie), to apply to our vision and our sacraments.

to Christ in every part of the law but especially in the whole
law as it distinguishes Jew from Gentile; practice, then,
doing the Word (Ro. 10.4-9), and prescription, like circum-
cision (Ro. 4.10-12), but also the guarantees of Israel's
salvific predominance, like the story of Sarah and Hagar
(Ga. 4.21-31).

For John, Moses' vision makes him the witness of the grace
and truth (i.e., of the true covenant); for Paul, the witness
of the new ministry of reconciliation. So also for Hebrews
Moses becomes a witness to a new covenant, "to the things that
would be spoken" (3.5) in God's son, to the "salvation which
had its beginning through being spoken by the Lord" (2.3). As
for John and Paul, this salvation replaces "the word spoken
through angels" (2.2), the law "given through angels, given by
the hand of a mediator" (Ga. 3.19), by fulfilling it.

As for John the law requires fulfillment by the truth
(not because it is false but because it lacks the fullness of
truth that comes to pass in the only son), and for
Paul the death-dealing letter must be swallowed up in the
lifegiving spirit, so also for Hebrews "the law, since it has
only the shadow of the good things to come, not the image
itself of the realities, never is able to perfect those who
approach it with the sacrifices they continually offer"
(10.1).

The problem of interpretation of the law thus stands on
its own ground more clearly in Hebrews than in the other two;
the question about the law is a soteriological question. The
question "what shall I do to be saved?" is no longer for
these authors to be answered "keep the commandments," but the
renunciation of that answer requires a transformation of the
question; it becomes "how are we saved in Christ?" In other
words, it becomes a question of soteriological Christology.
As the revelatory function of the law is shifted to Christ
in Christianity so also is its soteriological function.

The new Christian function of the vision of Moses makes
Moses' vision a testimony to the new salvation and an
exegetical principle for the law. The significant difference
of Hebrews' exegetical principle again appears in its application. For Hebrews, the fulfillment in Christ operates in

a combination of the two ways of Paul and of John: Christ
fulfills the law as the reality does the shadow, and at his
fulfillment of the law, it passes away. This is true for
Hebrews because of an element of this letter's Christology
which neither Paul nor John makes as explicit. For Hebrews
Christ fulfills the law by doing it.

In Hebrews also this principle is related to the vision
of Moses and the accompanying oracle.[95] John reads the vision
of Moses and the oracular name proclaimed before him on the
mount: "The Lord, the Lord, a God merciful and forgiving,
abounding in *steadfast love* and *faithfulness*" (Ex. 34.6). He
discovers that when God's glory passed by, Moses saw "the
Lord (Jesus)...full of grace and truth," whose being is "the
way, the truth and the life," in whom is our rebirth of God.
Hebrews too fastens upon Moses' witness to that fullness of
which we have all received, "that abundance of steadfast love
and faithfulness." Moses wrote the law, giving commandment
and penalty in the covenant which God bestowed upon Israel:

> Keeping steadfast love for thousands, forgiving ini-
> quity and transgression and sin, but who will by no
> means clear the guilty, visiting the iniquity of the
> fathers upon the children and the children's children,
> to the third and fourth generation.[96]

In the fulfillment of the precepts of that law the contradiction between forgiveness and retribution is resolved, or
perhaps overturned. Full forgiveness, the setting aside of
the sins of all who are guilty, now is offered to all in a
greater and more perfect salvation spoken by the Lord who

> was made like his brethren in every respect so that
> he might become a *merciful* and *faithful* high priest
> in the service of God to make expiation for the
> sins of the people.[97]

Thus grace and truth, a greater and more perfect salvation

---

[95]Ex. 34.6-7. Cf. Augustine, *Tract. in Ioh.* III.16. He
applies to John 1.17 the description of Moses' ministry
(ministerium; cf. He. 3.5, θεράπων...εἰς μαρτύριον) as that of
the "servant faithful in the house" He. 3.5).

[96]Ex. 34.7.

[97]He. 2.17.

are wrought on our behalf by Christ, that *merciful* and *faith-ful* high priest (ἐλεήμων...καὶ πιστός).

The witness of Moses to its fulfillment, to those things which would be spoken by the Lord, is found in his description of what the Lord does, of his ministry. For Hebrews more than for John or Paul, this witness consists in Moses' description through the law and its prescriptions of what he saw on the Mount. For the sake of this description, Moses was granted to be trusted and required to be faithful in all the house; for the sake of this description, he was led on high and told: "See." Thus when Hebrews comes to explain the relation between the two covenants, that explanation can be made through the testimonies that Moses gave in the first: the laws that he made, the rites that he did "according to the type that was shown to him on the mount" (He. 8.5).

Conclusion.

Investigation of the glory of Christ and of Moses has shown us that Moses' vision of God in Christ answers the two questions from which this chapter began; it reveals the like-ness between Christ and Moses and its source; it also tells us how Moses became a Christian. But the single answer it gives to both these questions also sheds light on many other significant and sometimes troublesome aspects of both the comparison and the letter. Not least important of these is the view it gives of the author's Christology and use of Christological testimonies. In this comparison the author articulates a theological decision about Christ, the decision that in Christ we have seen God unseeable. This decision (which, we repeat, is prior to the reading of the text) transcends the wording of any of the Christological testi-monies, either the oracle of the royal priest in 3 or the citations of 1, and determines in what sense the words "God" and "son" are applied to Jesus.

In addition this resolution of the comparison according to glory gives a coherent account of the multiple meanings of "house" and the relation of the house to Christ. In so doing it raises some questions about the author's understanding of the dispensation given or spoken through Moses, about the relation between Christ and the law. Chapter five will turn to these questions, examining the soteriological function of Moses' vision in the central chapters of the letter, asking how it illumines Hebrews' understanding of the law and of its fulfillment in Christ.

CHAPTER FIVE

MOSES LIKENED TO THE SON OF GOD ACCORDING TO HIS MINISTRY:
THE SOTERIOLOGICAL FUNCTION OF THE LAW

> ...let us first take up the question of what the law
> is and what the dispensation of the law is. For thus
> shall we know from the figure what the truth is and
> what is the freedom of the truth.

> The law given through Moses is a collection of varied
> and necessary teachings, a common feast of all good
> things of life, a mystic copy of the heavenly city,
> lamps and lampstands, fire and lights, the ornaments
> of the torch-light procession above. The law given
> through Moses is the symbolic and figurative epitome
> of the coming grace, declaring with like things the
> perfection of the coming truth: with sacrifices, the
> rite; with blood, the blood; with a lamb, the Lamb;
> with a dove, the dove from the heavens; with altars,
> the high priest; with the temple, the lodging of
> divinity below; with the fire upon the altar, the
> entirety of light from above the world.
> > *On the Pasch*[1]

In the first chapter of this study, we were faced with
the question of how Moses became a Christian martyr, not only
conformed to Christ in his suffering, but actually a witness
who shoulders his burden knowingly in the expectation of its
recompense. The examination of 3.1-6 has given us an answer
to that question: chapter two provided a view of the
determinative role of the Christological oracles in 3.1-6;
chapter three placed Hebrews' use of Nu. 12.7 in a tradition
which views Moses as a visionary who entered God's house, the
heavens, and carried off the law of fire; chapter four
uncovered in the point of the comparison according to glory
the conclusion that Moses' vision of God was a vision of
Christ in glory, of the dead and risen Lord. His seeing of
of the seeable of God unseen explains Hebrews' conviction that

---

[1]PG 59.738. This text has been credited to Chrysostom
and is included by Migne under *Spuria*. Apparently it was
first attributed to Hippolytus of Rome and, according to
Pierre Nautin, derives from his work. See Introduction,
Homélies Pascales I, SC 27 (Paris: Editions du Cerf, 1950),
7-9.

Moses wore the glory and bore the opprobrium of Christ. But
Hebrews' concern with the vision of Moses does not end with
that conviction; more significant still for the letter is the
ministry of Moses which also results from what he saw. By
examining Hebrews' discussion of Moses' ministry, we can
further specify the content and the function of his vision.

The vision of Moses is a vision of the law or rather of
the law's source. When Israel refused to hear any longer the
voice that spoke the ten words, or to continue to look on
the great fire, Moses ascended the mountain alone, to look on
God and to bring back the fiery law: he became "the servant
appointed in all God's house to the witnessing of what would
be said." But for the Christian author, the law becomes
problematic. What does it mean now in the light of Christ?
What was its source and function if in Christ it has come to
an end?

For Paul, John, and Hebrews, the law remains the record
of Moses' vision of God, written in figures (1 Co. 13.13),
allegory (Ga. 4.21-31) and type (1 Co. 10.1-10), for those
who could not bear the too great light that burned on Sinai
and shone on Moses' face.[2] For each of these authors, Christ
is the end of the law, in that all was written about him and
therefore all passes away into the fulfillment, into Christ.
But the meaning of the law differs in Paul and in Hebrews,
particularly with regard to its soteriological function and
to the way it comes to its end in Christ. For Paul, the
passing away of the law's requirement implies an opposition
between the two senses of the law: the letter (the prescription) kills; the commandment that is in itself good,
holy and perfect is fatal to me who am weak. But the spirit
(the risen spirit of the Lord discovering the meaning of the
law) gives life; I come to life, when it declares to me that
sin is dead. The two senses are opposed in Paul's experience;
the zeal out of which he persecuted the Church is the zeal for
doing the law, and only "when he turns to the Lord is the
veil removed" so that he knows that the word of the law is

_____

[2]2 Co. 3.3-7, cf. John 12.36-43, where the Jews are
accused of rejecting the light of God's glory according to the
prophecy of Isaiah (Is. 6.1-11).

near, not to be done but to be believed and confessed.

For the letter to the Hebrews, however, the prescriptive
and the predictive functions of the law are joined rather than
opposed. "The law has but a shadow of the good things to come,
and not the true image of these realities." Yet the coming
true of the image does not reverse the shadows of the law;
rather, it fills them out, fulfills them:

8.4 ...there are priests who offer gifts according
to the law.

.5 They serve a copy and a shadow of the heavenly
sanctuary; for when Moses was about to erect a
tent, he was instructed by God, saying: "See
that you make everything according to the
pattern that was shown you on the mountain."

.6 But as it is, Christ has obtained a ministry
which is as much more excellent than the old
as the covenant he mediates is better, since
it is enacted on better promises.

8.4 ...ὄντων τῶν προσφερόντων κατὰ νόμον τὰ δῶρα·

.5 οἵτινες ὑποδείγματι καὶ σκιᾷ λατρεύουσιν τῶν
ἐπουρανίων, καθὼς κεχρημάτισται Μωϋσῆς μέλλων
ἐπιτελεῖν τὴν σκηνήν· ὅρα γάρ φησιν, ποιήσεις
πάντα κατὰ τὸν τύπον τὸν δειχθέντα σοι ἐν τῷ
ὄρει.

.6 νῦν δὲ διαφορωτέρας τέτυχεν λειτουργίας ὅσῳ
καὶ κρείττονός ἐστιν διαθήκης μεσίτης, ἥτις
ἐπὶ κρείττοσιν ἐπαγγελίας νενομοθέτηται.

Hebrews, like Paul and John, explains the function of the
law by its derivation from Moses' vision; but, for this
author, Moses' "testimony to the things that would be said"
is brought to its end by being completed in Christ, fulfilled
by him in prescription as well as in prediction. This
exegetical principle is expressed by Hebrews through the
citation of Ex. 25.40.

Hebrews' understanding of the function of the law is
best approached through an examination of the application of
this text and of the principle. The function of the verse in
Hebrews has already been stated in a perfunctory fashion:
Ex. 25.40 attests the "shadowy" character of the Jewish
liturgy. However, the function of the verse as a proof-text
is complex. Hebrews' use of the Old Testament is far from
mechanical at any point. In case after case it proves to be
thoroughly integrated with a coherent exegetical tradition,

a major theological picture, or both. In this case, the
proof-text chosen is neither the only nor the most obvious
proof of the principle. It is rather the product of both
selection and revision. Further, its use raises wider
questions about the framework of Hebrews. It appears to explain the Jewish liturgy as the derivative result of a vision
of Moses. Is this vision directly connected with the traditions about Moses as visionary which have illumined other
passages about Moses in the letter? Were there a series of
visions? Does the author distinguish between the vision of
God's glory and the vision of the models of the tabernacle?
Of what objects did Moses see the *typos*, and what was the
typos that Moses saw? What does the vision of Moses imply
about the soteriological character of the law?

These larger questions can best be approached through a
series of questions more closely directed to the text: 1) Why
was Ex. 25.40 chosen and revised? 2) What was the antitype
which Moses made as a result of his vision? 3) What then was
the *typos* that Moses saw? These questions provide a useful
organizing principle for the discussion of the chapter
because they can be answered by examining in order 8.5, the
citation of Ex. 25.40; 9.1-16, the interpretation of the
tabernacle and cult; and 9.17-28, the interpretation of the
inauguration of the tabernacle.

This chapter will make three major assertions about Ex.
25.40, the function of Moses, and the interpretation of the
law in the Letter to the Hebrews:

1) The interpretive principle is Christ, in both theory
and practice. Not only does Hebrews subscribe to the Pauline
principle that "Christ is the end of the law," but it is also
clear that the biblical texts and the contemporary interpretations have been radically revised by the authors' understanding of the soteriological role of Christ.

2) The soteriological role of Moses is not only a
predictive role but also a real, though limited, dispensational one. In this regard Hebrews' understanding of the soteriological function of the law differs from that of Paul.
Whereas Paul regarded the glory of Moses as attendant upon
the "dispensation of death," for the Letter to the Hebrews

the law is not fatal, making sin the more irrevocably sinful,
but imperfect, unable to bring to perfection.

3) This high view of the vision of Moses and of the law
and its institutions does not depend upon the text of Ex.
25.40 or upon the tradition attached to that text, but upon
the author's conviction that Moses did see the seeable of the
Unseen, and thus ultimately upon the Christology of the
letter.

These assertions arise from and are borne out by the
examination of the function of Ex. 25.40 in the text of
Exodus, in the tradition of interpretation, and in the letter
to the Hebrews. The history of the Exodus text and its
interpretation is long and complex; only those aspects of it
to which Hebrews directs attention or raises questions can be
examined here.

The selection and revision of the oracle.

Why did Hebrews choose and revise Ex. 25.40 as a proof-
text for the exegetical principle employed in 8-9? If the
text of the LXX is being used, then the author has added
"all" (πάντα) and changed the perfect participle of δείκνύω
to an aorist. While it is possible to explain the whole as
another text or a variant reading, and to explain the second
change as a result of syntactical preference,[3] neither
solution is really satisfactory. Both the selection and the
revision of the text are best explained as highly deliberate,
as exegetical decisions probably made by the author of Hebrews
and certainly based upon the context of the verse in Exodus
and on the traditional interpretation of Exodus 25-31.

Exodus 25-31 recounts God's dictation to Moses of the
specifications for the furnishings of the tabernacle (25);
the tabernacle itself (26); the altar, court and lamp (27);
the vesture of the priests (28); the ordination of Aaron and
his sons (29); the altar of incense, the poll tax, the
anointing chrism and the incense itself (30); the call of
Bezalel, the appointment of workers, and the sabbath law (31).
Within these chapters there are four verses which suggest

---

[3] Cf. Williamson, *Philo and Hebrews*, 558.

that these instructions for Moses also included illustrations.
Upon Moses' ascent God said to him:

> And you shall make for me *according to all* whatever
> I show you on the mountain, the *paradigm* of the
> tent and the *paradigm* of its vessels; thus shall
> you make.
>
> καὶ ποιήσεις μοι κατὰ πάντα ὅσα σοι δεικνύω ἐν τῷ
> ὄρει, τὸ παράδειγμα τῆς σκηνῆς καὶ τὸ παράδειγμα
> τῶν πάντων τῶν σκευῶν αὐτῆς· οὕτως ποιήσεις.
>
> (Ex. 25.9 LXX)

There follow the specifications for the ark, the cherubim, the
table and the candlestick. The section on the candlestick
concludes:

> All these vessels shall be a talent of pure gold.
>
> πάντα τὰ σκεύη ταῦτα τάλαντον χρυσίου καθαροῦ.
>
> See, you shall make *according to the type* that has
> already been shown to you on the mount.
>
> ὅρα ποιήσεις κατὰ τὸν τύπον τὸν δεδειγμένον σοι ἐν
> τῷ ὄρει.
>
> (Ex. 25.39, 40)

Next the tabernacle and its covering and frame are described
and their description concludes with the command:

> And you shall erect the tabernacle *according to the
> appearance* that has been shown to you on the mount.
>
> καὶ ἀναστήσεις τὴν σκηνὴν κατὰ τὸ εἶδος τὸ
> δεδειγμένον σοι ἐν τῷ ὄρει.
>
> (Ex. 26.30)

There follows the description of the veil which "shall divide
between the holy and the holy of holies" (26.33) and of the
altar of sacrifice (27.1-8). The latter concludes with the
command:

> *According to what-was-shown-as-a-paradigm* to you on
> the mount thus shall you make it.
>
> ...κατὰ τὸ παραδειχθέν σοι ἐν τῷ ὄρει οὕτως ποιήσεις
> αὐτό.
>
> (Ex. 27.8)

Another reference to the idea that Moses was given a model for
his work is found in Nu. 8.4:

> *According to the appearance* which the Lord showed to
> Moses, thus he made the candlestick.

κατὰ τὸ εἶδος ὃ ἔδειξεν κύριος τῷ Μωϋσῇ οὕτως ἐποίησεν
τὴν λυχνίαν.

At the first reading, Ex. 25.19 would appear to be the
most suitable proof-text for the point being made in He. 8.5.
Why, then, did the author instead choose to use Ex. 25.40
and revise it? There are two significant differences between
the two verses, either of which might have provided the author
with a reason for choosing a text that had to be revised.

The first is the extra emphasis which is given or can be
given to the visionary aspect of this oracle by the form in
which it is put: ὅρα ποιήσεις the text reads, and Hebrews
emphasizes the ὅρα by the placing of the (very common)
introductory formula: ὅρα γάρ φησιν ποιήσεις--"look," it
says, "make...." Both rabbinic sources and Philo understand
the "look" or "see" as redundant, and therefore of special
significance. Philo's interpretation of it is the more
striking:

> He testifies to these things by saying "see," (there-
> by) admonishing (us) to keep the vision of the soul
> sleepless and ever wakeful in order to see incorporeal
> forms, since if it were (merely a question of) seeing
> the sense-perceptible with the eye of the body, it is
> clear that no (divine) command would be needed for
> this.[4]

A second reason for the choice of 25.40 is probably the
use of the word *typos*. In the other three verses from Exodus
and in Nu. 8.4 the LXX uses other words: in 25.9 παράδειγμα;
in 27.8 τὸ παραδειχθέν (both of which will be represented in
translation by "paradigm") and in Ex. 26.30 and Nu. 8.4 εἶδος
("appearance"). Although Philo is able to use both of these
terms and invest them with positive meaning,[5] both appear
to have pejorative meanings for Hebrews. The first is used
as a derogatory term in He. 6.6 ("they crucify the son of God
on their own account and hold him up to contempt"--

---

[4]*Qu. in Ex.* 82 on 25.40 (Loeb Supp. II, 132). For an
example of rabbinic comments of this sort, see *Ex. R.* 40.2
cited below, 211.

[5]Williamson, 558, contends that τύπος and παράδειγμα are
synonymous; however, this is not true even for Philo (see
discussion below, 219-220).

παραδειγματίζοντες). Further it is and looks nearly synonymous with the slightly pejorative "copy" (ὑπόδειγμα). The
second word, "appearance" (εἶδος), was at this time and in the
milieu of Hebrews used chiefly to mean "mere or hollow appearance" (2 Co. 5.7). The most common meaning of *typos*, however,
would not seem to be much better. The image which the word
usually (though not always) evokes is that of the impression
made by a seal; in other words it usually means print or
copy also. However, Hebrews has revised its meaning by
pairing it with *antitypos*, so that *typos* is understood as
analogous to the pattern in the seal, *antitypos* to the
impression. While the use of *typos* may be one of the major
reasons for the selection of the verse, it only emphasizes the
complex character of the choice.

The revision of the oracle by the addition of "all"
(πάντα) is clearly an attempt to put the other three verses
at the service of the interpreter, especially Ex. 25.9, the
opening instructions which command Moses to make "all"
according to the paradigm. Indeed, one suspects that the
revision aims at the inclusion of the whole context, 25-31,
for the author of Hebrews wishes to present not merely the
tent but actually the whole worship which took place in it
as a "copy and a shadow of the things to come" (He. 10.1).
Not only is Jesus minister of the true tent (8.2), of which
the tabernacle is an earthly copy (8.5, 9.1), but also his
ministry itself surpasses theirs (8.6).

Again, the reason for the revision is partially clear,
but its implications are manifold. It represents not a
single exegetical decision, but a choice between exegetical
traditions. The alternative interpretations proposed by the
tradition help to clarify some of the implications of both
the selection and the revision of the text.

The tradition of interpretation of Exodus 25-31 can be
divided along two lines. One point at which the division
begins to be apparent is at the interpretation of Ex. 25.40:
on the question of what Moses saw, interpreters divide into
those who limit or specify the items of which Moses saw an
actual image and those who extend Moses' vision.

R. Jose ben Judah is credited with the opinion that fiery

models of the ark, the table and the candlestick came down
from heaven and that Moses copied them. He explicitly rejects
the application of the same notion to the tabernacle on the
grounds that Ex. 26.30 does not use the word תבנית ("form" or
"model") as do 25.8 and 40, but instead uses the word משפטו
("fashion," Soncino; εἶδος LXX).[6] This verbal scrupulosity
accompanies a particular understanding of the revelation to
Moses: 1) Moses did not go up to heaven, but rather the
models came down; 2) the objects of the vision were heavenly
objects made of fire is as all the heavenly region; 3) these
three objects and only these three objects of the tabernacle
and temple furnishings are replicas of the heavenly furnishings.

The text is also cited in an opposing stream of the
rabbinic tradition:

> 'See and make' (He said to Him: 'How can I make one
> like this?' He replied:) '"*After their pattern*":
> as thou seest above, so make below.'[7]

This elliptical formulation also betrays the traces of a
more developed theory according to which Moses in ascending
the mount ascended on high, that is, to heaven, and that what
he saw there was the model for what he made below. This
"higher" picture extends rather than limits the application
of the verse.

An amplified version of the dictum appears among the
comments upon Nu. 7.1, "on the day that Moses finished setting
up the tabernacle...":

> 'If,' said the Holy One, Blessed be He, to Moses,
> 'you will make below the same as that which is above,
> I shall leave my counselors on high and, coming down
> below, will accommodate my *Shekinah* to the confined
> space in their midst below.'[8]

All the more clearly, the formula is a summary of the
commands given to Moses in Ex. 25-31 as they are understood
within the context of a much larger development arising from

---

[6]*B. Men.* 29a (Soncino, 187-188).

[7]*S. of S. R.* III, 11.2 (Soncino, 174).

[8]*Nu. R.* 12.8 (Soncino, 474).

the (originally naive) belief that God's heavenly dwelling is also a temple. Its most striking representations in the biblical text are the prophetic visions of God enthroned: Is. 6.1-8, Am. 9.1-2, 1 Ki. 22.19. In these earliest versions God's heavenly dwelling is pictured in terms of, and perhaps interpenetrates, the earthly temple. By the time it appears in the texts of the Hellenistic era, the conviction that the earthly temple corresponds to the heavenly dwelling place is well established.

> *The Place for Thee To Dwell In.* Corresponding to Thy dwellingplace. This is one of the statements to the effect that the throne below corresponds to and is the counterpart of the throne in heaven. And so it also says: "The Lord is in His holy temple, the Lord, His throne is in heaven." (Ps. 11.4). And it also says: "I have surely built Thee a house of habitation, a place for Thee to dwell in forever" (1 Kings 8.13).[9]

Within this development Ex. 25.40 and the principle to which it is attached in *Song of Songs Rabbah* are the means of filling out the description of the correspondence between the heavenly and earthly dwelling of God, particularly (but not necessarily) through Exodus 25-31. In both *Numbers Rabbah* and *Song of Songs Rabbah* the principle is illustrated with the example of the "boards of acacia wood standing up" (Ex. 26.15) which are like the "seraphim standing up" (Is. 6.2), and the reminiscence of R. Hiyya that the golden clasps of the tabernacle looked like the stars of the sky.[10] Both of the illustrations must have originated as independent comments, as did the comment of R. Levi given by R. Joshua of Siknin, which is recorded with them:

> When the Holy One, blessed be He, commanded Moses, 'Make me a Tabernacle,' he should have just put up four poles and spread out the Tabernacle over them.' We are therefore forced to infer that the Holy One, Blessed be He, showed Moses on high, red fire, green fire, black fire and white fire, and said to him: *Make it according to the fashion thereof, which hath been shown thee in the mount* (Ex. XXVI.30).[11]

---

[9]*Mekilta Shirata* 10 (Lauterbach II, 78).

[10]*Nu. R.* 12.8 (Soncino, 474); *S. of S. R.* III.11, 2.

[11]*Nu. R.* 12.8 (Soncino, 474).

A similar but more fully integrated collection of comments
appears in *Exodus Rabbah*.[12] There Ex. 25.2, "...that they
take for me an offering," introduces a much longer list of
correspondences between heavenly realities on the one hand and
what one finds upon earth--or actually within Israel--on the
other. The nucleus of the corresponding earthly realities
is clearly the details of tabernacle, temple and service. The
passage is intended to be a coherent interpretation, or perhaps illustration, of 25-31, showing that the prescriptions
which follow 25.2 were based upon the heavenly dwelling of
God and the service that is done in it. Thus the acacia
boards standing correspond to the attendant seraphim, the
cherubim on earth to the cherubim in heaven, the veil to the
firmament, but also the high-priest clothed in linen (for the
entry into the holy of holies) to the heavenly linen-clothed
attendant of Ez. 9.11; the high priest (on earth) is the
angel (messenger) of the Lord (Mal. 2.7) as the Lord has also
his angel in heaven. This particular passage does not
emphasize the vision of Moses as the medium for the correspondences but introduces the list by saying: "You will find
that everything God has created in heaven He has also created
on earth."[13] However another passage from *Exodus Rabbah* not
only extends the idea of heavenly illustration through the
whole list of commands but even insists that the "see" of
Ex. 31.2 be taken quite literally:

> Another explanation: It does not say "I have called
> by name Bezalel," but SEE, I HAVE CALLED. You find
> that when Moses ascended on high, God showed him all
> the vessels of the tabernacle and told him: 'Thus
> and thus shalt thou do. *And thou shalt make a
> menorah, a table; and thou shalt make an altar.*'
> --and so with all the work of the tabernacle.[14]

Likewise with the appointment of Bezalel God did not merely
announce the appointment to Moses but:

---

[12]*Ex. R.* 33.4.

[13]*Ex. R.* 33.4 (Soncino 416).

[14]*Ex. R.* 40.2 (Soncino 461).

> He brought him the book of Adam and showed him all
> the generations that would arise from Creation to
> Resurrection, each generation and its kings, its
> leaders, and its prophets, saying unto him: I have
> appointed all these for their destinies from that
> time [Creation], and Bezalel, too, I have appointed
> from that time.' This is why it says, 'SEE, I HAVE
> CALLED BY NAME BEZALEL.'[15]

In all these cases, comments, applications and framework
are likely to have arisen independently, as is shown by the
occurrence of multiple parallels, often in collections whose
function differs or which are applied to different texts. The
last collector may attach a particular story or saying to Ex.
31.2 when in fact it arose in a comment upon Ex. 26.30 or
Nu. 8.4, or create a consistent interpretation of Exodus 25-26
out of comments which originated from a variety of stories.
But the theological picture which begins from a correspondence
between the heavenly dwelling of God and the earth and/or
the tabernacle below is not the characteristic of the last
layer of the collections but is rather the presupposition
which raised the first questions or guided the first comments
on these texts.

The main features of the development of the theological
picture that lies behind the use of Ex. 25.40 in Hebrews are:

1) The decision to interpret Ex. 25.40 in an inclusive
fashion, extending its application to all, or rather, to any
of the commands of Ex. 25-31, or in fact to all the commands
about the cult, so that any of these can be understood as
illustrated by heavenly models.[16]

2) A "high" view of the vision of Moses, according to
which Moses ascended to heaven and there was shown the heavenly furnishings as the models for the tabernacle and its
furnishings.

3) The explanation of the correspondence between heavenly
and earthly realities as analogous rather than exact. The
"acacia boards standing up" represent the attendant seraphim,

---

[15]Ibid.

[16]On this see Spicq II, 236, where he also notes Wis.
9.8, Acts 7.44 and R. Jose ben Judah as respresentative of an
opposing view.

the "fashion" of the tabernacle is demonstrated to Moses by means of red, green, black and white fire.

With regard to this last point we must note another set of texts which use the image of a garment of God. The principle "As you have seen above, make below," is introduced by the following parable:

> R. Berekiah in the name of R. Bezalah likened the matter to a king who, possessing an exquisite robe worked in precious stones, said to a member of his house: 'Make me another one like it,' and the latter said to him: 'My Lord, the King! Am I able to make one like that?' Said the king to him: 'I with my glory and you with your dyes [will make a worthy robe].'[17]

In its context the point of the parable seems to be similar to the dictum of R. Joshua of Siknin or even the opposing view of R. Jose b. Judah: what is made of precious jewels or fire above, is represented in dyes or in earthly matter here below. The fullest sense of the parable is clearly that the true likeness between them is given by the glory of God inhabiting the patterned robe. It also seems to suggest that the work of the tabernacle is intended to convey something of Moses' vision of the glory of God, something of God in his attributes. This idea stands out more clearly in another parable of R. Joshua of Siknin:

> R. Joshua of Siknin said in the name of R. Levi: It can be compared to a prince whose tutor wanted to go in before the king to plead on behalf of his son, but was afraid of those who stood by lest one of them should attack him. What did the king do? He clothed him in his royal purple cloak, so that all who saw might be afraid of him. Similarly Aaron used to enter the holy of holies nearly hourly [on that day][18] and had it not been for the many merits which entered with him and helped him [in his petitions], he would have been unable to go in on account of the angels that were there. For this reason did God give unto him [garments] after the pattern of the holy garments, as it says, *And for Aaron's sons thou shalt make tunics*, etc. (Ex. XXVIII.40); just as it is written: *And He put on righteousness as a coat of mail and a helmet of salvation upon His head and he put on*

---

[17]*Nu. R.* 12.8 (Soncino, 474).

[18]The Day of Atonement.

garments of vengence for clothing and was clad with zeal as a cloak (Isa. LIX.17).[19]

These three features of the development reveal the outlines of a theological position in which the addition of "all" (πάντα) to Ex. 25.40 indicates not merely an accommodation of the text to Ex. 25.8 but actually an adaptation of the verse into an exegetical principle according to which all the features of the cult become clues to the revelation of heavenly realities. They also demonstrate two highly significant qualifications of the working of the exegetical principle. On the one hand, the text and its interpretation do not stand alone but rather function within a wider and to some extent independent body of tradition and theologies which they embody and extend. On the other hand, the use of the text does not automatically invoke a construct of interpretation complete in every detail; rather it provides for the interpreter an array of tools and a variety of opportunities for their application.

Philo.

Philo also uses Ex. 25.40 in the *Legum Allegoria* and comments upon it in the *Quaestiones in Exodum*. His use of the text shares the characteristics of the second set of rabbinic texts (the texts which extend rather than limit the application of Ex. 25.40), although it is of course older than either the sources or authorities cited above. Indeed these characteristics are the more pronounced in his work. Philo also explains the construction of the tabernacle and the institution of the cult as representations of realities revealed to Moses in his ascent and vision. He too understands the whole of Exodus 25-31 to have been oracles[20] illustrated on high for Moses. Like Hebrews he even adds the

---

[19]*Ex. R.* 38.8 (Soncino, 456-457).

[20]*Vita* II.67: "χρησμοῖς ἕκαστα τῶν εἰς τὰς λειτουργίας καὶ ἱερὰς ὑπερεσίας ἀναδιδασκόμενος." Williamson distinguishes Philo and Hebrews on this point on the grounds that Philo never uses χρηματίζω to refer to Ex. 25.40. This seems to me to miss the functional likeness which does exist between Philo and Hebrews.

word "all" (πάντα) to 25.40.[21] Further his emphasis in the
interpretation of 25-31 in the *De Vita Mosis* is on the cult
rather than on the building of the tabernacle. The vision of
Moses and the consequent institution of tabernacle and cult
are the testimony to his function as priest and mystic rather
than as legislator: he ascends the mountain to be initiated
into all the mysteries of the priesthood.[22]

Likewise the work of Philo presents fruitful ground for
the examination of the choice of vocabulary for the description of that which Moses saw. Philo uses all the words for
"model" that the LXX and Hebrews use, as well as words which
he has chosen or even created. He also seeks to explain and
specify the words that he uses: Philo cites 25.40 but
changes *typos* to *paradeigma*. Further, Philo demands a more
extended or perhaps figurative meaning for these words, or
rather he radically revises their use by what appears to be a
denial that Moses saw anything at all in the physical sense.[23]

This observation leads one to the most significant
features of Philo's work. His appropriation of the theological traditions connected with the verse provide what the
rabbinic commentaries do not provide: a fully worked out
theological theory within which the texts and the traditions
are applied in a highly consistent manner across the fabric
of a very considerable body of work. Although the theory and
text are applied piecemeal and in differing functions, four
substantial passages (in addition to a number of shorter
references) treat of the vision of Moses in such a way as to
make it possible to give a fairly complete construction of
the theory. The major passages are: *Leg. All.* III.95-103;
Vita II.66-151; *De Spec. Leg.* II.41 ff., *Qu. in Ex.* II passim,
but esp. 52 and 82.

Qu. in Ex. II.52 is perhaps the best introduction to this
theory; the comment begins where Philo seems to begin in the
construction of the theory:

---

[21]*Leg. All.* III.103.

[22]*Vita* II.67.

[23]*De Post. Caini* 15; *Leg. All.* III.103.

216

> 52.(Ex. XXV.8 [Heb. 9]) What is the meaning of the
> words: "Thou shalt make, according to all that I
> shall show thee on the mountain, the pattern of the
> tent and the vessels"?[24]

> That every sense-perceptible likeness has (as) its
> origin an intelligible pattern in nature (Scripture)
> has declared in many other passages as well as in
> the present one.

From this version of the Platonist tenet, Philo turns the
texts and traditions surrounding Moses' vision to the integration of his own Platonist theology with the biblical scheme
of creation and revelation, at the same time presenting Moses
as the model of the philosopher or in his own words, the
Master Theologian.[25]

The passages which expose this theory seem to regard
Moses' visions (at least those described between Ex. 19.3 and
Ex. 34.28) as a single vision. Whereas the text of Exodus
appears to speak of at least three separate occasions when
Moses ascended the mount (Ex. 19.3, 24.9, and 33.12), Philo
sees all three instances as a single event,[26] or, as is more
likely, gives every instance of Moses' speaking with God a
single continuous meaning. Amid his discussion of the
tabernacle and its furnishing Philo turns again to the
theological meaning of Moses' vision and interprets Exodus
25-31 with the aid of the group of theological texts about
Moses' vision which we encountered in chapters three and four
of this study. The tent, the worship, and even more the words
of Exodus 25-31 which describe them are for Philo the product
of Moses' vision of God, and so reveal its content. They tell
the result of Moses' search for the unseen things of God, as

---

[24]*Qu. in Ex.* II.52 (Loeb Supp. II, 99); the text is Ex.
25.8 LXX, Ex. 25.9 MT.

[25]*Qu. in Ex.* II.37, 74, 87, 88, 108, 117. See esp.
II.37 (Loeb Supp. II,78-80) in which the vision of Moses and
the elders (Ex. 24.9) is discussed. There Moses' exemplary
as theologian consists in making clear the unseeability of
God.

[26]Pseudo-Philo records the glorification of Moses' face
as a result of the first forty-day sojourn of Moses, and
connects it immediately with God's revelation of the pattern
of the tabernacle and his promise that his glory will dwell
among them (XI-XII).

Exodus 33-34 describes its character.[27]

According to his theory, Moses is "called and taken above" (Lev. 1.1, Ex. 19.4-24.9, traditional texts for inaugurating discussion of Moses' vision)[28] that "these forms of intelligible things" might be revealed to him "in order not to deprive the race of mortals of an incorruptible vision (Aucher: *facie*) and not to spread abroad and publish to the multitude these divine and holy essences."[29]

This call of Moses is distinct from that of Bezalel (who was entrusted with the actual construction of the tabernacle) in that Moses (who constructed the "archetypes"[30]) is the teacher (ὑφηγητής) of Bezalel, but God the teacher of Moses, as Ex. 25.40 testifies;[31] "Excellently moreover has it presented (as) the teacher of incorporeal and archetypal things not one who is begotten and created but the unbegotten and uncreated God."[32]

This singular privilege of having God alone as his teacher makes Moses the model of philosophers in his search for God; Philo reflects frequently on his petition:

> "Manifest thyself to me; let me see Thee that I may know Thee" (Ex. XXXIII.13 LXX), "For I would not that Thou shouldst be manifested to me by means of heaven or earth or water or air or any created thing at all, nor would I find the reflection of Thy being in aught else than Thee Who art God...."33

---

[27] Williamson distinguishes Hebrews and Philo here on the grounds that Philo sees the text as a warrant for explaining all sensible reality as the result of multiple intelligible patterns or models. While this is true (cf. esp. *Qu. in Ex.* II.52 actually on 25.9) we should also note the function of this text as a proof that God is the pattern of all sensible reality as himself the pattern of the ideas.

[28] See chapter three, above, 128-129.

[29] *Qu. in Ex.* II.52 (Loeb Supp. II, 100).

[30] *De Plant.*, 26.

[31] *Leg. All.* III.102.

[32] *Qu. in Ex.* II.52 (Loeb Supp. II, 99).

[33] *Leg. All.* III.101 (Loeb I, 369): cf. *De Spec. Leg.* I. 41-51; *De Post. Caini*, 13-16, 167-169; *De Mut. Nom.*, 8; *De Fuga*, 164.

In this search for the unseeable (ἀόρατον) of God, that which he is in his essence (κατὰ τὴν οὐσίαν)[34] he enters into the dark cloud (Ex. 20.21)[35] "which signifies unseen and unbodied essences."[36]

On the question of the outcome of this search, the consistency of Philo's interpretation seems to break down. The one point on which he seems to be fairly clear is that Moses saw nothing with the eyes of the body, but that the seeing in question is a contemplation or *theoria* (θεωρία) by the "unsleeping eyes of the soul"[37] whether of the paradigms, of the cult, or of God Himself.[38] However, the treatment of the them in *Legum Allegoria*[39] raises a question about the *theoria*. That passage seems to suggest that Moses was granted a perception of God that was direct and not through the world. Every other treatment of Moses' vision of God in Philo's work appears to deny exactly that possibility and to deny it explicitly.[40]

The references to Moses as theologian in *Quaestiones in Exodum* all occur in the later chapters of Exodus which discuss Moses' vision or its results. The passages we have just examined exemplify the two-fold function of Moses as Philo's Master Theologian: his search for "manifest" knowledge of the unseeable God; his writings which declare that which was revealed to him of the unseen. Philo's purpose and his Platonic cosmology make it impossible to classify his picture

---

[34]*De Spec. Leg.* I.41, 50; *De Post. Caini*, 15-16, 167-169; *De Mut. Nom.*, 7-9.

[35]*De Post. Caini*, 14, 15; *De Mut. Nom.*, 7; *Qu. in Ex.* II.52.

[36]*De Mut. Nom.*,7 (Loeb V, 145); cf. *De Post.*, 148. Ex. 20.21 also is concerned with the vision of God.

[37]Cf. *De Spec. Leg.* I.49. See also *Qu. in Ex.* II.52, 82, and 90 and *Vita* II.90.

[38]*De Spec. Leg.* I.49.

[39]III.95-103.

[40]See esp. *De Spec. Leg.* I.41 ff.

of Moses on the basis of whether or not he will admit to a
physical seeing of God. Rather, the Moses of Philo is one who
has obtained certain knowledge of the unseen God through
which other elect souls can likewise learn to contemplate his
powers.

The role as theologian which Philo bestows on Moses is
related to the vocabulary of paradigm-archetype-seal-image-
shadow-type which plays so prominent a part in these discussions. This vocabulary is complex and somewhat problematic,
for Philo finds part of it in the text of Exodus and Numbers,
but adds to and revises what he finds there according to his
own purpose. Depending on the text cited and the context in
which he wishes to place it, Philo may change the word he
finds in a text or redefine it to suit his philosophical
vocabulary. While a full examination of this process is too
large a task to be completed in this context, some of the
ground can be cleared by noting that Philo's use of the words
does not require him to make consistent applications of them
because he retains and even extends their figurative character.
For instance, "paradigm" means "original" for Philo, but
that which is a copy of one thing can become the original
of another. Therefore God is the paradigm, the Word, his
shadow (σκία), representation (ἀπεικόνισμα), and image (εἰκών),
but the Word, the paradigm of humanity made according to the
εἰκών of God (Gen. 1.27), the word.[41] A man in turn can be
the paradigm of a statue, for instance the Moses of Michel-
angelo, which is an image or copy of him (after our fiction,
of course).

While Philo is able to interpret the *paradeigma* of 25.8
in a way that is relatively consistent with the common usage
and also permits him the full play of his philosophical
vocabulary, the common meaning of the word *typos* which is
used in 25.40 does not suit his purpose as well. The word is
used of the impression produced by a seal; that image is
evocative and is readily adapted to Philo's categories, so
he uses it throughout his writings. For instance, in *De Spec.
Leg.* I.47 the powers of God (presumably not merely "the ideas

---

[41]*Leg. All.* III.95-96 (Loeb I.364-367).

of every sense-perceptible thing"[42] but even the "twofold
creative and ruling powers"[43]) are likened to seals and are
not to be perceived by human beings, whereas the "impress and
copy of their active working"(ἐκμαγεῖόν τι καὶ ἀπεικόνισμα τῆς
ἑαυτῶν ἐνεργείας)[44] is perceptible and is likened to the impression the seal produces. Likewise Moses "saw" the paradigms
of the tabernacle and carried away the *typos* in his head.[45]
Thus, if paradigm means primarily model, *typos* means primarily
copy. Therefore in *Qu. in Ex.* II.82 on 25.40, *typos* must be
applied to the intelligible pattern or paradigm, for that is
what Moses saw, as has already been established in *Qu. in Ex.*
II.52 on 25.8. It refers to the incorporeal heaven, which is
also a copy, but, as the pattern of the sense-perceptible
heaven, is not just the *typos* but also *archetypos*. Thus *typos*
as *archetypos* becomes a synonym for paradigm.

When Philo cites Ex. 25.40 in *Legum Allegoria*[46] he does
so as a summary of the commands of 25-31 and he therefore
accommodates it to his purpose: he uses for *typos* the
functional synonym "paradigm" (which he derives from 25.8)
which will indicate that Moses' vision was of an original, a
model. But the change is far more radical than it first
appears, for its true purpose is to claim that Moses saw not
a copy, an image, but the original: Moses who receives the
clear vision of God directly from himself uses for his
instructor God, as it says "according to the paradigm (God
is the paradigm[47]) which was shown to you on the mount shall
you make all." With regard to this vision it is said of
Moses that "he is made certain (appointed/faithful) in all
the house; mouth to mouth will he speak with him in vision
and not in figures."

This brief examination of Philo's theory about Ex. 25.40

---

[42]Cf. *Qu. in Ex.* II.52.

[43]*Vita* II.99, cf. *Qu. in Ex.* II.52.

[44]*De Spec. Leg.* I.47.

[45]*Vita* II.76.

[46]III.103.

[47]*Leg. All.* III.95-96; above, 219.

and the vision of Moses leads us to underline two features
of it in particular. At least in the context of this discussion, Philo considers all the visions of Moses to have been
one vision, or perhaps we should say one single *theoria*:
all or nearly all of the texts about Moses' vision of God are
applied to his vision of the tabernacle. On the basis of his
vision of God, the work of Moses (all that he makes and does
in regard to the tabernacle, but even more his verbal blueprint for tent and cult) is a *theologia*, a discourse about
God. Perhaps we should also note here that Philo's theory,
and his explication of the vision or rather of the tent and
cult, in no way rely on Ex. 25.40. It is almost fortuitous
to the theory that Philo was able to find in this verse (with
a little philosophical clarification) a proof-text written to
his own specifications.

Our observations about Philo also help to delineate some
features of the tradition of interpretation of this verse and
its cognates. The work of Philo and the rabbis when taken
together demonstrate two seemingly contradictory aspects of
25.40 in interpretation. On the one hand the text
brings with it a complex of theological ideas and associated
citations and interpretations to which the interpreter is
inevitably drawn. This is true whether the interpreter takes
a high or a low view of Moses' vision. Rabbi Jose ben Judah,
for instance, takes up a position on Moses' ascent when he
says that the models came down;[48] further, he too must work
out the question he is asking by the comparison of this text
with the other texts about the vision (actually with 25.8).
On the other hand, this somewhat fixed contribution of the
tradition is readily accommodated to the demands of the
individual interpreter's theology, even to the extent that
Philo's commentary on Exodus can become a cosmological primer.

Comparison between Philo and the rabbis also helps
distinguish those elements of this "high" version of Moses
which are relatively fixed from those which invite the special
efforts of the individual interpreter. The constant elements
of the high doctrine are: 1) the understanding of Moses'

---

[48] *B. Men.* 29a above, 255-256, n. 6.

ascent as an ascent to the heavens where God gave him a grand
tour of his dwelling; 2) the tendency to generalize or extend
and compound the invitation "See," so that the interpreter
conceives of 25-31 as a series of illustrated oracles; 3) the
construing of Ex. 25.40 (note especially the Hebrew תבניתם,
"*their* pattern") to mean that the tabernacle, the furnishing
and the rites are in some not quite literal way a revelation
of the heavenly furnishings, of the unseen world or simply of
the Unseen. At the extreme of this tradition are Philo and
some rabbis who tend to amalgamate Moses' ascents into a
single ascent and bring all the texts mentioning his vision
together, who regard the vision of God as the illustration of
the oracle (e.g. in the parables of the garment of God),[49]
or who discover metaphysical revelations in the tabernacle
and its furnishing.

These three elements provide the interpreter with a
framework for allegorizing the text. Precisely where they
are all present, the interpreter is free to select the
distinctive features of the narrative of Exodus 25-31 and
apply them or extend them even further. Thus they provide
the author or interpreter with a maximum of freedom in the
interpretation or application of individual texts. Within
the same framework, Philo is able both to cite the text of
Ex. 25.40 and apply it to the candlestick,[50] and to rewrite
it to give the fullest possible interpretation.[51]

Hebrews' application of the text and the theology.

Hebrews' addition of the word "all" (πάντα) then reveals
itself as an exegetical decision, one which extends the
interpretation of the oracle and thereby marks the author's
theological understanding of the vision of Moses in Exodus
25-31 as "high." Such an estimation of the author's theological position was of course suggested by the comparison
between the glory of Christ and the glory of Moses in

---

[49]*Nu. R.* 12.8; *Ex. R.* 38.8, above, 210, 211, 213-214.

[50]*Qu. in Ex.* II.82.

[51]*Leg. All.* III.103.

He. 3.1-6, which seems to entail a view that Moses ascended
into the heavenly dwelling of God. It is clear also that
Hebrews 9 reflects a conviction that the earthly tabernacle
is indeed a figurative representation of heavenly realities.

Philo's *Quaestiones in Exodum* provides a pattern for a
consistent interpretation of Exodus 25-31 in this high
tradition. It must be pointed out that the three major
characteristics of this tradition of interpretation really
amount to a rationale for the allegorization of these chapters and in practice for the whole body of Moses' teachings
about the tabernacle and the cult. Philo's version of these
tenets makes *Quaestiones* an allegory in what is very nearly
the fullest sense of that word: it is all about something
else. Moses ascended to not-place where he saw nothing with
the eyes of the body. Because of his "vision," the details
of the tabernacle can be interpreted as applying to other
things in a figurative rather than a representational way.
Philo's concern is not with whether the heavens look like the
tabernacle or the temple; rather the temple and its worship
communicate figuratively the realities of the noetic world.
Quaestiones is a sort of cosmological catechism, and while
the questions deal with the text in order they do not form an
exhaustive commentary upon it. Allegorical interpretation is
not the same as allegory in the writing of fabliaux; it does
not and cannot produce a one-to-one correspondence between
the details of the text and the realities they represent, so
that the code is continuous and consistent. It interprets
only those details which are clues: that which is unique,
disturbing, or strikingly suited to the theory of the interpreter. Thus there are two observations about the method of
interpretation in *Quaestiones* which illuminate the exegetical
enterprise in Hebrews: 1) the choice of that which is to be
interpreted is significant; 2) not only the prescriptions of
Exodus, but also their whole instantiation in temple and
tabernacle are available for interpretation.

One note should be added here in regard to the second
observation. It has often been remarked that Hebrews comments
upon the tabernacle and cult not as it is found in contemporary Jerusalem, or preserved in the halakah, but as it is

found in the books of Exodus, Leviticus and Numbers. This
however does not imply that the author knows nothing of the
halakah or of the contemporary cult. As we shall see, quite
the opposite is true. Hebrews (like Philo) awards pride of
place to the prescriptions of which Moses' witness consists.
Not every feature of the cult reveals the type in the same
way; quite certainly the cult that Hebrews describes never took
place in the temple of Jerusalem, but that is so because it is
only the antitypical features of that shadowy cult with which
our author is concerned.

Thus each author's picture of the cult will be highly
individual, and the great variety and complexity of this
exegetical tradition makes it clear that the details of the
picture can at no point be carried over wholesale from one
interpreter to another. However, the consistent elements of
the tradition help make clear the point at which the interpreter's individual theological interests come into play. This
point seems to be in the meaning and application of the word
that is used to indicate *what* Moses saw: in the case of
Hebrews, the word *typos*.

For Philo, the word *typos* is not completely satisfactory;
it normally means "copy" or "offprint," the image made by a
seal in wax. He uses it in this sense not only in other
contexts but also in his description of Moses' vision. Thus
its occurrence in Ex. 25.40 raises for Philo a problem which
he cannot resolve with complete consistency. As he comments
on Exodus verse by verse, in *Quaestiones in Exodum*, he prefers
to allow the word to stand in its place, but reinterprets it
as "archetype," which he understands as model, blueprint or
image on the seal.[52] In *Leg. All.* III.102, however, he
adjusts the text to suit what he believes is its meaning, by
borrowing the word "paradigm" from Ex. 25.8 LXX, or rather by
conflating Ex. 25.8 and 40 LXX.

The Letter to the Hebrews also understands the word *typos*
in Ex. 25.40 as "archetype," giving as synonym "image" (εἰκών)

---

[52]II.82. In fact, not every verse or every detail is
commented upon; nor can that have been Philo's intention (see
comments upon nature of allegory above); but the genre "commentary" makes some demands upon Philo all the same.

in 10.1. However, this use is consistent with the vocabulary
of Hebrews, or perhaps we should say, the vocabulary of Hebrews
is created in the service of this word. While Philo's vocabulary normally contrasts *typos* to *archetypos* ("pattern"),
Hebrews contrasts it to *antitypos* ("copy"). Thus according to
Hebrews Moses saw the *typos*, and the sanctuary that was
produced as a result of Moses' vision was the "antitype of the
true." This contrast becomes the vehicle of Hebrews' theory
of the meaning of "the holy things" of the old covenant. In
chapters 8-10, the author of Hebrews discusses the *antitypos*
and its fulfillment in Christ. Moses' vision of the *typos* is
invoked at the beginning of this passage to explain the
relation between the first covenant and its fulfillment; the
first covenant indicates the fulfillment by the antitypical
features of the institutions of Moses.

Thus we can discover the traits of the *typos* and the full
meaning of the reality Moses saw by examining the antitypical
features of the covenant of Moses as Hebrews describes it.
Hebrews 8-9 treats of three features of the old covenant in
particular: the tent itself, *teleiosis* according to the law
(9.9-16), and the inauguration of the covenant (9.16-22). We
shall be examining Hebrews' picture of each of these in order
to discover the character of the antitypes as this author
believes Moses to have constructed them.

Moses made a twofold tent, the antitype of the true.

Hebrews' interpretation of the tabernacle begins with a
list of the furnishings of the two tents which include not
only the furnishings named in 25-30 but also the two miraculous objects which Moses stores at the command of God: the
vase of manna and the staff of Aaron which had blossomed. All
of these things also could have provided the author of
Hebrews with material for interpretation. However, they are
dismissed as not within the range of this discussion. For
the commentator upon Hebrews, however, the inclusion of the
staff and vase offer the opportunity of clarifying one aspect
of the interpretation of Ex. 25.40. The biblical stories of
both these objects record that they were placed "before the
witness" at the command of God (Ex. 16.34, Nu. 17.26).

Nu. 17.26 concludes: "as the Lord *commanded* Moses, so they *did*." (καθὰ συνέταξεν κύριος τῷ Μωϋσῇ οὕτως ἐποίησαν). If these objects were included in the furnishing of the tent (or perhaps in its deposit of evidence) at the express command of an oracle from God to Moses, very probably God showed them to Moses also--as he showed him the clean from the unclean and the new moon.[53] The oracle cited by Hebrews 8.5 is then understood to apply to the things he did as well as to the things that he (had) made: "See, 'it says,' do (ποιήσεις)...." This is an insignificant point with regard to these particular furnishings of the tabernacle, but it applies also to the patterns for the cult which Moses described in Exodus 28-31 and also in the book of Leviticus. In other words not only what Moses commissions from Bezalel but also his own cultic actions and those of Aaron and his sons derive from oracles illustrated with the *typos* that Moses saw.

While similar observations on the interpretation of the letter might be made by examining the author's arrangement of the furniture of the tabernacle, this commentator will follow the example of Hebrews, passing over the details which the author also leaves aside with the observation that they have been treated elsewhere.[54]

The detail of the construction of the tabernacle which the author of Hebrews does wish to emphasize is then not any of these features, but rather the double tent, or rather, the two tents, and the double ministry for which they are built. This distinction seems to be the interpretandum for Hebrews, although the distinction is made in a peculiar way. The author includes in 9.2 and 3 the standard designations "holy place" and "holy of holies," but throughout the rest of the text they are distinguished as "first" and "second" tent. This picture of two tents rather than one divided tent seems to be derived from Ex. 26.1-6, which Hebrews thinks of as the holy of holies, and Ex. 26.7 ff, the description of the

---

[53]*B. Men.* 29a; for parallels see n. 68 below.

[54]For an extensive treatment of the way in which Hebrews envisages the furnishings of the tabernacle, see Spicq II, 249-252; also Buchanan (who includes a blueprint), 139-144; and Michel, 191-197.

coverings of the tabernacle, which Hebrews refers to the holy place. However, this application of the text by no means explains the peculiarities of Hebrews' interpretation. It rather raises another question: why is the holy of holies called the second tent, and the holy place the first? It would seem that both by honor and the order of the Exodus text, the holy of holies should claim the title of the first tent.

The application of the epithet seems to rest on a double circumstance. First, the author envisages the tent in use: the priest approaching the tabernacle from the court enters first the holy place, then the holy of holies. Second, the holy place is the first tent because a temporal sequence has intervened. Throughout Hebrews 8-10 there is a play of words and ideas on the adjectives "first" and "second." They are applied to two covenants (8.13, 9.1), two tents (9.2-10), two demands of God (10.9) which belong to two successive ages of salvation history. This dispensational identity of the items designated "first" and "second" is witnessed by the numerous scribes who were confused by it and were led to add "tent" (σκηνή) after "first" (πρώτη) in 9.1.[55] In the same chapter verse 18 could have led to a similar confusion: "For neither was the first inaugurated without blood." Out of context, the sentence could refer equally well to either the first tent or the first covenant, though the word "inaugurated" might be more commonly expected to be used of the tent. In context, the antecedent of "first" is the covenant. However, this passage makes clear the deliberation with which the ambiguity has been preserved by the author, for in the description of the inauguration of the covenant which follows, that rite proves to be also the inauguration of the tent.

The first tent, the holy place, becomes the visible sign of these other realities. At present accessible to all (the priests), it is comparable to (a parable of) the present age in which the way to the holy of holies is not yet open. It is likewise the symbol of the first covenant on whose laws the Aaronitic priesthood and the earthly sanctuary (τὸ ἅγιον

---

[55]Nestle cites 326 pm.

κοσμικόν 9.1) were founded. The characteristic by which this
first tent is comparable to the present age and to the first
covenant which has been revealed as old and coming to an end
(8.13) is that it does not continue to stand, to have existence
(9.8). In contrast to the true tent, it is made by hands, is
of the present creation. Together with the sacrifices that
are its service the first tent (covenant, demand) is taken
away in order that the second may stand (cf. 10.9). The
outer tent is the first tent because it signifies "this age"
which is destined to end, which lies under the eschatological
sentence in order that the age to come may be inaugurated.
Although the "earthly sanctuary" (τὸ ἅγιον κοσμικόν) belongs
to this first covenant and consequently passes away with it,
there seems to be no reference here to the destruction of the
Jerusalem temple. The end of the service belongs to the end
of this creation.[56]

A number of traditions link the tent as the whole tabernacle with the universe or the created world. Numerous
rabbinic comments on Nu. 8.4 liken the world as creation to a
tent. The most frequently repeated declares that on the day
that Moses finished setting up the tabernacle, he actually
completed two tents, for then the world also was made firm.[57]
A more elaborate comment on the same text pairs the products
of the seven days of creation with the features of the tabernacle and the worship.[58] Although the Jewish tradition has
provided the scheme of eschatology into which Hebrews makes
its comparison, these texts show no trace of it. No pejorative connotation, no mention of the passing character of the
creation attaches to its identification with the tabernacle
in the rabbinic tradition.[59]

---

[56]And therefore, no conjecture can be made about Hebrews'
date on the basis of the attitude to the temple worship.

[57]*Nu. R.* 12.11-12.

[58]*Nu. R.* 12.13.

[59]Sectarian traditions do associate the end or destruction of temple and cult with the end of the age. See II
Baruch 4.2-7; 32.2-4. N. B. Charles marks both passages as
interpolations (*Pseudepigrapha*, 482 and 499).

For Philo, the tabernacle as house is the symbol of
wisdom on the noetic level, the human soul on the anthropolog-
ical and the universe (τὸν δὲ τὸν κόσμον) on the sensible.[60]
Qu. in Ex. II.49 interprets the tabernacle as a set of cosmological illustrations, the details of its construction
indicating the qualities and elements of the universe, whether
noetic or sensible. Philo's interpretation of the tabernacle
makes the inner and outer tents of the tabernacle stand for
the immutable realities of the noetic world and the sensible,
mutable world respectively.[61] But while Philo invites the
philosopher to transcend the passing and the sensible world,
his cosmological ideas do not permit, let alone require, its
destruction.[62]

At the first examination, then, it appears that the shift
from a Jewish and Jewish-philosophical interpretation of the
tabernacle to the Christian interpretation made by Hebrews is
a switch from a cosmological to an eschatological application:
the holy place is this age, the holy of holies is the age to
come. The categories are not earthly-heavenly or sensible-
noetic but present-future. However, the application made by
Hebrews is in fact not as simple as this, for the first tent
is the figure of the present age, but the holy of holies is
the antitype of the heaven itself, where Christ has already
entered as the high priest of the good things that have come
to pass (9.11, 24).

Thus present-future is not the only category at work, nor
is it absolute. The author of Hebrews has combined the
temporal metaphor of a salvation history view with the spatial
metaphor of a heavenly-earthly view of reality. The combination is made by the application of the holy of holies to
heaven itself (not to the firmament or the skies), a reference
which is highly traditional--indeed almost automatic. The
heaven, the holy of holies: each is the place where God
dwells. Josephus' slender interpretive comments on the

---

[60]*De Cong.*, 117.

[61]*Qu. in Ex.* II.91.

[62]See Williamson, 143-144.

tabernacle remark that Moses proportioned the tabernacle in a
figurative way; two-thirds of the space (that is the holy
place) for all the priests, as the land and the sea are for
men, while the other third, the holy of holies like the
heavens, is for God alone.[63] In the rabbinic tradition the
firmament dividing between the waters below and the waters
above (on which God builds his dwelling) is likened to the
curtain dividing the holy place from the holy of holies.[64]
Although Philo wishes to make "not-place" the dwelling of God,
he also speaks of that which is within the curtain of the
tabernacle as "holy and truly divine," signifying "the heavenly region"[65] and "those things in the soul which are inward
and regard God" (τοῖς εἴσω πρὸς θεόν).[66]

This application of the spatial metaphor produces a
relatively simple and consistent picture in Josephus and even
in Philo, in whose work the inner/outer, heavenly/earthly
distinctions have multi-level applications. In Hebrews however the spatial metaphor is constantly interrupted by the
temporal scheme. The author has used the combination to
resolve the problematic of Christian eschatology that is
unresolved in the work of Paul. The combination of the temporal and spatial metaphor provides a framework which explains
how it is possible that the new age has begun in the resurrection of the just in Jesus while the old age continues.

Thus the metaphor cannot be consistently applied. The
earthly sanctuary provides a metaphor that is at every point
interrupted by the exchange: Christ traverses the (created?)
heavens, crosses the curtain of his flesh, crosses the greater
and more perfect tent which is not of this creation, in order
to enter into the true holy of holies, the heaven itself.
These crossings cannot be arranged in sequence, for they are
all a single crossing: by the transition of his death and
exaltation Christ has passed the boundary of his flesh,

---

[63]*Ant.* III.123, 181.

[64]*Nu. R.* 12.13.

[65]*Qu. in Ex.* II.99 on 26.31.

[66]*De Mut. Nom.*, 44.

passed the heavens or the firmament, crossed the heavenly
sanctuary. All of these are metaphors for the prelude of his
appearance across the veil before the face of God. This less
than perfect consistency of the metaphor's application
testifies to two things: first, it reveals it to be a metaphor
and not a cosmological theory; second, it strongly suggests
that the *typos* which Moses saw is also understood by the
author as conveyed in a metaphorical rather than in a direct
way by the earthly tabernacle.[67]

Thus the significant character of the *typos* of the tent
which Moses saw was conveyed by the divided tent, or according
to Hebrews, by the first and second tent of the earthly
sanctuary, whose holy of holies is the antitype of the very
heaven where Christ is come face to face with God. While the
combination of the spatial and temporal metaphor is clearly
one function and a deeply significant function of Hebrews'
interpretation of the tabernacle, it is not the focus of that
interpretation and indeed is made explicit only in asides and
parenthetic comments. The true focus of Hebrews' description
and interpretation of the tabernacle is the service done in it
by the priests, or more accurately, the unique service done
by the entry of the high priest into the holy of holies on
the Day of Atonement.

The antitype Moses made: the *teleiosis* of the sanctuary and
the priests.

As was remarked above, Hebrews belongs to that strain of
the tradition of interpretation which extends the application
of Ex. 25.40 to all or any of Exodus 25-31 which is of interest
to the interpreter. Thus the focus of the letter on the
unique service of the high priest on Yom Kippur ought to
reflect a conviction that of this also, or rather especially,
Moses saw the *typos* while he was on the mount. In fact, the
treatment of the cult in Hebrews 9 does reveal such a

---

[67]This discussion in particular has been framed by
discussion with R. A. Greer. His insistence upon the significance of the combined spatial and temporal metaphors and his
discussion of the Pauline theological metaphor were the
inspiration of these reflections on Hebrews' soteriological
framework.

conviction and the character of the *typos* that Moses saw
carries the influence of Hebrews' soteriology.

If the application of Ex. 25.40 is extended to all of
Exodus 25-31, Moses would have seen the pattern not only of
the tabernacle but also for the priests' vesture (Exodus 28),
the ordination of the priests (29.1-35), the atonement for the
altar (29.36-37), the perpetual offering (29.38-42) and the
prescription of the once yearly atonement for the altar of
incense (30.10). Each of these with the exception of the last,
is introduced with a demonstrative:

> 28.4 *These* are the garments which they shall *make*...
>
> καὶ <u>αὖται</u> αἱ στολαί, <u>ἃς ποιήσουσιν</u>...

> 29.1 And *these* are the things which you shall *do* to
> them to sanctify them to be priest to me.
>
> καὶ <u>ταῦτά</u> ἐστιν ἃ <u>ποιήσεις</u> αὐταῖς ἀγιάσαι
> αὐτοὺς ὥστε ἱερατεύειν μοι αὐτούς.

> 29.38 And *these* are the things you shall *do* upon the
> altar.
>
> καὶ <u>ταῦτά</u> ἐστιν ἃ <u>ποιήσεις</u> ἐπὶ τοῦ θυσιαστηρίου.

The description of the priestly ordination concludes:

> 29.35 And you shall *do* to Aaron and to his sons *thus*,
> according to all that I have commanded you.
>
> καὶ <u>ποιήσεις</u> ᾿Ααρων καὶ τοῖς υἱοῖς αὐτοῦ <u>οὕτως</u>
> κατὰ πάντα ὅσα ἐνετειλάμην σοι

The use of the demonstrative might easily suggest to the reader that God pointed to the model as he instructed Moses. In
conjunction with the repetition of the word ποιήσεις, "make"
or "do," it recalls 25.8 and 40. A comment credited to both
R. Simeon and R. Akiba tells that Moses found four things
difficult, which God showed him with his finger, saying:
"This is...."[68]

Thus the texts offer the interpreter grounds for infer-
ring that these commands are the specifics of 25.40, laying
out the details of the *typos*. However, drawing that conlusion
is a function of the author's purpose in writing, which

---

[68]To R. Akiba and R. Shimeon b. Yohai in *Mekilta Pisḥa* 2
(Lauterbach I.16); to R. Akiba in *Siphre Bemidbar Beha'alothka*
61 (on 8.4); to a Tanna of the school of R. Ishmael in *b. Men.*
29a. See also *Pesikta* 54b; *Pesikta Rabbathi* 15 (98b).

selects the details that are significant. Philo's work is an
example of the different ways in which the conclusion can be
drawn. When he treats of Moses as priest in the *Vita* II,[69]
he speaks of Moses' sojourn on the mount as instruction in the
sacred rites, but concentrates on the tent and its furnishings
in *Quaestiones in Exodum* II where his interest is in the
presentation of his cosmology.

The letter to the Hebrews reveals its focus by making a
still more specific claim in its interpretation of Ex. 25.40.
In 8.5, the verse is introduced as an oracle given to Moses
when he was about to "build" the tent, at least according to
the RSV. In fact, the Greek word rendered "to build" in
this verse appears to be so translated only because of the
context of Ex. 25.40. In itself ἐπιτελεῖν does not mean "to
build." The first two meanings given for it by LSJ are:
(I) *"complete, finish, accomplish"* or *"bring to perfection"*
and (II) *"discharge* a religious duty" or *"celebrate."* The
first of these two meanings appears in I Esdras 4.55, where
it is applied to the completion of the building (for which
οἰκοδομεῖν is used) of the temple. As an example of the
second LSJ cites He. 9.6: "the priests go in and out,
performing the rites" (τας λατρείας ἐπιτελοῦντες).

While neither meaning will fit Exodus 25-31, either
"complete" or "consecrate" will fit the meaning of the oracle
if it is understood as a prelude to the events described in
Exodus 40 and Nu. 7.1. The last of these two texts is (as we
have noticed) distinguished by extensive commenting in the
rabbinic sources: "On the day when Moses had brought to
completion (LXX συνετέλεσεν) the setting up of the tabernacle
and had anointed it and consecrated it with all its furnishings...." This verse combines the completion of the tent with
its anointing and consecration (sanctification), which were
done in a series of rites which accompanied the sanctification
of the priests (Ex. 40.1-8, 9-15). Both sets of unctions and
consecrations were performed by Moses: "And Moses did all,
as much as the Lord commanded him, so he did" (καὶ ἐποίησεν
Μωϋσῆς πάντα ὅσα ἐνετείλατο αὐτῷ κύριος, οὕτως ἐποίησεν.

---

[69]*Vita* II.66-76.

Ex. 40.16 LXX). According to the commands given to Moses in Exodus 25-31 and amplified in Leviticus 7-9, Moses erected and consecrated the tent.

At the very least, Hebrews can interpret the erection of the tent and its consecration as the fulfillment of the command, "See, do...." However, the introduction of the verse suggests something more. It suggests that Hebrews does not mean to cite Ex. 25.40 in 8.5 but rather refers to another oracle, or a repetition of this oracle on another occasion. This other oracle was given to Moses before he consecrated/ completed the tent, that is, it was given on 23 Adar, according to the traditional reckoning. This reckoning identifies "the day" of Nu. 7.1 as the eighth day of the consecration, 1 Nisan, the day on which Moses also stopped the daily erection and dismantling of the tent which the tradition finds that the verse implies.[70]

In the interpretation of the era this suggestion is less far-fetched than it seems. Philo who also remakes this verse both verbally and functionally understands the instructions given to Moses for the cult as oracles given for each detail of the cult.[71] The arrangement of the books of Exodus, Leviticus and Numbers presupposes the theory that Moses was given additional oracles for the ordination of the priests and the institution of the sacrifices especially for the Day of Atonement, barely mentioned in Ex. 30.10. Further, the rabbinic tradition shows a use of Ex. 25.40 which seems to suppose that it was spoken to Moses more than once, and that after he descended from the mount:

> R. Levi son of Rabbi says: a pure candlestick came
> down from heaven. For the Holy One, blessed be He,
> said to Moses: 'And thou shalt make a candlestick
> of pure gold' (Ex. 25.31). Moses asked Him: 'How
> shall we make it?' 'Of beaten work shall the candle-
> stick be made' (ib.) said He. Still Moses experienced
> difficulty and when he descended he forgot it. He
> went up again and said: 'Master.' I have forgotten
> it!' He then showed a model to Moses, but the latter
> still found it hard to construct. So He said to him:

---

[70] *Nu. R.* 12.15.

[71] *Vita* II.63.

'See it and make it' (ib. 40) and finally he took a candlestick of fire and showed him its construction.[72]

The most significant arguments in favor of this interpretation are, however, the ways in which it illumines the text of Hebrews. First, it suggests a substantive and very simple reason for the change from perfect to aorist in the ptc. of δεικνύω; the oracle is being spoken on a separate occasion after the *typos* was shown to Moses on the mount. Second, this interpretation fits into Hebrews' explication of the whole cult as a "copy and shadow"; for the consecration of priests, tabernacle and furnishings is precisely the inauguration of the cult, the eighth day of the consecration being the first day of the service. Thus the *typos* of the cult which Moses saw was a *typos* which instructed him precisely for the consecration. As the biblical author explains the inauguration and consecration of the tent in terms of the cult as he experienced it, so also the tradition used the account of the origins as an explanation of the contemporary cult. Thus the *typos* of the whole cult which Moses saw was a *typos* which also instructed him specifically for the consecration. In fact, the "oracles" given to Moses in 25-31 which deal with the cult deal mostly with the consecration of the priests and the first sacrifices. The *typos* that he saw was then the *typos* of these. Third, the explication of the *typos* as especially the *typos* of the inauguration (ἐγκαίνωσις) of the tent and the ordination of the priests helps to explain Hebrews' definition of the purpose of the service as to perfect or ordain the worshipper (τελειῶσαι τὸν λατρεύοντα). The prominence of the priestly consecration in the texts of Exodus and Leviticus, the use of the word *teleiosis* to refer to it in the LXX, and the paradeigmatic character of the ceremony in the halakah gives grounds for the focusing of the meaning of the cult in the *teleiosis* of the priest, rather than on the *enkainosis* of the tent. However, these are only a basis for the use of that word, which is then radically transformed by the demands of Hebrews' soteriology. Finally, the application of this oracle

---

[72]*Nu. R.* 15.10 (Soncino, 650). The comment seems to combine the view which limits and the view which extends the application of Ex. 25.40.

to the moment when Moses was about to complete/consecrate (ἐπιτελεῖν) the tent integrates the role of Moses in Hebrews, especially in 8-9, for the *typos* that Moses the mystic saw according to 8.5 is the *typos* of what Moses the minister did in 9.16 ff; it was also the *typos* of the inauguration of the tent.

Both of these last two points require further consider-ation. Two of the questions raised at the beginning of the discussion remain unanswered: what was the *typos* that Moses saw? what did Moses do in accordance with the *typos*? This suggestion brings into clearer focus the character of the *typos* Moses saw: it was the *typos* of the *teleiosis* of the priests, the *typos* of sacrifices and offerings whose purpose was "to perfect the worshipper."

Moses saw the *typos* of sacrifices and gifts whose purpose was τελειῶσαι τὸν λατρεύοντα.

Hebrews' interpretation of the tent in 9.1-10 gives the reader a description of the *typos* by telling the reader what the antitype was intended to convey: the two tents were intended to convey two succeeding ages, covenants, demands of God. Likewise the description of the cult in 9.1-10 empha-sizes certain details as antitypical. The feature of the cult which is the focus of Hebrews' interpretation is the once-yearly entry of the high priest into the holy of holies "not without blood which he offers on behalf of himself and the sins of the people (9.7)." Two aspects of this action become significant: first, it is the high priest alone who is allowed to enter (and that once a year only), indicating that the way is not open into the inner sanctuary (9.8) and therefore, as we have already remarked, indicating the transitory character of the outer sanctuary. Second, once a year continually the high priest *must* enter, offering once a year continually the sacrifices that give him access (10.1-3, 9.7, 9). This indicates the character of the worship of the present time or the law: it is unable to perfect the wor-shipper in conscience (κατὰ συνήδεισιν, 9.9).

An examination of the text of Hebrews reveals that the latter defect is a two-fold defect. The first and more

obvious aspect of it is the inability of the sacrifices for
sin to forgive deliberate and inward transgression. The
provisions for sacrifices for sin in Leviticus 4-5 are the
source of this conviction; the sacrifices effect ritual
purity and readmit the worshipper to the sacred precincts.
Against deliberate sin, sin "with a high hand," they effect no
remedy. In view of the biblical text only, this interpretation is correct. Indeed, the function of the Day of Atonement
itself was to cleanse the sanctuary of all impurities that it
might have contracted during the year from the entry (intentional or unconscious) of unclean persons into the sanctuary.[73]
However, this opinion directly contradicts the rabbinic
opinion which prescribes a variety of conditions under which
the Day does obtain forgiveness of sin when the latter is
sought with repentance.

The second defect is the necessity of repeating the
sacrifices which never bring forgetfulness of sin and never
are able to perfect the worshipper. This transformation of
the yearly repetition of the Day of Atonement into a defect of
that celebration appears at first to be a completely gratu-
itous intervention of the author's Christian soteriology.
While it is certain that the soteriology of the letter is
at work here, the full implication of the claim is understood
only in the light of the rabbinic interpretation of the texts
on the Day of Atonement and the ordination of the priests.

The former is treated in Leviticus 16 and 23.26-35,
Nu. 29.7-11 and 30.10; the latter in Ex. 29.1-46 and Leviticus 8 and 9. Leviticus 9 describes the eighth day of the
consecration on which Aaron and his sons perform the worship
for the first time; the central action of the ceremony is
that described in verses 6-7, given here according to the LXX:

> Lev. 9.6 This word/thing which the Lord has said, do,
> and there will appear to you the glory of
> the Lord.
>
> .7 And Moses said to Aaron: Go to the altar and
> make (or "do"--ποιήσον) your sin-offering and
> your burnt-offering and make atonement for

---

[73]Lev. 16.16; Nu. 19.13; see the article of M. L.
Margolis, "Atonement, Day of," *JE*.

> yourself and for your house and make the gifts
> of the people and make atonement on their
> behalf, as the Lord commanded Moses.

Such ceremonies as these appear to have been the early
form of the purification carried out on the Day of Atonement,
and were still the basis of those ceremonies in the last days
of the temple. Indeed, the Day was an annual feast of
rededication.[74]

More significant for Hebrews are the text and halakah
which prescribe an annual renewal of the ordination of the
high priest who actually enters the tabernacle. The verses
which inspire the requirement are:

Lev. 8.34 Just as he did on this day so the Lord has
           commanded to do so as to make atonement on
           your behalf.

     .35   And at the door of the tent of witness you
           shall sit seven days, day and night: you
           shall watch the watches of the Lord that you
           not die, as the Lord your God commanded (LXX).

The first prescription of the *Mishnah Yoma*[75] is the
prescription of the seven-day separation of the high priest
in preparation for the Day of Atonement, which is discussed
in conjunction with a similar prescription laid down for the
priest who performs the ritual of the red heifer. In the
Talmud two differing opinions are given as to *why* the
separation is required. According to the first opinion
(credited to Rabbi Johanan) the prescription is derived from
Lev. 9.34: "As has been done this day (i.e. the day of the
ordination of the priests and inauguration of the tent), so
the Lord commanded to do (for the occasion of the red heifer)
and to make atonement for you (on the Day of Atonement)."[76]
It is supported by the practice of sprinkling the priest
with water from the red heifer's ashes during the seven days
of the separation which is explained as analogous to the
seven days of sprinkling of blood in the ordination

---

[74]See once again Margolis, "Atonement, Day of," *JE*.

[75]1.1.

[76]This is the portion and the translation of the text
given in *b. Yoma* 2a (Soncino 2); parentheses are mine.

ceremony.[77] This opinion is given the support of an anonymous
Tanna through a baraitha which deduces the custom from Lev.
16.3, "With these (bezoth--redundant) shall he come into the
holy place: with a calf...." The "these" is taken to refer
to the ceremonies of ordination, but also to their renewal
in the seven day separation "so as to make atonement for you"
(cf. Lev. 8.34).[78]

The second opinion, that of Resh Lakish, derives the
practice from Ex. 24.16 and 18:

> And the glory of the Lord came down on mount Sinai and
> the cloud hid it for six days and the Lord called to
> Moses on the *seventh* day from the midst of the cloud....
> And Moses went into the midst of the cloud and went
> up the mountain.[79]

The LXX and English remove the ambiguity of the Hebrew in
which verse 16 can read: "...and the cloud covered *him* (i.e.
Moses) for six days...." However, the conclusion does not
really depend upon this ambiguity, for according to verse 15
Moses was already on the mountain when the cloud descended.
Thus Moses was sanctified for seven days for his entrance into
the presence of God. And so must the high priest also be
sanctified for seven days. The baraitha cited in favor of
Resh Lakish lays particular emphasis on the purpose of
sanctification:

> We have a teaching in accord with Resh Lakish: Moses
> went up in a cloud, was covered by the cloud, and was
> sanctified by the cloud in order that he might receive
> the Torah for Israel in sanctity as it is written,
> *And the glory of the Lord abode upon Mount Sinai.* [80]

---

[77]*B. Yoma* 2a-2b.

[78]*B. Yoma* 4a.

[79]See *ARNA* 1.1 (Goldin, *The Fathers*, 3). Elsewhere
Goldin points to the use of this text in the debate between R.
Akiba and R. Jose over the greatness of Moses (see "The First
Chapter....Appendix," 279-280). Even more significant both
for this debate and for Hebrews is the opening of *ARNB*, in
which Moses' exaltation and sanctification are attested by
Nu. 12.7 and accomplished by his entry into the cloud. To
ARNB 1.1 (Schecter, 1) cf. He. 5.5.

[80]*B. Yoma* 4a (Soncino, 13); Ex. 24.16.

Thus in the case of the priest who must be sanctified in
order to perform the ceremonies of sanctification in the
abode of God's glory on the Day, a week's sequestration is
required.

Because of a secondary dispute about halakah, the two
opinions are regarded by *b*. *Yoma* as mutually exclusive, but
this opposition does not seem to have been the origin of the
interpretation. In *Sifre Zuta*[81] the comment on Nu. 7.1 is a
list of the sanctifications required for the service of God's
dwelling: Moses' seven days in the cloud, the seven days of
anointing with blood and oil for Aaron and his sons, the
initiation of the Levites, the seven days of anointing, erection and dismantling which constituted the consecration of the
tabernacle. With the exception of the Levites all are consecrated for seven days, and the comment places an emphasis on
the number.[82] Moses' consecration, as the first, may well be
the pattern of the others. Thus the opposition seems to be if
not false at least secondary. The practice of the separation
of the high priest in preparation for his entry into the
presence of God is in fact derived from neither the consecration nor Sinai, but is explained by both events which also
explain each other. The seven days every year are a sanctification for the entry into the presence of God, as are the
ordination and Moses' sojourn in the cloud.

Sanctification is the explicit purpose of the preparation,
and the sanctification envisaged is more than a ritual concept.
While the removal of the high priest is at least at one level
a precaution against his disqualification for the service by
ritual impurity, and much of the discussion in *b*. *Yoma* is
either directed to or colored by that problem, the separation
is not as strict as that prescribed for the priest who
officiates in the rite of the red heifer. According to *b*.
Yoma the difference lies in the purpose of the two separations:
the priest who offers the heifer is separated for purity, but
the high priest for "greater holiness": he must be made holy
to enter the presence of the Holy One. The seven days are not

---

[81]*Sifre Zuta* 7.1 (Horowitz, 250-251).

[82]*B. Yoma* 8a-8b cf. also *b*. *Yoma* 4a cited above.

simply an isolation but a repetition of the seven days and
nights of watching whose purpose was "to make them holy in
order that they be priests to me" (Ex. 29.1).

The service of the Day of Atonement appears to be a
special fulfillment of this purpose of the ordination in a
comment attached by *Exodus Rabbah* to Ex. 29.1:

> (And these are the things which you shall do to them
> to make them holy that they may serve me as priests.)
>
> R. Ḥanina said: Let one that is holy come and enter
> the holy place, to sacrifice before the Holy One that
> he may atone for the holy ones. 'Let one that is holy
> come'--this refers to Aaron, because it says, *And of
> Aaron the holy one of the Lord* (Ps. CVI,16) 'and
> enter the holy place'--this refers to the sanctuary,
> for it says, *The sanctuary, O Lord, which Thy hands
> have established* (Ex. XV,7), 'To sacrifice before the
> Holy One'--this is God, who said: *For I the Lord your
> God am holy* (Lev. XIX,2); 'That he may atone for the
> holy ones' namely Israel to whom he said: *Ye shall be
> holy* (ib.).[83]

The comment, while attached to Ex. 29.1, seems also to reflect
Ex. 29.44: "I shall sanctify the tent of meeting and the
altar and Aaron and his sons shall I sanctify to serve me as
priests."

These details of the rabbinic interpretation of the Day
of Atonement and of the ordination of the priests help the
reader to reconstruct the logic and theology of Hebrews' use
of the word *teleiosis*. For the letter, *teleiosis* was the
ordination, consecration and preparation which allowed the
worshipper, the high priest, to enter the holiest place and
to come before the face of God, in the earthly sanctuary. It
was accomplished first through the ordination of the priest
with its sacrifices and sprinklings, then year by year
through the sprinkling of the red heifer's ashes and the
sacrifices of bulls and goats with whose blood the priest
gains access to the sanctuary (He. 9.7, 13).

According to Hebrews, then, the yearly celebration of
the Day of Atonement entailed a yearly *teleiosis* of the priest
who would enter to perform the liturgy, a *teleiosis* that never
was, was not *teleiosis* because it was in fact never perfect,

---

[83] *Ex. R.* 38.7 (Soncino, 455).

never complete. Thus there was no (real) *teleiosis* of the
Levitical priesthood, because the law that established that
priesthood was a "fleshly commandment," dealing only with the
flesh and blood of Aaron. In regard to the ordination and service also it is a fleshly commandment. The cleansing it brings
comes through the blood of bulls and goats (the sacrifices of
the consecration and the Day of Atonement) and the sprinkling
of the red heifer's ashes (in the seven days of preparation and
in the ordination of the Levites). It sanctifies only unto
cleanness of the flesh (He. 9.13), cleansing the body and the
sanctuary from the ritual impurity contracted by contact with
death (cf. Nu. 19.13). Finally it was a commandment of flesh,
an *imperfect* ordination in that those who underwent it were
prevented by death from an abiding service in the sanctuary
(He. 7.23). Possibly Hebrews by this refers not to the idea
that the priests died and succeeded each other but to the ruling of the *Mishnah* which did not permit the high priest to pro-
long his prayer within the sanctuary lest he should cause those
who awaited him to fear for his life.[84] In its assimilation of
the halakic decisions and haggadic expansions of the cultic
prescriptions of the Pentateuch, Hebrews has evolved a theory
about the meaning of the first covenant. The yearly ceremonies
of the Day of Atonement are a re-ordination of the priest and
a re-inauguration of the tent; that is, year by year, tent and
priest are re-consecrated so that "one that is holy" may "come
and enter the holy place to sacrifice before the Holy One that
he may atone for the holy ones." The service is the end, the
reality of the first covenant, and the inauguration of the
(earthly) tent is simultaneous with the inauguration of the
first covenant, or rather, as we shall see, they are one event.
The purpose of the service and covenant is the perfection or
ordination which permits the priest (the worshipper--τὸν
λατρεύοντα 9.9) to enter God's presence in the holy of holies,
the perfection which brings forgiveness and admits to communion. But Hebrews' focus on perfection as the end of the law
is based on the discovery that the perfection is incomplete,
the law does not reach its end, and brings nothing to perfection. Its defects are the same as those which Paul discerns

---

[84]*Yoma* 5.1, cf. *b. Yoma* 53b.

in the law's righteousness: it is external and exclusive. For Paul, the law is good, holy and perfect, but we are unable to bear it; for Hebrews, the law itself is incomplete--it does not reach to the cleansing of the conscience, it is able to admit no worshipper to the presence except the high priest, and him only in a dim and incomplete fashion, once a year.

This theory about perfection as the end of the law relies at every point upon the biblical text and the contemporary halakah,[85] but both have been radically revised; questions have been answered and changed, and also answers reversed at every point, because the author of Hebrews has recognized the ordination of the levitical priesthood and the sanctification of the Day of Atonement as the high point but also as the full extent of the first covenant, and as no more than the antitype of the true. It was able to bring nothing to perfection.

The antitype Moses made: the inauguration of the covenant.

Hebrews' interpretation of the tabernacle, the *teleiosis* and the ministry of the high priest in 8-9 is already an indirect interpretation of Moses' ministry, for the cult is being interpreted precisely as the product of Moses' vision. However, in 9.16-21, the author turns to the direct interpretation of what Moses did when he inaugurated the first covenant. Hebrews' treatment of the ordination and the Day of Atonement includes a revision of both text and halakah, but the revision is principally a matter of rearranging the emphasis and the application in light of the unexpected fulfillment. However, when the letter describes the inauguration of the covenant, the revision of the text is both drastic and startling. What looks like interpretation of Ex. 24.1-8 and indeed claims simply to cite the precedent of that event has in fact remade it.

Ex. 24.1-8 is an account of the covenant ceremony. Moses recites the laws he has been given and obtains the commitment of the people. He then writes the laws in a book and builds the altar and commands sacrifices. He takes half the blood

---

[85]Indeed, Hebrews appears to be a witness to the antiquity of the halakah on these particular points.

and reserves it and pours the rest out on the altar. He
reads the book, the affirmation of the people is repeated
and Moses sprinkles the people with the reserved blood,
expressing God's commitment with the words: "Lo, the blood
of the covenant which the Lord is making with you concerning
all these words" (Ex. 24.8 LXX).

In the account of Hebrews, Moses speaks the law, takes
"the blood of bulls and goats with water and red wool and
hyssop," then sprinkles the book and all the people, saying,
"This is the blood of the covenant which the Lord has
commanded for you." He then sprinkles the tent and all the
vessels of the service with blood, and the sprinkling is
explained as a cleansing (9.22-23).[86]

The most striking element of the revision is that the
inauguration of the covenant and the inauguration of the
tent and the worship have become a single event; the covenant
ceremony of 24.1-8 has as its end the ceremony of consecration described in Nu. 7.1. In a sense, the covenant ceremony
is the beginning of the ceremony which culminates in Nu. 7.1,
which begins the religious life of the people. Even if the
author of Hebrews is not trying to suggest that the consecration of the tent took place as part of the covenant ceremony,
he certainly intends it to be understood as an extension of
that ceremony.[87] However, a number of details in He. 9.16-21
suggest that the former is indeed the intent of the author.

First of all the word "was inaugurated" (ἐγκεκαίνισται,
16) applies in the LXX and the New Testament not to the covenant but to the altar (Nu. 7.10, 88), the temple (3 Ki. 8.63,
2 Chr. 7.5), the sanctuary (1 Macc. 5.1), an ordinary house
(Dt. 20.5) or a reign (1 Ki. 11.14). Primarily it applies to

[86]The fullest account of the revision of the inauguration
of the tent is given by James Moffatt (*Epistle to the Hebrews*,
ICC, 129-130). Revisions are also noted by Spicq II, 263-264;
Héring, 80-81; and Buchanan, 151-152.

[87]On the identity between inauguration of the tent and
ratification of the covenant, see N. A. Dahl, "A New and
Living Way: The Approach to God According to Hebrews 10:19-
25," *Interpretation* 5, 1951, 403-404. See also Buchanan, 152.

objects of cult (even the gold image of LXX Dan. 3).[88]

Secondly, there is no mention of a division of blood or of the pouring out of blood upon the altar. While the account of Hebrews is certainly an abridgement, this omission is not for the sake of brevity but is a deliberate revision. Ex. 24.6, which describes this part of the covenant ceremony, is replaced by He. 9.21, a description of the inauguration of the tent. The latter includes the consecration of the altar in which Moses does what he also does in Ex. 24.6--pours blood upon the base of the altar.[89] In other words, the author assumes that Ex. 24.6 refers to the inauguration of the altar and therefore the tent; the covenant ceremonies take place on the altar that is constructed according to the directives of Ex. 27.1-8. The covenant ceremony becomes a prelude, even a means for the inauguration of the tent even as the end of the first covenant, the lesser promises on which it is based are the right-wisings, *dikaiomata*, of the service, fleshly *dikaiomata* which are never able to put the conscience right.[90]

Third, this combination gives a special prominence to the use of blood in the ceremony being described, and the meaning of the "blood of the covenant" is different from its meaning in Ex. 24.1-8. The change is achieved through the altering of a series of details which also testify to the deliberateness of the revision. The blood is no longer the blood from sacrifices of calves only[91] but "the blood of bulls and goats,"

---

[88]Cf. Spicq II, 263.

[89]Lev. 8.15. Cf. the sacrifices of the ordination (Ex. 29.16, 21; Lev. 8.19, 23-24) and the eighth day of the consecration (Lev. 9.8, 18).

[90]Spicq, 264, and Buchanan, 152, in particular remark the changes in regard to the sprinkling of the tent with the blood of the covenant. Both refer to Josephus' description of the inauguration of the tent with blood (*Ant.* III.206). Josephus and Hebrews seem to testify that the contemporary halakah for Yom Kippur prescribed that the tent be sprinkled with blood and explained the ceremony as a rededication.

[91]Ex. 24.5; N. B. Philo marks out the use of this animal only for comment (*Qu. in Ex.* II.32).

that is the animals used in the sacrifices of the consecration,
of Yom Kippur and of the sin-offerings (Leviticus 4); the
animals used for expiatory offerings. In company with the
blood Moses uses "water, red wool and hyssop"; the exact
reference here is difficult to specify, but presumably the
hyssop was bound with the red wool and used to sprinkle the
water and the blood as in the sacrifices for the cleansing of
leprosy especially of a house, or for the sprinkling of the
water from the red heifer's ashes to cleanse from contact with
death.[92] This is borne out in that the blood is not dashed
against the altar but sprinkled on people, book and tent in a
gesture of cleansing. The rabbinic interpretation of the
Exodus account emphasizes and explicates the division of the
blood as a step in binding the people to the covenant. The
portion designated "God's portion" is sprinkled on the people
and is designated the blood of the covenant: "He (Moses) said
to them, Now you are bound, held and tied; tomorrow, come and
receive the commandments."[93] In Hebrews, there is no division
of the blood, but Moses declares of the blood sprinkled not
only upon the people but on the book, the tent and its
furnishings (including the altar): "This is the blood of the
covenant which the Lord has commanded for you." Thus the
covenant and the ceremony which inaugurates it (as well as
its realization in the fulfillment of the commanded "right-
wisings," δικαιώματα) are done by Moses at the command of God.

Thus the purpose of the blood in the ceremony is refocus-
ed, and with it the purpose of the covenant-making itself. No
longer is the purpose binding; rather in Hebrews the blood of
the covenant is a cleansing. The people, the book and the
tent and vessels of the service are all cleansed by it in
order that the covenant may be enacted and its services, those
sacrifices able only to cleanse the flesh, might begin.

---

[92]Leviticus 14, esp. 51-53; Nu. 19.18; Spicq II, 264,
points out also the very significant use of the bundle of
hyssop for sprinkling of the blood of the Paschal sacrifice.

[93]*Mekilta Baḥodesh* 3 (Lauterbach II, 211). I have taken
this description of the covenant ceremony as a representative
rabbinic description; it is credited by the text to R. Ishmael.

Moses' inauguration of the covenant has become the antitype of the cleansing of the heavenly sanctuary, which must
be cleansed with better sacrifices than these, that is,
through the entry of Christ into the holy of holies in his own
self-offering with his own blood. However, the author does
not emphasize or even mention that Moses entered the sanctuary
to cleanse it.[94] The two antitypical features of this account
are rather the "bloodshed" and the uniqueness of the ceremony,
this first of the yearly cleansings. The *typos* which both
details convey is the death of Christ as the beginning of the
new covenant which holds out the better promises of true
right-wisings, the forgiveness and even oblivion of sins and
the knowledge of God. This is very nearly self-evident, for
the event is reported as a testimony to exactly this function
of Christ's death. The event appears to be rather a lame
proof, for the statement that the will goes into effect only
on the death of the testator is but poorly illustrated by the
Sinai covenant. In Exodus 24 the testator (ὁ διαθέμενος He.
9.16) is God or rather, the Lord (ἧς διέθετο κύριος Ex. 24.8
LXX). The text shows only that the covenant ceremony required
bloodshed, and that Moses presented to the people "the blood
of the covenant." This declaration of Moses is seen by the
author of Hebrews as a sort of "death certificate" under
which the testament can be enacted. It applies in Exodus to
the blood designated by the rabbinic interpreters as "God's
portion." Although the blood is not allotted into two portions
in Hebrews, it seems that blood indicates the enactment of
the covenant on the part of God. To provide the blood of the
covenant, the sacrificial animals die vicariously, or rather
antitypically. For the "blood of bulls and goats" which
enacts this covenant is only a substitute, a fleshly command,
which is in force only until the advent of the true son and
heir, the Lord and testator, who enacts the new covenant by
his own death.

The highly traditional explanation of Jesus' death as
the shedding of the blood of the covenant is thus brought forward and explicated. Hebrews cites a form of Ex. 24.8 which

---

[94]Philo, however, does draw this picture (*Vita* II.153).

appears to be influenced by the Christian tradition, for its
opening words are those of the form of this verse connected by
Paul and the synoptics with the cup of the Lord's supper
rather than those of the LXX.[95] The word "sprinkling"
(ῥαντισμός) is left aside in 9.22 for the word "bloodshed"
(αἱματεκχυσία) which is usually regarded as Hebrews' creation.[96] For Hebrews as for the other accounts (with the
possible exception of Matthew) the forgiveness of sins is not
the primary purpose of the bloodshed. While it does effect
"cleansing from dead works" the cleansing is only the preliminary, the first step of the liturgy through which the entry
is effected and by which Christ offers himself, appearing
before God "to do his will" not by offering sacrifices, but
seated on the right hand of God, awaiting the time when all
things shall be put under his feet, when the outer tent will
be removed and he will appear a second time to those who
await him unto salvation (10.9, 13; 9.8, 28). The antitype
of the suffering of Christ, his death and sacrifice, is not
the slaughter of the sacrificial animals but the entry of the
high priest into the holy of holies.

In the process of discussing the antitypical features of
Moses' institution, we have come to the conclusion that the
typos that Moses saw on the mount was the *teleiosis* of Jesus,
the dead and risen Lord. Startling as this conclusion might
have been if drawn out of context, all the observations we
have made not only about the antitypical character of the cult
as described by Hebrews but also about the function of Moses'
vision in the "high" tradition of interpretation draw us to
this conclusion. Our discussion of the "high" tradition of
interpretation of Ex. 25.40 showed that the vision of the
pattern is interpreted in that tradition as a vision of God
and in fact as the same as or continuous with the vision of

---

[95]τοῦτο τὸ αἷμα τῆς διαθήκης ἧς ἐνετείλατο πρὸς ὑμᾶς ὁ
θεός instead of ἰδοὺ τὸ αἷμα τῆς διαθήκης ἧς διέθετο κύριος
πρὸς ὑμᾶς (Ex. 24.8 LXX). Cf. Spicq II, 264, and on the
meaning of the blood, his "Excursus VIII--La Théologie et
liturgie du précieux Sang" (II, 271-285).

[96]Spicq II, 265.

Exodus 33-34. Further, in Hebrews *typos* is synonymous with image (10.1) and should therefore be related to the vision of God and also be identified with reality rather than copy. A still more positive assertion of this observation can be made when we have reviewed the meaning of the word *teleiosis* and its function in the soteriology of Hebrews and summarized the function of the word *typos* in the New Testament. These two areas clarify the possibility of interpreting the *typos* of 8.5 as a vision of the perfection, the passage of Christ from death to life. We are then left with the question of whether the vision of the unseen God, the glory of God can have been interpreted by the letter as the vision of Christ's passage.

The *typos* that Moses saw was the *teleiosis* of Jesus.

At the first reading of the letter, it is clear that the word *teleiosis* has a specifically Christian content, or even a specifically Christological content, for Hebrews. The meaning of the Greek word itself invites each theologian to appropriate it fully; as "completion" and "perfection" it becomes the designation for the writer's religious ideal or, more properly, end. For Hebrews, *teleiosis* of the believer is a concept similar to the Pauline "conformity to Christ"; for both Christ and the believer, perfection means what was done in Jesus. The discovery that the ordination of the high priest for his entry into the holy of holies is the skeleton (or the shadow) through which Hebrews explicates perfection only shows the way in which this perfection is that which was done in Jesus. The defects of the old perfection are the excellencies of the new: the true *teleiosis* which permits the priest to remain always before God pleading on behalf of the people, which perfects the worshipper according to conscience, which perfects not only the priest who enters, but cleanses, sanctifies, gives admission to all who approach: this is the perfection of Christ, "the son perfected forever according to the order of Melchisedech" (7.28).

The theologies of Hebrews' near contemporaries provide parallels to some of these expectations of *teleiosis* and of the liturgy. The halakah explains under what conditions the Day of Atonement brings the forgiveness of sins (that is,

beyond the forgiveness of ritual transgressions).[97] Philo's
mystic doctrine offers a *teleiosis* and admission to the
presence of God to all who proselytize themselves to philosophy. Philo even considers *teleiosis* a permanent matter:
for him Aaron's death is his true perfection, his translation
into light.[98] The unique feature of Hebrews' understanding of
teleiosis is no single one of these explanations but rather
their revision by the unique Christian soteriology. The
teleiosis of the Christian is through that of Christ, there is
really only the one *teleiosis*: "with one offering he has
perfected for all time those who are to be sanctified" (10.14).

Once those who were to be sanctified were Aaron and his
sons (Ex. 29.1-4). The sacrifice which the high priest
offered on his own behalf was for himself and his house, the
latter interpreted by the liturgy of the Day as the children
of Aaron, the priests.[99] But Christ the true priest is
clearly not a descendent of Aaron, being of the tribe of Judah,
but is rather the heir of Abraham (6. 2,16), with all who
draw near by faith. His kinship is not through the flesh of
Aaron but through his sharing in flesh and blood, as do all
the children, so that "sanctifier and sanctified are all of
one" (2.10). The *archegos* and *teleiotes* of our salvation is
perfected in the way appropriate to our common familial
mortality: through παθήματα, through what he suffered, "in
order through death to destroy the one who holds the power
of death" (2.16). Like the *teleiosis* of the Levitical priesthood his is accomplished through blood, but also through the
oath accompanying his session: "The Lord has sworn and he
shall not repent: you are a priest forever according to the
order of Melchisedek."[100] This perfection, his passion, is

---

[97]*Mishnah, Yoma* 8.8 and 9, *b. Yoma* 85b-87a.

[98]*Leg. All.* III.45: "when Aaron dies, that is when he is
made perfect" (...Ἀαρων ὅταν τελευτᾷ τουτέστιν ὅταν τελειωθῇ).

[99]See *Mishnah, Yoma* 4.2 also 1.1 where "his house" is
explained as the priest's wife. Also *b. Yoma* 2a.

[100]Ps. 110.4 in He. 5.6; cf. Hebrews 7, esp. 7.28: "the
word of the oath [establishes] the son forever perfected/or-
dained" (...ὁ λόγος δὲ τῆς ὁρκωμοσίας τῆς μετὰ τὸν νόμον
καθίστησιν υἱὸν εἰς τὴν αἰῶνα τετελειωμένον).

the crossing of the veil, that is his flesh, but also of the
heavens and of the greater and more perfect tent. "What he
suffered" is for Hebrews what we are now accustomed to refer
to as "the paschal mystery"; that is not the pains of death
but rather the undergoing of obedience, the *transitus* through
death to life.

The picture of Moses' ministry given in 11.28 likewise
suggests that the type according to which Moses did all was
the death of Christ. Again the meaning of that event is
extended to include the crossing of the veil of his flesh/of
the heavens. "By faith he instituted the pasch and the out-
pouring of blood...." Hebrews' use of παθεῖν and παθήματα
to designate not merely the suffering and death of Jesus but
also his entry across the veil suggest that for this author
the word *pascha* has already acquired the Christian etymology
which transforms the meaning of both words, by the interchange
of meaning (as has already been suggested in the case of 1
Peter). It is based in part on the Jewish etymology which
explains *pascha* as crossing (διαβατήρια).[101] This meaning
appears to be invoked by the following verse: "By faith they
crossed (διέβησαν) the Red Sea as (though) dry land, though
the Egyptians when they essayed it were drowned." This passage too is antitypical for Hebrews, reflecting the "new and
living road beyond the veil"..."inaugurated for us" (10.20),
when Christ traversed (διεληλυθότα) the heavens as the great
high priest of our confession (4.14, cf. 6.19). So too the
bloodshed which preserved their first born from the touch of
the destroyer foretold--or reflected--our redemption "...from
the one who holds the power of death (He. 2.17)..." "by the
blood of a spotless and unblemished lamb (1 P. 1.19)."
1 Peter and Hebrews appear to use the word πάσχειν in the
same sense,[102] and in Hebrews τελειῶσαι is a synonym: "It
was fitting to perfect through suffering...(He. 2.10)."

The cultic law and the ordination which established the

---

[101]Cf. Philo *De Spec. Leg.* II.145-147.

[102]On the meaning of the word in 1 Peter, see Frank L.
Cross, *1 Peter, a Paschal Liturgy* (London: A. R. Mowbray,
1954).

levitical priesthood are the antitype of the true, the perfection of Christ which is their *typos*. That *typos*, that pattern
which Moses saw and according to which he did in fulfillment of
the oracles must then be the perfection of Christ, his death
and exaltation.

The New Testament offers three basic meanings of *typos*.
The first is infrequent and of minor importance in our discussion. It is the literal use of *typos* to mean "mark" or
"impression" (Jn. 20.25, Acts 23.25). The second is a metaphorical use, that use on which the discussion in this chapter
has concentrated: the use of *typos* to mean "pattern," "model"
or "copy" especially as a term in the interpretation of scripture. The most important instances of this are in Paul and
Hebrews (Acts 7.42-44 also uses the word, but the discussion
of this passage can be postponed). Paul's use of the word
seems to have determined its meaning in the development of
theories of exegesis: Adam is a type of the one to come (Ro.
5.14), the cloud was a type of baptism (1 Corinthians 10):
this imagery stays close to the literal meaning; *typos* is the
mark rather than the stamp that makes the mark. Hebrews and 1
Peter have revised the usage in order to produce their understanding of the word and its use: the ark was the antitype of
baptism, the earthly holy of holies is the antitype of the
true, heaven itself. The word *typos* can thus be reserved for
the reality which can be described through (only) the significant characteristics of the antitype. Of the tabernacle, this
characteristic is its construction as two tents which are
successive. Of the cult, and the *teleiosis*, it is the entry
of the high priest into the presence of God in the holy of
holies through the blood of the sacrifices. In both cases,
the *typos* being conveyed through the antitypical details is
the death of Christ and his enthronement, his entry into the
good things which are new but already come. Likewise the
antitypical burning of the cadavers of the sacrificial animals
outside the camp conveys the historical but theologized
circumstance of Jesus' death outside the city walls (13.11-13).

The third meaning of *typos* in the New Testament is also
a metaphorical meaning and seems to have some bearing on the
revision of the imagery in Hebrews and 1 Peter. *Typos* is

used in Paul, the Pastorals and 1 Peter as a moral term, to
mean a model or example of behavior. This meaning retains the
imagery of model or pattern and copy that was noted in *Legum
Allegoria*;[103] however, *typos* in this scheme in the New Testament seems always to be used to mean model rather than copy:
e.g. in 1 Th. 1.6-7, the Thessalonians, having become imita-
tors of Paul and his companions and of the Lord, also themselves have become *typoi* for all the believers of Asia and
Macedonia. The model is always a person, either the apostle
or the addressees. Ro. 6.17 is sometimes considered an
exception to this usage: "but thanks be to God, because you
were slaves of sin, but you have obeyed from the heart the one
unto whom you have been delivered as a "type of teaching"
(τύπον διδαχῆς). It has been suggested that this phrase
refers to a traditional code; however, when Paul cites tradition as the ground of conduct, he does not cite *haustafeln*,
but rather Christological teaching, or the example of Christ
(1 Co. 11.2 ff; 23 ff; Ro. 15.1-6, 7-13; Ph. 2.1-11), or his
own living example (1 Th. 3.6-9).

The use of the word *typos* to mean moral example or model
may well explain the favorable connotations of the word for
Hebrews and the consequent preference for *antitypos* to refer
to the old dispensation. 1 Peter, which also shows this
preference, uses *typos* in this way (5.3).

Hebrews certainly does focus upon the exemplary character of Christ's death and resurrection. The author could
well borrow the phrase from Paul: "you have obeyed the *typon
didaches*"..."who learned obedience through what he suffered
and once perfected became the cause of salvation to all who
obey him" (5.8-9). Whether or not the vocabulary can be
generalized to Hebrews, in that letter the dead and risen
Lord, the beginner and perfecter of our salvation, is surely
the type to whom the believer must look.

This study began from the observation that Moses had
turned into a Christian in the Letter to the Hebrews and into
a Christian martyr at that. Although "not perfected without
us," Moses is a witness to our contest as one who himself has

---

[103]*Leg. All.* III.95-96.

chosen maltreatment with the people of God and the reproach
of Christ. He is the model of the Christian and the imitator
of Christ in his (unnecessary) choice of the contest alloted
to the people of God (cf. 12.1-2). His choice was made
because he looked ahead (ἀπέβλεπεν) to the recompense, as we
are called upon to look ahead (ἀφορῶντες) to the beginner and
perfector of our faith. As the glory of Moses was the result
of the glory he saw, his endurance (11.27), his bearing of the
reproach of Christ and his expectation of a better resurrection
is the result of his vision of the unseeable. He is conformed
to the cross and exaltation of Jesus, because as faithful, as
believer, he fulfills the command, "See, do all according to
the *typos* that was shown to you on the mount...."

Thus we discover that in Hebrews the *teleiosis* of Jesus
is both the end and the pattern of the cult and that *typos* in
the theological, or rather parenetic function which would best
suit the milieu of Hebrews' thought not only can but even
should refer to a person. Thus in our passage its likely
application is to the person of Christ as the dead and risen
Lord, whose person is the image of our creation and whose
passage is the pattern of our reforming, whose reproach Moses
bore and whose glory he wore as a result of his vision.

Moses' vision of God as soteriological.

We have already pointed out that Hebrews' interpretation
of the vision of Moses belongs to a stream of the tradition
in which the tendency is to merge rather than to distinguish
the instances or episodes in which Moses spoke with God face
to face and beheld the glory of the Lord. But even more
significant for our argument than this general theological
tendency is the role of Moses' vision in Hebrews' explication
of the saving role of Christ and the soteriological function
of the law. In order further to describe that role, we must
return briefly to Moses' vision of God as it is described in
Exodus 33-34, the vision which Moses seeks. In these chapters
Moses seeks the sight of God's glory as an assurance of his
own favor with God, the favor which will permit him to
complete the ministry to which he has been appointed. The
glory that he asks to see is a guarantee of the relationship

between God and Israel of which he himself is both mediator
and guarantor; that is, of the covenant. Moses seeks his
vision as a testimony to the covenant which has been broken
by Israel and which God has agreed to reinstate at the inter-
cession of Moses, who has offered his life in place of
Israel's (Ex. 32.32). And God accedes to all Moses' requests
in so far as Moses is able to bear them (cf. Ex. 33.17).
As he makes all his glory pass by (Ex. 33.19, 22; 34.5), he
proclaims the covenantal name which is the guarantee of his
relation to Israel:

> The Lord, the Lord a God...full of steadfast love
> and fidelity, keeping steadfast love for thousands,
> forgiving iniquity and transgression and sin...
> (Ex. 34.6-7, cf. 33.19).

For the halakah, this promise of covenanted love and
inexhaustible forgiveness is fulfilled on the Day of Atonement,
when the ineffable name pleads on behalf of the guilty in the
abode of his glory. The Talmud explains at length the conditions under which the Day and repentance bring forgiveness
for "iniquity, transgression and sin," as promised in the
oracle.[104]

For Christian authors also, the oracle pronounced before
Moses is a promise of the forgiveness of sin. But for these
authors, the dispensation instituted by Moses is still a
dispensation of death, though attended by glory; under this
dispensation, God will "by no means clear the guilty (Ex.
34.7)." It is a dispensation of precept and ritual, never
able to clear the guilty according to their conscience.[105]

But at least for the author of Hebrews, it is by no
means without purpose: for the precepts of the law and its
ministry are enacted as a testimony to the "grace and truth"

---

[104]*B. Yoma* 36b, 85b-86a.

[105]Cf. Aug. *Tract. in Ioh.* III.16 (CCL 36,27):

*Lex per Moysen data est, gratia et veritas per Iesum
Christum facta est.* Per servum lex data est; reos fecit;
per imperatorem indulgentia data est, reos liberavit.
Lex per Moysen data est. Non sibi aliquid amplius
servis assignet, quam quod per illum factum est. Electus
ad magnum ministerium tamquam fidelis in domo, sed tamen
servus, agere secundum legem potest, solvere a reatu
legis non potest.

that was to be. In the vision which inspired the law, when
the Lord made his glory pass by,[106] Moses saw in clear vision
"the death of the testator" (He. 9.16), bringing the true
covenant into force; he saw the Lord, the testator, "the Lord
full of steadfast love and fidelity," whose deed of covenant
love is the deed of the "high priest *merciful and faithful*, to
propitiate the sins of the people" (He. 2.17). And about
this vision Moses wrote the law in antitypes and riddles, as
his hearers were able to bear. But the riddles are not lies;
although the ritual cannot cleanse the conscience, although
it is a fleshly law, limiting the access to the sanctuary to
the son of Aaron and weakened by the debility which will not
allow him to remain in the glorious presence, still the incomplete fleshly cleansing, the dim momentary contact, is real.

Thus the tent and its service are given a positive
soteriological function in Hebrews both in the new dispensation and in the old. The law, the fleshly commandment which
established the service of the tent is ἐπεισαγωγὴ τῆς
κρείττονος ἐλπίδος, "conduct to a better hope," and in the
old order was able to accomplish at least (though only) the
cleansing of the flesh while preparing for the better promise
in which the Lord declares: "I will be merciful to them and
forget all their sins" (He. 8.12, Jer. 31.32). Unlike the
Pauline understanding of the Law, the Law in Hebrews is not
"holy, righteous, good" and death-dealing. It is imperfect,
itself incomplete and unable to bring about the *teleiosis* so
as to bring an amnesia of sin and the knowledge of God.
Hebrews' view of the law stresses the continuity between the
two covenants, whereas Paul stresses the discontinuity. The
view of Moses' role as the receiver and deliverer of the
oracles of God, Moses' institution of the antitypical role of

---

[106]Cf. Augustine, *De Trinitate* II.29, (CCL 50, 120). He
applies the word *transiet* in Exodus 33 and 34 to the *transitus*,
passage, of Christ from death to life--to the pasch:

Inde non vult nisi cum transierit videri posteriora sua
ut in eius resurrectionem credatur. Pascha enim
hebraeum verbum dicitur quod transitum interpretamur.
Unde et Iohannes Evangelista dicit: *Ante diem autem
festum paschae sciens Iesus quia venit eius hora ut
transeat de hoc mundo ad patrem.*

the high priest, the inauguration of the covenant all explicate the soteriological role of Jesus insofar as they derive
from it. They are all alike the result of Moses' unique
position, the servant "appointed/faithful in all the house who
speaks face to face with the Lord." In other words, the
dispensational role of Moses is the result of a "high Mosesology." Likewise the three assertions made at the beginning
of this chapter hold true because of the "high" picture of
Moses. The conviction that when Moses ascended to receive
the law, he saw the unseeable God is the real basis of the
exegetical theory. This theory then uses rather than depends
upon Ex. 25.40. This is the more evident when we recall that
the author of Luke-Acts also uses both the word *typos* and
Ex. 25.40 in his discussion of the cult. The citation occurs
in Acts 7.44, in the speech of Stephen: "The tent of witness was with our fathers in the desert, as he commanded who
spoke with Moses (telling him) to make it according to the
typos he had seen." But the function of the type and the
role of both tabernacle and temple are quite different in
Luke-Acts. The tent is a witness against them, rather than
a promise of the greater things to come, for it is hardly
distinguished from the tent of Moloch and the *typoi* (idols)
which they worshipped in the desert. The temple is not an
efficacious sign of God's dwelling among them but rather a
sign of their misunderstanding of the God who dwells not in
a house made by hands.[107] And linked to this low view of the
law and its institutions is the view which Luke-Acts takes of
Moses' prophecy. For "the one who spoke with Moses" for this
author is an angel, a messenger and not the Lord himself.

In contrast, the author of Hebrews takes a high view of
the dispensation of Moses not because of Ex. 25.40, but
because of the high Christology which brings out a correspondingly high view of Moses: because the one we have seen
is *visibilis invisibilis Dei Filii*, so also Moses gazed on
the Unseen and endured.

---

[107] Héring, 66-67, gives the same estimate of Acts 7.44,
but links Hebrews with Luke-Acts.

Conclusion

The discussion of what Moses did as a result of his
vision has already remarked the degree to which the biblical
role of Moses, the events of the exodus and the lawgiving and
the halakah of the temple service have been revised by the
Christian soteriology. For Hebrews, Christ is the end of the
law as its *typos*; it was all written about him, all that was
done was done about him. For Philo, Moses is the Master
Theologian, who from his vision of God and of the archetypal
essences made the archetypes according to which Bezalel constructed the tent in the wilderness. Hebrews too explains
the role of Moses as theological. But Moses constructed or
wrote or performed not as "Master Theologian" but "servant
unto the witnessing (place) of the things that would be
said" (3.5). However, although Moses' role as witness is
primarily predictive, it is not only antitypical. Melchisedech
in Hebrews and Adam in Romans 5 also play a predictive role
as antitypes. The former is "likened to the son of God": the
latter "*typos* of the one who is to come." While Moses is
also antitypical in the details of his life, his likeness to
the son of God is not simply a result of the instantiation
of the pattern in his creation (although it is surely also
that) but also is a result of his vision.[108] His martyrdom
is a Christian martyrdom, his glory is the reflection of that
which he saw, and especially his witness which is embodied in
the tent (of witness, σκηνὴ τοῦ μαρτυρίου or simply τὸ
μαρτύριον, Ex. 16.34) is also the result of his vision.

The same conviction makes Christ the exegetical principle,
affirming that Christ is the *typos* and therefore the *telos* of
the law in its prescriptions. So also by reason of the vision
he is the *archegos* as well as the *teleiotes*, the beginner as
well as the perfecter of our salvation. By the vision, the
soteriological role of Moses is guaranteed; his institutions
become ἐπεισαγωγή, the conduct of a better hope, but also the
lesser, weaker, and debilitated dispensation of the law is
still salvific, although only partial.

---

[108]Cf. Philo, for whom God is paradigm of his own creation, but also through Moses' vision, of the description
written about him in the law, above, p. 219.

CONCLUSION

This study of Moses in the letter to the Hebrews, can appropriately be brought to a close with some observations about the relation of Christology and the interpretation of the scriptures in Hebrews and in the New Testament as a whole.

We have remarked that the picture of Moses in Hebrews is basically the picture of Moses as a visionary conformed to his vision of the son of God. Not only the glory of Moses which is compared to that of Christ in 3.1-6, but also Moses' enduring faith praised in 11.23-27 and his ministry of witness described in 8-9 are the result of his vision of the dead and risen Lord. This picture of Moses as visionary is in part a traditional picture associated with specific scriptural texts. But the picture of Moses in Hebrews is not determined by the scriptural citations with which these passages of the letter are concerned. This is evident when we recall that two of the citations involved--Ex. 2.11 ff and Ex. 25.40--also occur in the portrait of Moses in Acts. There Moses the prophetic martyr foretells by his career the fate of the prophet-martyr Christ, and Moses the architect of the tent beholds its pattern and institutes its worship. Hebrews also uses both texts and images of Moses, but their meaning is filled out and transformed through another picture, the picture of Moses the theologian; or rather, through the theological discussion which is articulated in terms of Moses' vision as it is described in Exodus 33-34. For Hebrews, Moses the martyr is a Christian witness who endured as seeing the seeable of God the Unseen; Moses the theologian inaugurated the tent and instituted the Pasch as the antitype of the passage of God which he saw; they declare for us the salvation wrought by Christ our high priest who has traversed the heavens. This picture of Moses is determined by a Christological decision on the part of the author of Hebrews. This decision is the solution to two sets of questions about God, the first concerned with the problem of transcendence,

259

creation and revelation, the second with the problem of
retribution and salvation, of justice and forgiveness.

For our author the resolution of these problems is in
Christ, and the answers given to the questions they pose are
Christological statements. If we ask how God unseeable is
known, the answer is in Christ, the effulgence of God's glory,
the character of his unseeable substance, by whom he also made
the worlds, and in whom he has at last spoken to us (1.3, 1).
The solution is the solution of John: "the only begotten God,
he has revealed him." If we ask how justice shall be
satisfied and mercy shown to thousands when no one is without
sin, the answer is in Christ whose deed on our behalf out-
weighs the debt of proliferated iniquity because in Paul's
words it is "the gift of God and the free gift of the one man
Jesus Christ." This is also Hebrews' resolution; the son whom
God leads to the world commanding, "let all God's angels
worship him" (1.6), becomes fully partaker of our flesh and
blood, "that he might become our merciful and faithful high
priest before God, to expiate the sins of the people" (2.17
cf. 14).

These convictions are also articulated through the vision
of Moses, which has already been the locus in which the
problems have been addressed by other theologians. Beginning
from the resolution in Christ, the author of Hebrews reads
the text of Exodus and discovers that that glory of God whom
Moses saw, that seeable of God unseen is the son, the Lord
who has spoken the beginning of our salvation (2.2). The
promise of forgiveness and communion that accompanied his
vision, and was so imperfectly fulfilled in the celebration
of the Day of Atonement, is fulfilled in Christ our high
priest, the Lord full of mercy and faithfulness, who by one
offering has for all time perfected those who are to be
sanctified.

Thus for the author of Hebrews, the principle of exegesis is Christ, and Christ explained in a definite theological
fashion. But the process of interpretation according to that
principle is not to be thought of as a process of uncritical
and violent exegesis. Rather, Hebrews relies upon the
scholarly methods and the theological discussions of the

period, as well as the tradition of interpretation. There can be no question but that this author is familiar with the haggadic elaboration and halakic decision which we normally characterize as the predecessors of normative rabbinic tradition, as well as with the interpretive theories credited to Alexandria. These provide the author of Hebrews with an approach to the scripture which includes both methods and questions which are raised by or at least attached to the text.[1] That their resolution is in Christ is indeed a foregone conclusion. This does not however mean that the text and methods are violated or questions slighted. Rather for the author these elements of the understanding of the scripture want filling out as the shadow wants completion in the true image. The strong light of Christ reveals the true objects by which the shadows are cast and so reorganizes the shadows.

Thus our approach to the letter to the Hebrews through Moses has given us some ideas about the Christology of the letter, its theories about soteriology and the meaning of the law, and its relation to the history of interpretation. It also seems to have some implications for the scholarly study of the New Testament, for it offers another way of looking at the relation between the Old Testament and the writing of the New Testament. Much attention has already been given to the theory that community reflections on the Old Testament text have influenced the picture of Jesus and his history, producing stories about Jesus or explaining his role in terms of Israel's past. Attention has also been given to the accommodation of the scriptures to history, or rather to

---

[1] Cf. R. A. Greer:

...theology, itself derived from the Scriptures...shapes exegesis in the sense that it determines the questions asked of the text. The correlation between theology and exegesis is to be defined as that between the question posed and the answer obtained from the text. Furthermore, the role of theology is not only decisive in shaping exegetical results, it is of great importance in the formulation of exegetical methods.

The Captain of Our Salvation: A Study in the Patristic Exegesis of Hebrews (Tübingen: J. C. B. Mohr [Paul Siebeck], 1973), 5.

the mutual accommodation of history and scriptures in the reflection of the community.[2] The description which we have given of Hebrews' Moses is a description which seeks out the role of theology in interpretation; perhaps we should say of Christology, so as to recognize the intervention of history with the theological questions which have illuminated and transformed it. This descriptive approach appears to be a fruitful one and one which has not received much explicit attention.[3]

Perhaps it is also appropriate to say something about the relevance of Moses and his search for God for continuing theological reflection. Other than the illumination of the New Testament text, what relevance has this completely fictive story of Moses' request for the vision, or the thoroughly metaphorical descriptions of the means of his prophecy, for the Christian theologian, for whom salvation had its beginning by being spoken through the Lord?

One answer to this is to look at the function of the text in the New Testament. As we pointed out above, Moses' vision is used in a variety of ways to help define the Christian reality, for it continues to speak to the theological issues with which it was originally concerned, the issues of transcendence, revelation and salvation. Thus it is used by Paul to define the difference between our present and our future experience of God: "We see now in a glass darkly, then face to face; now I know in part, then I shall know even as I have been known." The vision once granted to one only now is extended to the whole people. Thus as Moses saw, so also shall we one day see. Hebrews also uses Moses' vision in a comparison between old and new covenants in 12.18-24.

---

[2]Notably by Mr. Dahl in his article, "History and Eschatology in Light of the Qumran Texts," *The Crucified Messiah* (Minneapolis: Augsburg Publishing House, 1974).

[3]This descriptive approach has been mapped out for the study of Patristic exegesis by Mr. Greer in *The Captain of Our Salvation*. He has also suggested an extension of this approach, consisting in tracing "high roads" of theology and exegesis through the New Testament and early Christian literature in an unpublished paper called "A Trajectory from Paradise" (delivered at the Harvard Divinity School, May, 1974).

There in place of the fearful vision of Sinai which the people rejected and Moses bore in fear and trembling, we are offered a new communion in the festival of angels and saints on Sion, our approach guaranteed by the redeeming blood that speaks better than Abel's. For Hebrews, this offer is both eschatological and actual; Paul and Chrysostom, on the other hand claim for our present the immediacy of the vision of Moses and more:

> Do you wish to learn from another example as well how much greater is the lot of which you have been judged worthy? The Jews then were not able to see the face of Moses glorified, and this although he was their fellow slave and kinsman. But you have seen the face of Christ in his glory. And Paul cries out: "We with unveiled faces gaze upon the glory of the Lord." They had Christ following then, but how much more does he now follow us. For the Lord followed them on account of the grace of Moses, but us not on account of Moses' favor alone, but also because of your own proper obedience.[4]

John also when he declared "*we* have seen his glory" makes the common claim of Christianity that in coming face to face with Christ we have joined Moses on the mount. The claim is itself of course only the beginning of a theology; it is theology's task to expound that claim. But the claim itself represents a decision about Christ and about Moses which as in the first century and at Chalcedon and Nicea, is a decision at once about God and about humanity. The high view of Christ and of Moses is an estimation of human possibility as well as a decision about God's self-revelation; we see in Christ the God who became partaker of our humanity in so far as we are also able to hope to become partakers of his divinity. And with possibility comes the obligation, the imperative we see in Moses' search and his transfiguration: "Gloria enim Dei vivens homo; vita autem hominis visio Dei."[5]

---

[4] John Chrysostom, *Catechesis* III, 25 from *Huit Catéchèses Baptismales*, A. Wenger, SC 50 (Paris: Editions du Cerf, 1950).

[5] Irenaeus, *Adv. Haer.* IV, 20,7.

BIBLIOGRAPHY

Texts and translations: Judaica.

Aboth de Rabbi Nathan. Ed. Solomon Schechter. New York:
Philipp Feldheim, Publisher, 1945.

*Apocrypha and Pseudepigrapha of the Old Testament in
English*. 2 vols. Tr. R. H. Charles. Oxford:
Clarendon Press, 1913.

The Babylonian Talmud. Tr. under the editorship of
Isidore Epstein. London: The Soncino Press, 1948.

The Bible in Aramaic. 5 vols. Ed. Alexander Sperber.
Leiden: E. J. Brill, 1959.

The Biblical Antiquities of Philo. Tr. M. R. James.
London: SPCK and New York: Macmillan, 1917; reprint
ed., New York: KTAV Publishing House, 1971.

The Dead Sea Scrolls in English. Tr. Geza Vermes.
Baltimore: Penguin Books, 1968.

The Fathers According to Rabbi Nathan. Yale Judaica
Series X. Tr. Judah Goldin. New Haven: Yale
University Press, 1955.

The Hebrew-English Edition of the Babylonian Talmud. Ed.
Isidore Epstein. London: The Soncino Press,
[1960-].

Josephus; With an English Translation. Loeb Classical
Library. 8 vols. Tr. H. St. J. Thackeray. London:
William Heinnemann Ltd. and Cambridge, MA: Harvard
University Press, 1966.

The Life and Works of Flavius Josephus. Tr. William
Whiston. Philadelphia: J. C. Winston, 1957.

Mekilta de Rabbi Ishmael. 3 vols. Ed. and tr. Jacob
Lauterbach. Philadelphia: The Jewish Publication
Society of America, 1976.

Midrash 'Agadah Wayyikra'. Ed. Solomon Buber. Jerusalem,
1961.

The Midrash on Psalms. Yale Judaica Series VI. 2 vols.
Tr. William G. Braude. New Haven: Yale University
Press, 1959.

Midrash Rabbah. Printed edition. Jerusalem, 1956.

Midrash Rabbah. Tr. under the editorship of H. Freedman
and Maurice Simon. London: The Soncino Press, 1939.

*Midrash Siphre on Numbers: Selections from Early Rabbinic
Interpretation*. Tr. Paul Levertoff. London: SPCK,
1926.

Midrash Tehillim. Ed. Solomon Buber. Jerusalem, 1965.

265

The Mishnah. Tr. Herbert Danby. Oxford: Clarendon Press, 1933.

Neofiti I. 5 vols. Ed. and tr. Alejandro Diez-Macho. Madrid-Barcelona, 1970.

Philo; With an English Translation. Loeb Classical Library. 10 vols., 2 supplements. F. H. Colson and R. H. Whitaker, *et al.* London: William Heinneman Ltd. and Cambridge, MA: Harvard University Press, 1968.

Pseudo-Philo's Liber Antiquitatum Biblicarum. Ed. Guido Kisch. Notre Dame, IN: University of Notre Dame, 1949.

The Samaritan Liturgy. 2 vols. Ed. A. E. Cowley. Oxford: Clarendon Press, 1909.

Siphre ad Deuteronomium. Ed. L. Finkelstein. Berlin: Gesellschaft zur Förderung des Wissenschaft des Judentums, 1939; reprint ed., New York: Jewish Theological Seminary of America, 1969.

Siphre ad Numeros adjecto Siphre Zutta. Ed. H. S. Horowitz. Leipzig: Gesellschaft zur Förderung des Wissenschaft des Judentums, 1918; reprint ed., Jerusalem: Wahrmann Books, 1966.

Le Talmud de Jerusalem. 6 vols. Tr. Moïse Schwab. Paris: Editions G. P. Maisonneuve, 1960.

Pseudo-Jonathan. Targum Jonathan ben 'Uzi'el on the Pentateuch. Ed. David Rieder. Jerusalem: Rieder, 1974.

The Targums of Onkelos and Jonathan ben Uzziel on the Pentateuch with the Fragments of the Jerusalem Targum from the Chaldee. Tr. J. W. Etheridge, M. A. London: Longman, Green, Longman and Roberts, 1862-1865; reprint ed., New York: KTAV Publishing House, 1968.

The Zadokite Documents. Ed. and tr. Chaim Rabin. Oxford: Clarendon Press, 1954.

Texts and translations: Early Christian Writers.

Athanasius. *Expositio in Psalmos.* PG 27.

Augustine. *Enarrationes in Psalmos LI-C.* Ed. D. Eligius Dekkers and Johannes Fraipont. CCL 39. Turnhout, 1956.

_____. *In Iohannis Evangelium Tractatus CXXIV.* Ed. D. Radbodus Willems. CCL 36. Turnhout, 1954.

_____. *De Trinitate Libri XXV.* Ed. W. J. Mountain and Fr. Glorie. CCL 50. Turnhout, 1968.

John Chrysostom. *Homiliae in Epistula S. Pauli ad Hebraeos.* PG 63.

_____. *Homiliae in Evangelium S. Iohannis.* PG 59.

_____. *Homilies on the Gospel of St. John and the Epistle to the Hebrews*. Tr. Philip Schaff and Frederic Gardiner. NPNF 14. New York: Charles Scribner's Sons, 1889.

_____. *Huit Catéchèses Baptismales*. A. Wenger. SC 50. Paris, 1950.

Clement of Rome, *The Apostolic Fathers II, First and Second Clement*. Ed. and tr. Robert M. Grant and Holt H. Graham. New York: Thomas Nelson and Sons, 1965.

_____. *Clément de Rome, Épitre aux Corinthiens*. Ed. and tr. Annie Jaubert. SC 167. Paris: Editions du Cerf, 1971.

_____. *Épitre aux Corinthiens, Homélie du IIe Siècle*. Les Pères Apostoliques II. Hippolyte Hemmer. Paris, 1926.

Eusebius of Caesaea. *Commentaria in Psalmos*. PG 23.

_____. *Praeparatio Evangelica*. PG 21.

Hesychius (Pseudo-Athanasius). *De Titulis Psalmorum*. PG 27, 650-1344.

Homélies Pascales I: Une Homélie inspirée du traité sur la Pâque d'Hippolyte. Sc 27. Tr. Pierre Nautin. Paris: Editions du Cerf, 1950.

In Pascha VI. (Chrysostom, *Spuria*). PG 59, 735-746.

Irenaeus. *Libros Quinque adversus Haereses*. 2 vols. Ed. W. Wigan Harvey, S. T. B. Cambridge: Typis Adademicis, 1870; reprint ed., Ridgewood, NJ: Gregg Press Inc., 1965.

Jerome. *Tractatus de Psalmis*. D. Germanus Morin. CCL 78. Turnhout, 1958.

Lactantius. *Divine Institutes*. Tr. Rev. William Fletcher. ANF 7. New York: The Christian Literature Company, 1896.

Origen. *Die Homilien zu Numeri, Josua und Judices*. Ed. W. A. Baehrens. GCS 7. Leipzig: J. C. Hinrichs'sche Buchhandlung, 1921.

_____. *Selecta in Psalmos*. PG 12.

On the Pasch, see *In Pascha VI*.

Proclus of Constantinople. *Oratio XIII: In Sanctum Pascha*. PG 65.

Theodore of Mopsuestia. *Le Commentaire de Théodore de Mopsueste sur les Psaumes* (I-LXXX), Studi e testi 93. Ed. Robert Devréesse. Vatican City: Biblioteca Apostolica Vaticana, 1939.

Theodoret. *Interpretatio Epistulae ad Hebraeos*. PG 82.

Commentaries and studies.

Aalen, Sverre. "'Reign' and 'House' in the Kingdom of God. Supplement: 'Kingdom' and 'House' in Pre-Christian Judaism," *NTS* 8, 1961, 215-240.

Abelson, J. *The Immanence of God in Rabbinical Literature.* London: Macmillan and Co. Limited, 1912.

Aquinas, Thomas, O. P. "Ad Hebraeos," *Super Epistolas S. Pauli Lectura.* Ed. Raphael Cai. Turin and Rome: Marietti, 1953.

Barrett, Charles Kingsley. "The Eschatology of the Epistle to the Hebrews," *The Background of the New Testament and Its Eschatology.* Ed. W. D. Davies and David Daube. Cambridge: University Press, 1956, 363-393.

Brown, Raymond E., S. S. *The Gospel According to John.* AB 29. 2 vols. Garden City, NY: Doubleday and Company, Inc., 1966.

Bruce, Frederick Fyvie. *The Epistle to the Hebrews.* Grand Rapids, MI: William B. Eerdmans Publishing Co., 1964.

Buchanan, George Wesley. *To the Hebrews.* AB 36. Garden City, NY: Doubleday and Company, Inc., 1972.

Bultmann, Rudolf. *Der Zweite Brief an die Korinther.* Göttingen: Vandenhoeck und Ruprecht, 1976.

Callan, Terrance Dennis, Jr. "The Law and the Mediator: Ga. 3.19b-20." Ph. D. Dissertation, Yale University, December, 1976.

Combrink, H. J. B. "Some Thoughts on the Old Testament Citations in the Epistle to the Hebrews," *Neotestamentica 5.* Proceedings of Die Neuw-Testamentiese Werkgemeenskap van Suid-Afrika, 1972, 22-36.

Cross, Frank Leslie. *I Peter: A Paschal Liturgy.* London: A. R. Mowbray, 1954.

Dahl, Nils Alstrup. "A New and Living Way: The Approach to God According to Hebrews 10.19-25," *Interpretation* 5, 1951, 401-412.

_____. *The Crucified Messiah.* Publishing House, 1974.

_____. *Jesus in the Memory of the Early Church.* Minneapolis: Augsburg Publishing House, 1974.

Friesen, Isaac I. *The Glory of the Ministry of Jesus Christ, Illustrated by a Study of 2 Co. 2.14-3.18.* Basel: Friedrich Reinhardt Kommisionsverlag, 1971.

Goldin, Judah S. "The First Chapter of Abot de Rabbi Nathan," *Mordecai M. Kaplan: Jubilee Volume on the Occasion of his Seventieth Birthday.* New York: Jewish Theological Seminary of America, 1953, 263-280.

_____. "Not by Means of an Angel and not by Means of a Messenger," *Religions in Antiquity: Essays in Memory of Erwin Ramsdell Goodenough*. Ed. Jacob Neusner. Leiden: E. J. Brill, 1968, 412-424.

_____. *The Song at the Sea: Being a Commentary upon a Commentary in Two Parts*. New Haven: Yale University Press, 1971.

Greer, Rowan Allan. *The Captain of our Salvation: A Study in the Patristic Exegesis of Hebrews*. Tübingen: J. C. B. Mohr (Paul Siebeck), 1973.

_____. "A Trajectory from Paradise." Paper presented at the Harvard Divinity School. May, 1974.

Hanson, A. T. "Christ in the Old Testament according to Hebrews," *Studia Evangelica* II, 1964, 393-407.

Hay, David M. *Glory at the Right Hand: Psalm 110 in Early Christianity*. Nashville and New York: Abingdon Press, 1973.

Héring, Jean. *The Epistle to the Hebrews*. London: Epworth Press, 1970.

_____. *The Second Epistle of Saint Paul to the Corinthians*. London: Epworth Press, 1967.

Hoppin, Ruth. *Priscilla, Author of the Epistle to the Hebrews and other essays*. New York: Exposition Press, 1969.

Jastrow, Marcus. *A Dictionary of the Targumim, the Talmud Babli and Yerushalmi and the Midrashic Literature*. New York: Pardes Publishing House, Inc., 1950.

Jervell, Jacob. *Imago Dei: Gen. 1.26 f. im Spätjudentum, in der Gnosis und in der Paulinischen Briefen*. Göttingen: Vandenhoeck und Ruprecht, 1960.

Kosmala, Hans. *Hebräer, Essener, Christen*. Leiden: E. J. Brill, 1959.

Krauss, Samuel. *Griechische und Lateinische Lehnworte im Talmud, Midrasch und Targum*. 2 vols. Hildesheim: Georg Olms Verlagsbuchhandlung, 1964.

Küss, Otto. *Der Brief an die Hebräer*. Regensburg: Verlag Friedrich Pustet, 1966.

Le Déaut, Roger. *La Nuit Pascale*. Rome: Institute Biblique Pontificale, 1963.

Mac Donald, John. *The Theology of the Samaritans*. London: SCM Press Ltd., 1964.

Mc Namara, Martin. *Targum and Testament*. Grand Rapids: William B. Eerdmans Publishing Co., 1972.

Meeks, Wayne Atherton. "Moses as God and King," *Religions in Antiquity: Essays in Memory of Erwin Ramsdell Goodenough*. Ed. Jacob Neusner. Leiden: E. J. Brill, 1968, 354-371.

_____. *The Prophet King: Moses Tradition and the Johannine Christology*. Leiden: E. J. Brill, 1967.

Michel, Otto. *Der Brief an die Hebräer*. Göttingen: Vandenhoeck und Ruprecht, 1955.

Moffat, James. *A Critical and Exegetical Commentary on the Epistle to the Hebrews*. ICC. New York: Charles Scribner's Sons, 1924.

Moïse, l'Homme de l'Alliance. Cahiers Sioniens. Paris: Desclée et Cie, 1955.

Soffer, Arthur. "Anthropomorphisms and Anthropopathisms in the Septuagint of Psalms," *Studies in the Septuagint: Origins, Rescensions and Interpretations. Selected Essays with a Prolegomenon*. Ed. Sidney Jellicoe. New York: KTAV Publishing House, 1974.

Spicq, Céslaus. *L'Épitre aux Hébreux*. 2 vols. Paris: J. Gabalda et Cie, 1952.

Stauffer, Ethelbert. *Theology of the New Testament*. Tr. John Marsh. London: SCM Press, Ltd., 1955.

Strack, Hermann L. and Paul Billerbeck. *Kommentar zum Neuen Testament aus Talmud und Midrasch*. Munich: Beck, 1922-1956.

Williamson, Ronald. *Philo and the Epistle to the Hebrews*. Leiden: E. J. Brill, 1970.

Windisch, Hans. *Der Hebräerbrief*, Handbuch zum Neuen Testament 14. Tübingen: Verlag von J. C. B. Mohr (Paul Siebeck), 1931.